ISOLATIONISM

OPPOSING VIEWPOINTS®

Other Books in the American History Series:

ISOLATIONISM
O P P O S I N G V I E W P O I N T S®

David L. Bender, *Publisher*
Bruno Leone, *Executive Editor*

William Dudley, *Series Editor*
John C. Chalberg, Ph.D., professor of history,
   Normandale Community College, *Consulting
   Editor*

John C. Chalberg, *Book Editor*

AMERICAN HISTORY SERIES

Greenhaven Press, Inc.
San Diego, California

Library of Congress Cataloging-in-Publication Data

Isolationism : opposing viewpoints / John C. Chalberg, book editor.
    p.   cm. — (American history series)
    Includes bibliographical references and index.
    ISBN 1-56510-223-1 (lib.) — ISBN 1-56510-222-3 (pbk.)
    1. United States—Foreign relations—20th century. 2. United States—Foreign relations—20th century—Sources. 3. Neutrality —United States—History—20th century. 4. Neutrality—United States—History—20th century—Sources. I. Chalberg, John C., 1942-   . II. Series: American history series (San Diego, Calif.)
E744.C415   1995   94-5112
327.73—dc20   CIP

© 1995 by Greenhaven Press, Inc., PO Box 289009,
San Diego, CA 92198-9009

Printed in the U.S.A.

Every effort has been made to trace the owners of copyrighted material.

"America was born of revolt, flourished in dissent, became great through experimentation."

Henry Steele Commager, American Historian, 1902-1984

Contents

Foreword

Aboard the *Arbella* as it lurched across the cold, gray Atlantic, John Winthrop was as calm as the waters surrounding him were wild. With the confidence of a leader, Winthrop gathered his Puritan companions around him. It was time to offer a sermon. England lay behind them, and years of strife and persecution for their religious beliefs were over, he said. But the Puritan abandonment of England, he reminded his followers, did not mean that England was beyond redemption. Winthrop wanted his followers to remember England even as they were leaving it behind. Their goal should be to create a new England, one far removed from the authority of the Anglican church and King Charles I. In Winthrop's words, their settlement in the New World ought to be "a city upon a hill," a just society for corrupt England to emulate.

A Chance to Start Over

One June 8, 1630, John Winthrop and his company of refugees had their first glimpse of what they came to call New England. High on the surrounding hills stood a welcoming band of fir trees whose fragrance drifted to the *Arbella* on a morning breeze. To Winthrop, the "smell off the shore [was] like the smell of a garden." This new world would, in fact, often be compared to the Garden of Eden. Here, John Winthrop would have his opportunity to start life over again. So would his family and his shipmates. So would all those who came after them. These victims of conflict in old England hoped to find peace in New England.

Winthrop, for one, had experienced much conflict in his life. As a Puritan, he was opposed to Catholicism and Anglicanism, both of which, he believed, were burdened by distracting rituals and distant hierarchies. A parliamentarian by conviction, he despised Charles I, who had spurned Parliament and created a private army to do his bidding. Winthrop believed in individual responsibility and fought against the loss of religious and political freedom. A gentleman landowner, he feared the rising economic power of a merchant class that seemed to value only money. Once Winthrop stepped aboard the *Arbella*, he hoped, these conflicts would not be a part of his American future.

Yet his Puritan religion told Winthrop that human beings are fallen creatures and that perfection, whether communal or individual, is unachievable on this earth. Therefore, he faced a paradox: On the one hand, his religion demanded that he attempt to

9

live a perfect life in an imperfect world. On the other hand, it told him that he was destined to fail.

Soon after Winthrop disembarked from the *Arbella*, he came face-to-face with this maddening dilemma. He found himself presiding not over a utopia but over a colony caught up in disputes as troubling as any he had confronted in his English past. John Winthrop, it seems, was not the only Puritan with a dream of a heaven on earth. But others in the community saw the dream differently. They wanted greater political and religious freedom than their leader was prepared to grant. Often, Winthrop was able to handle this conflict diplomatically. For example, he expanded, participation in elections and allowed the voters of Massachusetts Bay greater power.

But religious conflict was another matter because it was grounded in competing visions of the Puritan utopia. In Roger Williams and Anne Hutchinson, two of his fellow colonists, John Winthrop faced rivals unprepared to accept his definition of the perfect community. To Williams, perfection demanded that he separate himself from the Puritan institutions in his community and create an even "purer" church. Winthrop, however, disagreed and exiled Williams to Rhode Island. Hutchinson presumed that she could interpret God's will without a minister. Again, Winthrop did not agree. Hutchinson was tried on charges of heresy, convicted, and banished from Massachusetts.

John Winthrop's Massachusetts colony was the first but far from the last American attempt to build a unified, peaceful community that, in the end, only provoked a discord. This glimpse at its history reveals what Winthrop confronted: the unavoidable presence of conflict in American life.

American Assumptions

From America's origins in the early seventeenth century, Americans have often held several interrelated assumptions about their country. First, people believe that to be American is to be free. Second, because Americans did not have to free themselves from feudal lords or an entrenched aristocracy, America has been seen as a perpetual haven from the troubles and disputes that are found in the Old World.

John Winthrop lived his life as though these assumptions were true. But the opposing viewpoints presented in the American History Series should reveal that for many Americans, these assumptions were and are myths. Indeed, for numerous Americans, liberty has not always been guaranteed, and disputes have been an integral, sometimes welcome part of their life.

The American landscape has been torn apart again and again by a great variety of clashes—theological, ideological, political, economic, geographical, and social. But such a landscape is not necessarily a hopelessly divided country. If the editors hope to prove anything during the course of this series, it is not that the United States has been destroyed by conflict but rather that it has been enlivened, enriched, and even strengthened by Americans who have disagreed with one another.

Thomas Jefferson was one of the least confrontational of Americans, but he boldly and irrevocably enriched American life with his individualistic views. Like John Winthrop before him, he had a notion of an American Eden. Like Winthrop, he offered a vision of a harmonious society. And like Winthrop, he not only became enmeshed in conflict but eventually presided over a people beset by it. But unlike Winthrop, Jefferson believed this Eden was not located in a specific community but in each individual American. His Declaration of Independence from Great Britain could also be read as a declaration of independence for each individual in American society.

Jefferson's Ideal

Jefferson's ideal world was composed of "yeoman farmers," each of whom was roughly equal to the others in society's eyes, each of whom was free from the restrictions of both government and fellow citizens. Throughout his life, Jefferson offered a continuing challenge to Americans: Advance individualism and equality or see the death of the American experiment. Jefferson believed that the strength of this experiment depended upon a society of autonomous individuals and a society without great gaps between rich and poor. His challenge to his fellow Americans to create—and sustain—such a society has itself produced both economic and political conflict.

A society whose guiding document is the Declaration of Independence is a society assured of the freedom to dream—and to disagree. We know that Jefferson hated conflict, both personal and political. His tendency was to avoid confrontations of any sort, to squirrel himself away and write rather than to stand up and speak his mind. It is only through his written words that we can grasp Jefferson's utopian dream of a society of independent farmers, all pursuing their private dreams and all leading lives of middling prosperity.

Jefferson, this man of wealth and intellect, lived an essentially happy private life. But his public life was much more troublesome. From the first rumblings of the American Revolution in the 1760s to the North-South skirmishes of the 1820s that ultimately produced the Civil War, Jefferson was at or near the center of American political history. The issues were almost too many—and too crucial—for one lifetime: Jefferson had to choose between sup-

11

porting or rejecting the path of revolution. During and after the ensuing war, he was at the forefront of the battle for religious liberty. After endorsing the Constitution, he opposed the economic plans of Alexander Hamilton. At the end of the century, he fought the infamous Alien and Sedition Acts, which limited civil liberties. As president, he opposed the Federalist court, conspiracies to divide the union, and calls for a new war against England. Throughout his life, Thomas Jefferson, slaveholder, pondered the conflict between American freedom and American slavery. And from retirement at his Monticello retreat, he frowned at the rising spirit of commercialism he feared was dividing Americans and destroying his dream of American harmony.

No matter the issue, however, Thomas Jefferson invariably supported the rights of the individual. Worried as he was about the excesses of commercialism, he accepted them because his main concern was to live in a society where liberty and individualism could flourish. To Jefferson, Americans had to be free to worship as they desired. They also deserved to be free from an over-reaching government. To Jefferson, Americans should also be free to possess slaves.

Harmony, an Elusive Goal

Before reading the articles in this anthology, the editors ask readers to ponder the lives of John Winthrop and Thomas Jefferson. Each held a utopian vision, one based upon the demands of community and the other on the autonomy of the individual. Each dreamed of a country of perpetual new beginnings. Each found himself thrust into a position of leadership and found that conflict could not be avoided. Harmony, whether communal or individual, was a forever elusive goal.

The opposing visions of Winthrop and Jefferson have been at the heart of many differences among Americans from many backgrounds through the whole of American history. Moreover, their visions have provoked important responses that have helped shape American society, the American character, and many an American battle.

The editors of the American History Series have done extensive research to find representative opinions on the issues included in these volumes. They have found numerous outstanding opposing viewpoints from people of all times, classes, and genders in American history. From those, they have selected commentaries that best fit the nature and flavor of the period and topic under consideration. Every attempt was made to include the most important and relevant viewpoints in each chapter. Obviously, not every notable viewpoint could be included. Therefore, a selective, annotated bibliography has been provided at the end of each book to aid readers in seeking additional information.

The editors are confident that as this series reveals past conflicts, it will help revitalize the reader's views of the American present. In that spirit, the American History Series is dedicated to the proposition that American history is more complicated, more fascinating, and more troubling than John Winthrop or Thomas Jefferson ever dared to imagine.

John C. Chalberg
Consulting Editor

Introduction

"U.S. history in the first half of the twentieth century is marked by a long, painful, and controversial transition from isolationism to significant U.S. political involvement in global affairs."

The United States has had a profound influence on global political affairs in the twentieth century—arguably more than any other nation. This influence can be seen in innumerable instances and events. Three key decisions stand out, however: the decision to enter World War I against Germany, Austria-Hungary, and the Ottoman Empire (Turkey) in 1917; the decision in 1941 to fight in World War II against Germany, Japan, and Italy; and finally the decision in the late 1940s to enter a state of "cold war" against the communist nations of the Soviet Union and China. All three of these conflicts reshaped the world order and enlarged America's place in it. All three could be easily classified as "victories" for the United States. Yet American participation in these conflicts was bitterly opposed by many who argued that such involvement in foreign affairs was not merely inadvisable, but antithetical to the essence of what the United States had stood for as a nation since its founding. The philosophy behind such opposition has become known as "isolationism" and its proponents as "isolationists."

Isolationism refers to a set of beliefs about the United States and its place in the world that exerted significant influence on American foreign policy from the end of the eighteenth century to the beginning of the twentieth. U.S. history in the first half of the twentieth century is marked by a long, painful, and controversial transition from isolationism to significant U.S. political involvement in global affairs—an involvement the United States maintains to this day. To understand the dynamics of the debates over this transition, which are the primary focus of the viewpoints in this volume, it helps to be familiar with the elements of American isolationism.

Defining isolationism in American history is a complex question that has itself elicited disagreement and controversy. People have used the term in various ways to describe differing people and courses of action. However, some basic aspects and elements can be roughly identified. One way to begin is to explain what American isolationism is not, because the United States has never been an isolationist nation in the strictest sense of the term—in the way of, to take one example, Japan from the 1630s to 1854. A comparison between the two nations during this time period is revealing. Japan, during this span of Tokugawa shogun rule, excluded all foreigners and expelled or killed shipwrecked sailors and others who landed by accident on its shores. The United States, during colonial times and after, was by contrast a nation of immigrants from many different countries and ethnic groups. The Japanese government sought to purge the country of all foreign religions and other cultural influences; the United States government had no comparable policy. Japan sought to restrict trade with foreign nations to a bare minimum; the United States aggressively pursued foreign commerce with many nations (indeed, it was an 1854 U.S. naval mission to Japan designed to promote trade, led by Commodore Matthew C. Perry, that forced Japan to emerge from its isolationist posture). The United States, unlike Japan, thus was neither culturally isolationist nor economically isolationist.

Many historians, in describing isolationism in the American context, qualify it by describing the United States as *politically* isolationist. However, to define political isolationism as simply the avoidance of all diplomatic, political, and military contact with other nations does not quite describe the United States either. The United States went to war with Great Britain in 1812, with Mexico in 1846, and with Spain in 1898; it did not hesitate to aggressively confront these countries (and Russia) in its quest for territorial expansion in the North American continent; and by the end of the nineteenth century it was forcefully pursuing military and political influence in Asia. Historian Wayne S. Cole writes:

> Isolationists . . . never favored cutting off the United States from the rest of the world, nor did they rule out the possibilities of American expansion—territorial, commercial, financial, ideological, or military—particularly in the Western Hemisphere, the Pacific, and East Asia.

A more accurate description of America's political isolationism is the avoidance of *alliances*. Historian Leroy N. Rieselbach explains American isolationism to mean

> an attitude of opposition to binding commitments by the United States government that would create new, or expand existing, obligations to foreign nations.

Foreign alliances create obligations, which create limits on American power to determine its own foreign policy. The isolationists' greatest fear was that America could be obligated by some foreign alliance to enter a war it would otherwise avoid. Some commentators have argued that Americans have historically been opposed not to involvement in foreign affairs and diplomacy as such, but to foreign restrictions on American freedom of action. Historian Walter LaFeber emphasizes this point in *The American Age*.

> "Isolationism". . . means in U.S. history not withdrawal from world affairs (a people does not conquer a continent and become the world's greatest power by withdrawal or by assuming it enjoys "free security"), but maintaining a maximum amount of freedom of action. Americans who have professed to believe in individualism at home not surprisingly have often professed the same abroad.

Some historians have argued that "unilateralist" describes this concept of maximizing America's freedom of action better than "isolationist," with its implications of seclusion like that of pre-Perry Japan.

In addition to this element of unilateralism, another important element of American isolationist thought is its focus on, and fear of, Europe. Europe at the time of the American Revolution was the center of world power, a collection of monarchies and empires engaged in constant warfare and diplomatic intrigue. Declaring independence from Great Britain meant achieving independence from Europe's wars as well, many revolutionary leaders argued. Such a separation was desirable because the United States, in the eyes of many Americans, was different. Unlike Europe, America would have no standing armies that threatened civil liberties. Unlike Europe, America would have no kings but rather a republican form of government, with political power decentralized among its states. Unlike Europe, America would have none of the secret diplomacy and power politics and wars caused by entangling alliances. Unlike Europe, America would not have religious wars pitting Protestant against Catholic. Unlike Europe, America would be a shining beacon of freedom and democracy in an otherwise unfree world.

But how was America to be such a beacon—how was it to contribute to what many people in the nineteenth century viewed as the inevitable spread of world democracy and peace? Not by foreign diplomacy, isolationists argued, and certainly not by fighting in foreign wars. America instead would avoid the European scene and lead by example. A good illustration of this reasoning comes from Silas Wood, a representative from New York, speaking in Congress on January 21, 1824, against a congressional resolution to make an official gesture of support for the Greeks revolting against the Ottoman Empire. Wood states:

Because the world is full of oppression, is this Government the Hercules that is to free it from the monsters of tyranny and slavery? And are we bound to emulate the chivalrous achievements of the renowned Knight of La Mancha, by engaging in conflict with every windmill that we may, in the delirium of our frenzy, imagine ourselves to be a tyrant?

It will be asked, is our Government to be of no use to mankind? I answer yes; but not by its fleets and armies—not by embarking in a military crusade to establish the empire of our principles—not by establishing a corps of diplomatic apostles of liberty, but by the moral influence of its example.

It presents to the world a model by which the rights of men may be secured. . . . The knowledge of it will be conveyed, by our flag, to every region of the earth.

The foundations of a policy of avoiding political and military alliances (most notably with the powers of Europe) were laid by George Washington, America's first president, who during his presidency maintained a difficult neutrality during a war between Great Britain and France, and who in his famous Farewell Address published in 1796 urged the United States "to steer clear of permanent alliances with any portion of the foreign world." Rieselbach writes that Washington's words influenced American foreign policy for many years.

Staying clear of European entanglements, generalized to an aversion to all contact with foreign nations, was a guiding tenet of American policy for 140 years. Except for one brief interlude—the Spanish-American War, which pointed toward Asia, not Europe, and which did not involve this country in European politics or entangling alliances—this policy remained inviolate until World War I, and after that conflict isolationism regained its dominant position.

In the years between 1797 and 1917, the idea of isolation was reaffirmed on many occasions, the most widely known being the promulgation of the Monroe Doctrine in December, 1823. While warning the European powers to keep clear of the Western Hemisphere, President [James] Monroe reiterated that "our policy in regard to Europe, which was adopted at an early stage of the wars which have so long agitated that quarter of the globe, nevertheless remains the same, which is, not to interfere in the internal concerns of any of its powers."

This isolationist (or unilateralist) approach to foreign policy was, in the words of historian Samuel Flagg Bemis, "remarkably successful throughout the 19th century and well into the 20th." America was able to avoid European wars, expand its boundaries to the Pacific Ocean, attract millions of immigrants, and survive a major civil war without serious diplomatic repercussions. Bemis and other historians have attributed the successes of American isolationism to several external factors. The United States was physically separated from Europe by the Atlantic Ocean; Europe was embroiled in its own internal conflicts and in colonial pursuits in Africa and Asia; the interests of the United States and Great Britain, then the world's leading naval power and the only one with the capability to threaten the United States, were for the most part congruent (and Canada was, in effect, a hostage for peaceful Great Britain–U.S. relations). Whether these external conditions had changed enough so as to make isolationism obsolete was the focus of much twentieth-century debate.

These then were some of the identifiable elements of what American isolationism was and what it was not. Isolationism did *not* entail the cultural, economic, or even political separation of the United States from the rest of the world; it was not opposed to territorial expansion in the North American continent or, later, in the Pacific. It did cite George Washington's "Farewell Address" and the Monroe Doctrine as touchstones of U.S. foreign policy; it sought to maximize American freedom of action in determining foreign policy by avoiding entangling alliances, especially with European nations; it viewed America as a special beacon of freedom for the world (freedom to be spread by example, not military force); it was opposed to standing armies and a centralized and militarized federal government; and it viewed America as advantageously located far from potential enemies, and thus safe from direct attack.

This general view of America and the world was directly challenged by the momentous events of the twentieth century, beginning with World War I. President Woodrow Wilson, in full keeping with American isolationist traditions, proclaimed American neutrality and sought to keep American soldiers out of the conflict. However, when faced with a choice between supporting Great Britain, a parliamentary democracy with whom the United States had over the course of decades developed a cordial relationship, and Germany, a new military power that was not democratic and that threatened to militarily dominate most of Europe, Wilson and most of his advisers leaned toward the former. Wilson finally led the United States into war on the side of Great Britain and the Allies, as an "associated power."

Having broken with part of America's isolationist tradition of avoiding foreign wars, Wilson after World War I sought to replace the entire isolationist vision with his own vision of a peaceful postwar world—a world where freedom and democracy would be universal, where all peoples could control their political destinies, where the seas were opened to unrestricted use, where an international organization would maintain international law, and where nations could no longer threaten other nations by use of force. In a sense, Wilson was merely restating American nostrums about the United States' being a beacon of light and liberty for the world. But instead of the United States' leading merely by example, Wilson was willing to contribute American diplomatic muscle and, in the case of World War I, American soldiers to the causes of "making the world safe for democracy" and creating a League of Nations with the power to enforce peace.

Opponents of Wilson's decisions to go to war and to press for a new order in the postwar world for the most part emphasized America's isolationist tradition, but they split in emphasizing different aspects of that tradition. Some refused to make distinctions between Great Britain and Germany, labeling the entire continent of Europe a morass for the United States to avoid. Others reiterated the advice of Silas Wood—the United States should spread democracy by example only. One group emphasized the need to protect American freedom of action; they were willing for the United States to take more action on the global stage as a world power, but were unwilling to place power in a supranational organization. Some pointed back to George Washington's Farewell Address as reason enough to oppose foreign intervention. Some simply opposed all war and use of force. Under their combined weight, Wilson's crusade to remake world politics failed, and the United States returned to its tradition of isolationism. The divisions within the isolationist camp, as well as between isolationists and opponents of isolationism, would continue to affect foreign policy debates over the following years. The issues set into motion by the "Great Debate" after World War I did not go away; they returned with a vengeance when war broke out again in Europe two decades later.

Ultimately, when America made its three critical decisions, it chose each time to intervene in world politics. Yet isolationists, although they lost the great debate over America's role in the world, were right in one sense: U.S. participation in World War I, World War II, and the Cold War did massively transform the nation. Whether these changes were positive and/or worth the results of these wars is one of many questions to consider when reading the opposing viewpoints of this volume.

John C. Chalberg
Consulting Editor

CHAPTER 1

George Washington and America's Isolationist Tradition

Chapter Preface

For approximately 150 years, one of the most influential and frequently quoted documents in American history was George Washington's Farewell Address. First published in 1796 to announce Washington's retirement from public life at the end of his second presidential term, the essay by America's first president sought to advise the new nation on domestic and foreign policy.

The most enduring part of his advice concerned foreign affairs and the necessity for America to isolate itself politically from Europe and its wars. After his long public and military career, George Washington was personally familiar with European wars and diplomacy. He fought for the British against the French in the French and Indian War. He fought against the British as commander of the Continental Army in the American Revolution. As America's first president from 1789 to 1797, he sought to keep the fledgling nation secure and in peace amidst war and intrigue among Great Britain, France, and Spain, the European powers whose territories surrounded the United States. Although Washington's experience was more extensive than most, many other Americans shared his opinions about Europe and America's place in the world. Historian Wayne S. Cole writes in *The Reader's Companion to American History* that Washington's advice for Americans to separate themselves from Europe was influential in part because such ideas were already well established in American thought:

> The roots of isolationism extended back to the colonial period. Settlers came to escape religious persecution, economic hardship, wars, or personal problems in Europe. From the beginning there was the assumption (or the hope) that the New World would be better than the Old. The long and dangerous journey magnified the geographic (and moral) separateness of America. Despite the alliance with France during the American Revolution, the attitudes undergirding isolationism were well established long before independence.

> When George Washington in his Farewell Address asserted that Europe had "a set of primary interests which to us have none or a very remote relation" and advised America "to steer clear of permanent alliances," he was advancing views that were already old and widely accepted.

The isolationist impulse found in Washington's address is also reflected in two other presidential pronouncements from America's early history. In Thomas Jefferson's first inaugural address, made in 1801, he warned against all "entangling alliances" with other nations—a warning that would be frequently repeated (and misattributed to Washington) in coming decades. President James Monroe issued a proclamation of foreign policy in 1823 that most famously warned against European attempts to colonize Latin America, but it also echoed the prescriptions of Washington and Jefferson.

> In the wars of the European powers, in matters relating to themselves, we have never taken any part, nor does it comport with our policy so to do. It is only when our rights are invaded, or seriously menaced, that we resent injuries, or make preparation for our defense.

Throughout the nineteenth century the words of Washington, Jefferson, and Monroe were frequently cited to explain U.S. foreign policy. During that century revolutions in Greece, Hungary, and other nations in Europe elicited some enthusiasm from the American people and calls for official recognition or support, but the American government, citing Washington's warning among other reasons, refused to take such actions. As late as 1885 President Grover Cleveland summarized American foreign policy as

> the policy of independence, favored by our position and defended by our known love of justice and by our power. It is the policy of peace suitable to our interests. It is the policy of neutrality, rejecting any share in foreign broils and ambitions upon other continents and rejecting their intrusion here. It is the policy of Monroe and of Washington and Jefferson—"Peace, commerce and honest friendship with all nations; entangling alliances with none."

As the twentieth century approached, however, some American observers began to question the relevance of Washington's eighteenth-century advice. America was no longer a weak nation surrounded by stronger ones as in Washington's time, they argued, but one of the world's great powers. Washington's Farewell Address continued to be ceremoniously read in Congress every February, but more people were arguing about what it meant. The arguments foreshadowed the intense controversies of the twentieth century when America abandoned its policy of political isolationism.

VIEWPOINT 1

"The Great Rule of conduct for us, in regard to foreign nations, is in extending our commercial relations to have with them as little political connection as possible."

The United States Should Remain Aloof from Europe

George Washington (1732-1799)

For many Americans isolationism is synonymous with George Washington's famous Farewell Address. Written in collaboration with James Madison and Alexander Hamilton, the address was never orally delivered by Washington himself. It was instead published in the *American Daily Advertiser* on September 19, 1796, to announce to the American people his decision not to run for a third term as president, and to offer some final words of advice. Among the first president's main points were a plea for unity and a warning against sectionalism, a condemnation of the "baneful effects" of political parties, and a call for recognizing the importance of religion and morality in American life. The most lasting and influential part of Washington's counsel to the nation was the section on foreign affairs, reprinted here.

Washington's advice is reflective of the difficulties of his second term as president. In 1793 war broke out between Great Britain and France, and the United States was caught in a precarious balance of neutrality between the world's two leading powers. Washington's secretary of the treasury, Alexander Hamilton, was a sympathizer with Great Britain and argued that America should renounce its security alliance made during the Revolutionary War with King Louis XVI of France in 1778. He argued

Excerpted from George Washington's farewell address as published in the *American Daily Advertiser*, September 19, 1796. Reprinted in *The Writings of George Washington*, Worthington C. Ford, ed., vol. 13. New York: n.p., 1893.

that the alliance did not carry over to the revolutionary French government (which had beheaded Louis XVI in 1793). Thomas Jefferson, Washington's secretary of state, supported neutrality in the war between the two European powers, but spoke against renouncing the treaty. Washington did not formally renounce the treaty, but he did issue a Proclamation of Neutrality calling for "conduct friendly and impartial" to all warring nations and forbidding American ships from carrying war supplies to such nations. (America eventually formally ended its security alliance with France in 1800.)

The divisions between the pro-British Hamilton and the pro-French Jefferson, who disagreed on many other foreign and domestic issues, developed into the beginnings of America's two-party system, with Jefferson leading the Democratic-Republicans and Hamilton leading the Federalists. Washington at first attempted to reconcile the two factions and to remain above the fray of politics. However, he eventually found himself the target of withering criticism, mostly from the Democratic-Republicans—a development that stung him personally and that accounts for the attacks on political parties in his address.

Washington's foreign policy strictures were to prove far more lasting than his warnings against political parties, which quickly became entrenched American political institutions. His injunction to steer clear of Europe and its wars and troubles dovetailed very nicely with the American temper of the times. Washington's address was read in Congress every February 22 throughout the nineteenth and well into the twentieth centuries. Its "Great Rule" of avoiding political entanglements with European nations was repeatedly cited by those who argued against American involvement in European affairs, making the address a logical starting point for the study of American isolationism.

Friends and Fellow Citizens:

The period for a new election of a citizen to administer the executive government of the United States being not far distant, and the time actually arrived when your thoughts must be employed in designating the person who is to be clothed with that important trust, it appears to me proper, especially as it may conduce to a more distinct expression of the public voice, that I should now apprise you of the resolution I have formed to decline being considered among the number of those out of whom a choice is to be made. . . .

A solicitude for your welfare, which cannot end but with my life, and the apprehension of danger natural to that solicitude, urge me, on an occasion like the present, to offer to your solemn contemplation, and to recommend to your frequent review, some sentiments which are the result of much reflection, of no inconsiderable observation, and which appear to me all-important to the permanency of your felicity as a people. These will be offered to you with the more freedom as you can only see in them the disinterested warnings of a parting friend who can possibly have no personal motive to bias his counsels. . . .

Advice on Foreign Relations

Observe good faith and justice toward all nations. Cultivate peace and harmony with all. Religion and morality enjoin this conduct; and can it be that good policy does not equally enjoin it? It will be worthy of a free, enlightened, and, at no distant period, a great nation to give to mankind the magnanimous and too novel example of a people always guided by an exalted justice and benevolence. Who can doubt that in the course of time and things the fruits of such a plan would richly repay any temporary advantages which might be lost by a steady adherence to it? Can it be that Providence has not connected the permanent felicity of a nation with its virtue? The experiment, at least, is recommended by every sentiment which ennobles human nature. Alas! is it rendered impossible by its vices?

In the execution of such a plan nothing is more essential than that permanent, inveterate antipathies against particular nations and passionate attachments for others should be excluded and that in place of them just and amicable feelings toward all should be cultivated. The nation which indulges toward another an habitual hatred or an habitual fondness is in some degree a slave. It is a slave to its animosity or to its affection, either of which is sufficient to lead it astray from its duty and its interest. Antipathy in one nation against another disposes each more readily to offer insult and injury, to lay hold of slight causes of umbrage, and to be haughty and intractable when accidental or trifling occasions of dispute occur.

Hence, frequent collisions, obstinate, envenomed, and bloody contests. The nation prompted by ill will and resentment sometimes impels to war the government, contrary to the best calculations of policy. The government sometimes participates in the national propensity, and adopts, through passion, what reason would reject; at other times, it makes the animosity of the nation subservient to projects of hostility instigated by pride, ambition, and other sinister and pernicious motives. The peace often, sometimes perhaps the liberty, of nations has been the victim.

So, likewise, a passionate attachment of one nation for another produces a variety of evils. Sympathy for the favorite nation, facilitating the illusion of an imaginary common interest in cases where no real common interest exists, and infusing into one the enmities of the other, betrays the former into a participation in the quarrels and wars of the latter without adequate inducement or justification. It leads also to concessions to the favorite nation of privileges denied to others, which is apt doubly to injure the nation making the concessions, by unnecessarily parting with what ought to have been retained, and by exciting jealousy, ill will, and disposition to retaliate in the parties from whom equal privileges are withheld.

America's Response to Revolution in Europe

America flirted with ending its official noninvolvement in European affairs in the mid-nineteenth century, when a series of revolutions swept Europe. In 1852 Louis Kossuth, the leader of a failed revolution in Hungary, traveled to the United States seeking aid against the armies of Austria and Russia. Henry Clay, longtime senator from Kentucky, responded to Kossuth on January 9, 1852, arguing that America could best serve the cause of liberty in the world by staying out of European wars.

I trust you will believe me, too, when I tell you that I entertain the liveliest sympathies in every struggle for liberty in Hungary, and in every country, and in this I believe I express the universal sentiment of my countrymen. But, sir, for the sake of my country, you must allow me to protest against the policy you propose to her. . . .

By the policy to which we have adhered since the days of [George] Washington, we have prospered beyond precedent—we have done more for the cause of liberty in the world than arms could effect. We have showed to other nations the way to greatness and happiness; and, if we but continue united as one people, and persevere in the policy which our experience has so clearly and triumphantly vindicated, we may in another quarter of a century furnish an example which the reason of the world can not resist. But if we should involve ourselves in the tangled web of European politics, in a war in which we could effect nothing, and if in that struggle Hungary should go down, and we should go down with her, where, then, would be the last hope of the friends of freedom throughout the world? Far better is it for ourselves, for Hungary, and for the cause of liberty, that, adhering to our wise, pacific system, and avoiding the distant wars of Europe, we should keep our lamp burning brightly on this western shore as a light to all nations, than to hazard its utter extinction amid the ruins of fallen or falling republics in Europe.

And it gives to ambitious, corrupted, or deluded citizens (who devote themselves to the favorite nation) facility to betray or sacrifice the interests of their own country, without odium, sometimes even with popularity, gilding with the appearances of a virtuous sense of obligation, a commendable deference for public opinion, or a laudable zeal for public good, the base or foolish compliances of ambition, corruption, or infatuation. As avenues to foreign influence in innumerable ways, such attachments are particularly alarming to the truly enlightened and independent patriot. How many opportunities do they afford to tamper with domestic factions, to practise the arts of seduction, to mislead public opinion, to influence or awe the public councils! Such an attachment of a small or weak toward a great and powerful nation dooms the former to be the satellite of the latter.

Against the insidious wiles of foreign influence, I conjure you to believe me, fellow citizens, the jealousy of a free people ought to be *constantly* awake, since history and experience prove that foreign influence is one of the most baneful foes of republican government. But that jealousy, to be useful, must be impartial, else it becomes the instrument of the very influence to be avoided instead of a defense against it. Excessive partiality for one foreign nation and excessive dislike of another cause those whom they actuate to see danger only on one side and serve to veil and even second the arts of influence on the other. Real patriots, who may resist the intrigues of the favorite, are liable to become suspected and odious, while its tools and dupes usurp the applause and confidence of the people to surrender their interests.

The Great Rule of Conduct

The great rule of conduct for us, in regard to foreign nations, is in extending our commercial relations to have with them as little political connection as possible. So far as we have already formed engagements, let them be fulfilled with perfect good faith. Here let us stop.

Europe has a set of primary interests which to us have none, or a very remote relation. Hence she must be engaged in frequent controversies, the causes of which are essentially foreign to our concerns. Hence, therefore, it must be unwise in us to implicate ourselves, by artificial ties, in the ordinary vicissitudes of her politics or the ordinary combinations and collisions of her friendships or enmities.

Our detached and distant situation invites and enables us to pursue a different course. If we remain one people, under an efficient government, the period is not far off when we may defy material injury from external annoyance; when we may take such an attitude as will cause the neutrality we may at any time resolve upon to be scrupulously respected; when belligerent nations, under the impossibility of making acquisitions upon us, will not lightly hazard the giving us provocation; when we may choose peace or war, as our interest guided by our justice shall counsel.

Why forgo the advantages of so peculiar a situation? Why quit our own to stand upon foreign ground? Why, by interweaving our destiny with that of any part of Europe, entangle our peace and prosperity in the toils of European ambition, rivalship, interest, humor, or caprice?

Alliances Should Be Temporary

It is our true policy to steer clear of permanent alliances with any portion of the foreign world. So far, I mean, as we are now at liberty to do it, for let me not be understood as capable of patronizing infidelity to existing engagements (I hold the maxim no less applicable to public than to private affairs that honesty is always the best policy). I repeat it, therefore: let those engagements be observed in their genuine sense. But, in my opinion, it is unnecessary and would be unwise to extend them.

Taking care always to keep ourselves, by suitable establishments, on a respectably defensive posture, we may safely trust to temporary alliances for extraordinary emergencies.

Harmony, liberal intercourse with all nations are recommended by policy, humanity, and interest. But even our commercial policy should hold an equal and impartial hand, neither seeking nor granting exclusive favors or preferences; consulting the natural course of things; diffusing and diversifying by gentle means the streams of commerce but forcing nothing; establishing with powers so disposed, in order to give to trade a stable course, to define the rights of our merchants, and to enable the government to support them, conventional rules of intercourse, the best that present circumstances and mutual opinion will permit, but temporary and liable to be from time to time abandoned or varied, as experience and circumstances shall dictate; constantly keeping in view that it is folly in one nation to look for disinterested favors from another; that it must pay with a portion of its independence for whatever it may accept under that character; that, by such acceptance, it may place itself in the condition of having given equivalents for nominal favors and yet of being reproached with ingratitude for not giving more. There can be no greater error than to expect, or calculate, upon real favors from nation to nation. It is an illusion which experience must cure, which a just pride ought to discard.

"Nothing can be more obvious . . . than that the conditions for which Washington made his rule no longer exist."

Washington's Farewell Address No Longer Applies to the United States

Richard Olney (1835-1917)

Richard Olney served as U.S. secretary of state under President Grover Cleveland from 1895 to 1897. The Massachusetts lawyer oversaw the foreign policy of a nation that had changed much in the century since George Washington's Farewell Address. The United States had grown from a small strip of former colonies surrounded by the world's great powers into a great power itself. Its population had grown from four million in 1790 to sixty-three million in 1890; over the same time period its area expanded from less than 900,000 to 3.6 million square miles, stretching from the Atlantic to the Pacific Oceans. The small agrarian country had transformed itself into an industrial and trading powerhouse that produced much of the world's oil and steel—key resources in the industrial age.

America during much of the nineteenth century was immersed in domestic affairs—most notably the Civil War. In foreign policy the United States, in the 1823 Monroe Doctrine and other actions, had asserted its interests in the Western Hemisphere against Europe, and had also taken steps to increase its influence in the Pacific. But many Americans, often citing Washington's Farewell

Excerpted from Richard Olney, "International Isolation of the United States," *The Atlantic Monthly*, May 1898.

Address, still placed a relatively low priority on political relations with other nations. Historian Jerald A. Combs writes in *The History of American Foreign Policy*:

> American politics of the post-Civil War period revolved around domestic issues. . . .
>
> Evidence of the relative lack of concern for aggressive diplomacy and overseas expansion can be seen in Congress's neglect of the instruments needed for such a policy—the army, the navy, and the diplomatic corps. At the end of the Civil War, the American army had been the most powerful in the world. Soon afterward it averaged only about 28,000 men, most of whom were scattered in frontier forts and Indian territories. None were serving outside the borders of the nation. . . .
>
> America neglected its diplomatic corps even more than the armed forces. In the nineteenth century, most diplomats were selected not for knowledge and competence, but as rewards for partisan service. . . . Scandal and contempt surrounded American representatives abroad. . . . America's diplomats were woefully underpaid by a Congress that sometimes asked seriously whether the United States needed a diplomatic service at all.

Toward the end of the nineteenth century a growing number of people concerned with American foreign policy questioned what George Washington had meant in his Farewell Address, as well as its applicability decades later. One example of such questioning comes from a speech given by Olney at Harvard College on March 2, 1898. In his address, Olney argues that Washington's Farewell Address has been misused by those who seek to keep the United States out of all foreign agreements. He argues that Washington's advice was meant for its own time and circumstances, when the United States was a weak nation. Now that it is a world power, it has a responsibility to involve itself in world affairs. The argument over the relevance of Washington's Farewell Address was to be repeated many times in the next century.

The foreign policy of the country is one of the things a citizen should study and understand and aim to have studied and understood by the community generally—and I therefore do not hesitate to invite you to consider for a few moments a feature of our foreign policy which may be described as the "international isolation of the United States."

What is meant by the phrase "international isolation" as thus used is this. The United States is certainly now entitled to rank

America Must Fight for the Cause of Liberty

Richard Olney's arguments were foreshadowed in a speech from almost five decades earlier. In 1851 Louis Kossuth, the leader of a failed revolution in Hungary, went on a speaking tour of the United States asking for American aid for his cause. Kossuth's plea gained the support of William Sweetser, a Democratic congressman from Ohio. In a speech on January 3, 1852, on behalf of Kossuth and Hungarian independence, Sweetser suggests that America has grown in strength and should use that power to fight for liberty in the world. Most members of Congress, however, politely rejected Kossuth's request.

I believe that the time has come, in this nineteenth century, when the power of this nation, with its twenty-five million people, is not only to be felt in a moral point of view, but is to be felt with all the force we can command. Two of the counties that compose the Congressional district which I have the honor to represent upon this floor, being the central countries of the great State of Ohio, have spoken out upon this subject and while they, in common with the whole people of this country, understand the issue which Kossuth desires to make in coming here, they have, by their resolutions, instructed me to say in my place here that so far as relates to the mission of this man to our country—so far as relates to the principles which he maintains, they are prepared to declare not only to this Congress, but to the world, that the time has come when the American nation, with twenty-five millions of people, will enter their protest against such atrocities as characterized the interference of Russia in the recent contest between Hungary and Austria. They have, by their resolutions, authorized me to say this; and in saying it they have not been unmindful of the precepts given to us by the Father of his Country. Prudential motives alone stimulated that illustrious man and the patriots of his day to recommend that policy. . . . The condition of the nation has changed since that time.

among the great Powers of the world. Yet, while its place among the nations is assured, it purposely takes its stand outside the European family circle to which it belongs, and neither accepts the responsibilities of its place nor secures its advantages. It avowedly restricts its activities to the American continents and intentionally assumes an attitude of absolute aloofness to everything outside those continents. This rule of policy is not infrequently associated with another which is known as the Monroe doctrine—as if the former grew out of the Monroe doctrine or were, in a sense, a kind of consideration for that doctrine, or a sort of complement to it. In reality the rule of isolation originated and was applied many years before the Monroe doctrine was proclaimed. No doubt consistency requires that the conduct toward

America which America expects of Europe should be observed by America toward Europe. Nor is there any more doubt that such reciprocal conduct is required of us not only by consistency but by both principle and expediency. The vital feature of the Monroe doctrine is that no European Power shall forcibly possess itself of American soil and forcibly control the political fortunes and destinies of its people. Assuredly America can have no difficulty in governing its behavior toward Europe on the same lines.

Washington's Address

Tradition and precedent are a potent force in the New World as well as in the Old and dominate the counsels of modern democracies as well as those of ancient monarchies. The rule of international isolation for America was formulated by Washington, was embalmed in the earnest and solemn periods of the Farewell Address, and has come down to succeeding generations with all the immense prestige attaching to the injunctions of the Father of his Country and of the statesmen and soldiers who having first aided him to free the people of thirteen independent communities, then joined him in the even greater task of welding the incoherent mass into one united nation. The Washington rule, in the sense in which it has been commonly understood and actually applied, could hardly have been adhered to more faithfully if it had formed part of the text of the Constitution. But there can be no question that such common understanding and practical application have given an extension to the rule quite in excess of its terms as well as of its true spirit and meaning. Washington conveyed his celebrated warning to his countrymen in these words:—

> The great rule of conduct for us in regard to foreign nations is, in extending our commercial relations, to have with them as little political connection as possible. . . .
>
> Europe has a set of primary interests which to us have none or a very remote relation. Hence she must be engaged in frequent controversies the causes of which are essentially foreign to our concerns. Hence, therefore, it must be unwise in us to implicate ourselves by artificial ties in the ordinary vicissitudes of her politics or the ordinary combinations and collisions of her friendships or enmities.
>
> Our detached and distant situation invites and enables us to pursue a different course. . . .
>
> Why forego the advantages of so peculiar a situation? Why quit our own to stand upon foreign ground? Why, by interweaving our destiny with that of any part of Europe, entangle our peace and prosperity in the toils of European ambition, rivalship, interest, humor, or caprice?
>
> It is our true policy to steer clear of permanent alliances with

any portion of the foreign world; . . .

Taking care always to keep ourselves by suitable establishments on a respectable defensive posture, we may safely trust to temporary alliances for extraordinary emergencies.

Now what is it that these utterances enjoin us not to do? What rule of abstinence do they lay down for this country? The rule is stated with entire explicitness. It is that this country shall not participate in the ordinary vicissitudes of European politics and shall not make a permanent alliance with any foreign power. It is coupled with the express declaration that extraordinary emergencies may arise to which the rule does not apply, and that when they do arise temporary alliances with foreign powers may be properly resorted to. Further, not only are proper exceptions to the rule explicitly recognized, but its author, with characteristic caution and wisdom, carefully limits the field which it covers by bounds which in practice are either accidentally or intentionally disregarded. For example, it cannot be intermeddling with the current course of European politics to protect American interests wherever in the world they may need such protection. It cannot be such intermeddling to guard our trade and commerce and to see that its natural development is not fraudulently or forcibly or unfairly arrested. It is as open to America as to Europe to undertake the colonization of uninhabited and unappropriated portions of the globe, and if the United States were to enter upon such a policy, it would not be implicating ourselves in the ordinary vicissitudes of European politics. In short, the rule of the Farewell Address does not include many important subjects-matter its application to which is commonly taken for granted, and does not excuse the inaction of this government in many classes of cases in which the rule is pleaded as a sufficient justification. Take, for instance, the case of American missions and American missionaries in Turkey, and assume for present purposes that missionaries have been maltreated and their property destroyed under circumstances which call upon Turkey to make reparation. The duty of government to exact the reparation is clear—it can be exonerated from its discharge only by some invincible obstacle, such, for example, as the concert of Europe. Suppose that concert did not exist or were broken, and that by joining hands with some competent Power, having perhaps similar grievances, the government could assert its rights and could obtain redress for American citizens. Does the rule of the Farewell Address inhibit such an alliance in such a case for such a purpose? Nothing can be clearer than that it does not. To protect American citizens wherever they lawfully are, instead of being an impertinent intrusion into foreign politics, is to accomplish one of the chief ends for which the national government is instituted—

33

and if the government can do its duty with an ally where it must fail without, and even if it can more securely and efficiently do that duty with an ally than it can without, it would be not merely folly, but recreancy as well, not to made the alliance. . . .

Circumstances Have Changed

The Washington rule of isolation, then, proves on examination to have a much narrower scope than the generally accepted versions give to it. Those versions of it may and undoubtedly do find countenance in loose and general and unconsidered statements of public men both of the Washington era and of later times. Nevertheless it is the rule of Washington, and not that of any other man or men, that is authoritative with the American people, so that the inquiry what were Washington's reasons for the rule and how far those reasons are applicable to the facts of the present day is both pertinent and important. Washington states his reasons with singular clearness and force. "This nation," he says in substance, "is young and weak. Its remote and detached geographical situation exempts it from any necessary or natural connection with the ordinary politics or quarrels of European states. Let it therefore stand aloof from such politics and quarrels and avoid any alliances that might connect it with them. This the nation should do that it may gain time—that the country may have peace during such period as is necessary to enable it to settle and mature its institutions and to reach without interruption that degree of strength and consistency which will give it the command of its own fortunes." Such is the whole theory of the Washington rule of isolation. Its simple statements show that the considerations justifying the rule to his mind can no longer be urged in support of it. Time has been gained—our institutions are proven to have a stability and to work with a success exceeding all expectation—and though the nation is still young, it has long since ceased to be feeble or to lack the power to command its own fortunes. It is just as true that the achievements of modern science have annihilated the time and space that once separated the Old World from the New. In these days of telephones and railroads and ocean cables and ocean steamships, it is difficult to realize that Washington could write to the French Ambassador at London in 1790, "We at this great distance from the northern parts of Europe hear of wars and rumors of wars as if they were the events or reports of another planet." It was an ever present fact to his mind, of course, and is of the first importance in connection with this subject, that notwithstanding our remoteness from Europe, not merely one, as now, but three of the great Powers of Europe had large adjoining possessions on this continent—a feature of the situation so vital and so menacing in the eyes of the statesmen of that day as to force [Thomas] Jefferson to buy Louisiana despite the national poverty and despite plausible, if not conclusive, constitutional objections. Nothing can be more obvious, therefore, than the conditions for which Washington made his rule no longer exist. The logical, if not the necessary result is that the rule itself should now be considered non-existent also. Washington himself, it is believed, had no doubt and made no mistake upon that point. That he was of opinion that the regimen suitable to the struggling infancy of the nation would be adapted to its lusty manhood is unsupported by a particle of evidence. On the contrary, there is authority of the highest character for the statement that he entertained an exactly opposite view and "thought a time might come, when, our institutions being firmly consolidated and working with complete success, we might safely and perhaps beneficially take part in the consultations held by foreign states for the common advantage of the nations." Without further elaboration of the argument in favor of the position that the rule of the Farewell Address cannot be regarded as applicable to present conditions—an argument which might be protracted indefinitely—the inquiry at once arising is, What follows? What are the consequences if the argument be assumed to be sound? Let us begin by realizing that certain results which at first blush might be apprehended as dangerous do not necessarily follow and are not likely to follow.

It is a mistake to suppose, for example, that if the doctrine of the Farewell Address had never been formally promulgated or if it were now to be deemed no longer extant, the United States would have heretofore embroiled itself or would now proceed to embroil itself in all sorts of controversies with foreign nations. We are now, as always, under the restraint of the principles of international law, which bid us respect the sovereignty of every other nation and forbid our intermeddling in its internal affairs. The dynastic disputes of European countries have been, and would still be, of no possible practical concern to us. We covet no portion of European soil, and, if we had it, should be at a loss what to do with it. And it may be taken for granted with reasonable certainty that no Executive and Senate are likely to bind us to any foreign Power by such an alliance as Washington deprecated—by a permanent alliance, that is, offensive and defensive, and for all purposes of war as well as peace. The temptation sufficient to induce any administration to propose such a partnership is hardly conceivable—while an attempt to bring it about would irretrievably ruin the men or the party committed to it, and would as certainly be frustrated by that reserve of good sense and practical wisdom which in the last resort the American people never fail to bring to bear upon public affairs.

Outliving Its Usefulness

On these grounds, it is possible to regard the isolation rule under consideration as having outlived its usefulness without exposing ourselves to any serious hazards. But it is to be and should be so regarded on affirmative grounds—because the continuance of its supposed authoritativeness is hurtful in its tendency—hurtful in many directions and large interests. To begin with, it is necessarily unfortunate and injurious, in various occult as well as open ways, that a maxim stripped by time and events of its original virtue should continue current in the community under the guise of a living rule of action. The greater the prestige of such a maxim by reason of its age or its origin, the greater the mischief. Human affairs take their shape and color hardly more from reason and selfish interest than from imagination and sentiment. A rule of policy originating with Washington, preeminently wise for his epoch, ever since taught in schools, lauded on the platform, preached in the pulpit, and displayed in capitals and italics in innumerable political manuals and popular histories, almost becomes part of the mental constitution of the generations to which it descends. They accept it without knowing why and they act upon it without the least regard to their wholly new environment.

The practical results of such an ingrained habit of thought, and of the attempt to govern one set of circumstances by a rule made for another totally unlike, are as unfortunate as might be expected, and might be illustrated quite indefinitely. The example most deserving of attention, however, is found in the commercial policy of the government. What Washington favored was political isolation, not commercial. . . .

Political isolation may in a special case coexist with entire freedom of commercial intercourse—as where a country is weak and small and its resources, natural and artificial, are too insignificant to excite jealousy. Such was the case with the United States immediately after the war of independence, when its inhabited territory consisted of a strip of Atlantic seaboard and its people numbered less than four million souls. But a policy of political isolation for a continental Power, rapidly rising in population, wealth, and all the elements of strength, and able to cope with the foremost in the struggle for the trade of the world, naturally fosters, if it does not entail, a policy of commercial isolation also. The two policies are naturally allied in spirit and in the underlying considerations which can be urged in their defense, and being once adopted render each other mutual support. Political isolation deliberately resolved upon by a great Power denotes its self-confidence and its indifference to the opinion or friendship of other nations; in like manner the commercial isolation of such a Power denotes its conviction that in matters of trade and commerce it is sufficient unto itself and need ask nothing of the world beyond. In the case of the United States, the policy of political seclusion has been intensified by a somewhat prevalent theory that we are a sort of chosen people; possessed of superior qualities natural and acquired; rejoicing in superior institutions and superior ideals; and bound to be careful how we connect ourselves with other nations lest we get contaminated and deteriorate. This conception of ourselves has asserted itself in opposition to international arrangements even when . . . the only object and effect were to open a new region to commerce and to give our merchants equal privileges with those of any other country. We accept the privileges but at the same time decline to become a party to the compact which secures them to us as to all nations. The transaction is on a par with various others in which, with great flourish of trumpets and much apparent satisfaction at the felicity of our attitude, we tender or furnish what we call our "moral support." Do we want the Armenian butcheries stopped? To any power that will send its fleet through the Dardanelles and knock the Sultan's palace about his ears, we boldly tender our "moral support." Do we want the same rights and facilities of trade in Chinese ports and territory that are accorded to the people of any other country? We loudly hark Great Britain on to the task of achieving that result, but come to the rescue ourselves with not a gun, nor a man, nor a ship, with nothing but our "moral support." But, not to tarry too long on details, what are the general results of these twin policies—of this foreign policy of thorough isolation combined with a domestic policy of thorough protection? So far as our foreign relations are concerned, the result is that we stand without a friend among the great Powers of the world and that we impress them, however unjustly, as a nation of sympathizers and sermonizers and swaggerers—without purpose or power to turn our words into deeds and not above the sharp practice of accepting advantages for which we refuse to pay our share of the price. . . .

A Shirking of Responsibilities

A nation is as much a member of a society as an individual. Its membership, as in the case of an individual, involves duties which call for something more than mere abstention from violations of positive law. The individual who should deliberately undertake to ignore society and social obligations, to mix with his kind only under compulsion, to abstain from all effort to make men wiser or happier, to resist all appeals to charity, to get the most possible and enjoy the most possible consistent with the least possible intercourse with his fellows, would be universally condemned as shaping his life by a low and unworthy standard. Yet, what is true of the individual in his relations to his fellow men is equally true of every nation in its relations to other nations. In this matter, we have fallen into habits which, however excusable in their origin, are without present justification. Does a foreign question or controversy present itself appealing however forcibly to our sympathies or sense of right—what happens the moment it is suggested that the United States should seriously participate in its settlement? A shiver runs through all the ranks of capital lest the uninterrupted course of money-making be interfered with; the cry of "Jingo!" comes up in various quarters; advocates of peace at any price make themselves heard from innumerable pulpits and rostrums; while practical politicians invoke the doctrine of the Farewell Address as an absolute bar to all positive action. The upshot is more or less explosions of sympathy or antipathy at more or less public meetings, and, if the case is a very strong one, a more or less tardy tender by the government of its "moral support." Is that a creditable part for a great nation to play in the affairs of the world? The pioneer in the wilderness, with a roof to build over his head and a patch of ground to cultivate and wife and children to provide for and secure against savage beasts and yet more savage men, finds in the great law of self-preservation ample excuse for not expending either his feelings or his energies upon the joys or the sorrows of his neighbors. But surely he is no pattern for the modern millionaire, who can sell nine tenths of all he has and give to the poor, and yet not miss a single comfort or luxury of life. This country was once the pioneer and is now the millionaire. It behooves it to recognize the changed conditions and to realize its great place among the Powers of the earth. It behooves it to accept the commanding position belonging to it, with all its advantages on the one hand and all its burdens on the other. It is not enough for it to vaunt its greatness and superiority and to call upon the rest of the world to admire and be duly impressed. Posing before less favored peoples as an exemplar of the superiority of American institutions may be justified and may have its uses. But posing alone is like answering the appeal of a mendicant by bidding him admire your own sleekness, your own fine clothes and handsome house and your generally comfortable and prosperous condition. He possibly should do that and be grateful for the spectacle, but what he really asks and needs is a helping hand. The mission of this country, if it has one, as I verily believe it has, is not merely to pose but to act—and, while always governing itself by the rules of prudence and common sense and making its own special interests the first and paramount objects of its care, to forego no fitting opportunity to further the progress of civilization practically as well as theoretically, by timely deeds as well as by eloquent words. There is such a thing for a nation as a "splendid isolation"—as when for a worthy cause, for its own independence, or dignity, or vital interests, it unshrinkingly opposes itself to a hostile world. But isolation that is nothing but a shirking of the responsibilities of high place and great power is simply ignominious. If we shall sooner or later—and we certainly shall—shake off the spell of the Washington legend and cease to act the rôle of a sort of international recluse, it will not follow that formal alliances with other nations for permanent or even temporary purposes will soon or often be found expedient. On the other hand, with which of them we shall as a rule practically cooperate cannot be doubtful. From the point of view of our material interests alone, our best friend as well as most formidable foe is that world-wide empire [Great Britain] whose navies rule the seas and which on our northern frontier controls a dominion itself imperial in extent and capabilities. There is the same result if we consider the present crying need of our commercial interests. . . . But our material interests only point in the same direction as considerations of a higher and less selfish character. There is a patriotism of race as well as of country and the Anglo-American is as little likely to be indifferent to the one as to the other. Family quarrels there have been heretofore and doubtless will be again, and the two peoples, at the safe distance which the broad Atlantic interposes, take with each other liberties of speech which only the fondest and dearest relatives indulge in. Nevertheless, that they would be found standing together against any alien foe by whom either was menaced with destruction or irreparably calamity, it is not permissible to doubt. Nothing less could be expected of the close community between them in origin, speech, thought, literature, institutions, ideals—in the kind and degree of the civilization enjoyed by both. In that same community, and in that coöperation in good works which should result from it, lies, it is not too much to say, the best hope for the future not only of the two kindred peoples but of the human race itself.

CHAPTER 2

World War I and American Isolationism

Chapter Preface

When war erupted in Europe in the summer of 1914, the prospect that the United States would join the conflict seemed remote. For nearly 120 years Americans has followed the maxims contained in Washington's Farewell Address warning against involvement with European nations and their wars. European quarrels, Americans assumed, ought to be solved by Europeans. The fight in 1914 between the Allied Powers (England, France, and Russia) and the Central Powers (Germany, Austria-Hungary, and the Ottoman Empire) was just another European quarrel that the United States should avoid. That this did not turn out to be the case—that before the war would end, two million American soldiers would be sent to fight in Europe—marks a significant turning point in American history. The years of World War I and the peace that followed were marked by significant debates among Americans over their country's place in the world.

The central figure of these debates was Woodrow Wilson, a scholar and former governor who was elected U.S. president in 1912. Wilson's response to the outbreak of World War I was at first consistent with long-established American foreign policy traditions. He proclaimed U.S. neutrality and asked Americans to be neutral in thought and action and to be an example of peace and prosperity in a war-torn world. At the same time, he insisted that the United States possessed historic neutral rights in international law (rights it had claimed since 1776) that he as president did not intend to relinquish. Neutral rights, which had evolved in international law in the eighteenth and nineteenth centuries and were formally negotiated and codified in the 1856 Declaration of Paris and the 1909 Declaration of London, established rules for international conduct in times of war. Under these rules nations not at war (neutrals) were not to sell military arms and munitions (contraband) to nations at war (belligerents). In return, belligerents had to concede neutrals the right to sell non-military goods to all nations. Many Americans believed that the United States should, as a neutral trading nation, be in a position to take advantage of Europe's predicaments. If Europeans chose to fight among themselves, so the argument went, the United States had the right to profit from trade with the warring nations.

Initially, Wilson saw no contradiction between maintaining American neutrality and asserting American rights as a neutral trader. But his policy resulted in conflict with two of the warring nations—Great Britain and Germany—that both sought to restrict American goods from reaching the ports of their enemies.

Great Britain, with the world's largest navy, launched a blockade that intercepted and harassed American shipping, and confiscated foodstuffs and other goods it designated as contraband under a broad definition. Wilson formally protested these British violations of American neutral rights, but Britain's promises to pay for lost and damaged property, as well as the belief of Wilson and his advisers that a German victory was undesirable for American interests, prevented any break in relations between the two countries. Great Britain's blockade reduced U.S.-German trade from $345 million in 1914 to $29 million in 1916. During the same period American trade with the Allied Powers rose from $753 million to almost $3 billion. The United States was in effect supporting the Allied war effort, although its government remained officially neutral.

Germany, with a weaker navy, resorted to a new invention—the submarine—to interdict shipping to Great Britain. The submarine proved itself a lethal weapon for sinking ships, but because it depended on surprise for its effectiveness, Germany was unable to warn ships of attack or otherwise conform with international laws designed to protect neutrals and noncombatants. In February 1915 the German government announced the creation of a war zone around Great Britain and warned that enemy ships entering the zone would be sunk. Wilson responded by informing German leaders that Germany would be held to "strict accountability" if American lives and property were lost in the war zone.

German submarine warfare created a crisis in May 1915 with the sinking of the *Lusitania*, a British passenger liner. The attack killed 1,198 people, including 128 Americans. Former U.S. president Theodore Roosevelt and others argued that the time had come for the United States to enter the war on the side of the Allied Powers. Others, including Secretary of State William Jennings Bryan, thought the time had come for the American government to stop its citizens from traveling on ships of Great Britain and other warring nations. In other words, Bryan was willing to give up one of America's neutral rights in order to ensure that the country stayed out of war.

President Wilson tried to steer a middle ground between Roosevelt and Bryan. He refused to declare war over the incident, but he also harshly condemned Germany's actions and insisted on the right of Americans to travel on all passenger ships. Roosevelt continued to attack Wilson, and Bryan resigned as secretary of state. Germany, however, pledged not to attack passenger ships. On March 16, following another crisis caused by the sinking of the *Sussex*, a French ship, Germany pledged not to attack merchant ships without warning (in effect, to suspend its submarine warfare). American anger about the *Lusitania* incident subsided, and Wilson won reelection in November 1916 with the slogan "He kept us out of war."

Wilson used his victory to work for American mediation rather than American entry into the conflict. The culmination of that effort was a speech appealing to the peoples of Europe to ask their leaders to settle on the basis of "peace without victory." A few days later Germany, feeling the pinch of Great Britain's blockade and gambling that it could win the war before America could intervene, renewed its unrestricted submarine warfare. Wilson cut off diplomatic relations with Germany, and two months later went before Congress to ask for a formal declaration of war.

That request provoked intense debate within Congress and the rest of the nation. In the end, six senators and fifty representatives voted against their president's request for war. While far from enough to block American entry into the war, those fifty-six votes were the most ever cast in opposition to a war resolution in American history. They represented a severe rebuke to the president, as well as serious concerns about the course of American foreign policy. A country peopled by refugees from European wars, European armies, and European draft laws was about to send an army to Europe. What had been completely unthinkable a few years earlier was suddenly a troubling reality.

Wilson sought to overcome American ambivalence over the war with numerous speeches in which he sought to link American involvement with his vision for a postwar world. Historian George Moss writes in *America in the Twentieth Century:*

> Wilson himself provided the most potent ideological defense of the war when he called it a struggle to preserve democracy. Linking the war to democracy made it a crusade, tying it to the ancient doctrine of American mission. World War I became a war to save democracy, to save Europe from itself, and to redeem mankind. . . . Most Americans embraced the notion of a great war to make the world a safe place for democratic governments.

After the Allied Powers, with the help of the United States, emerged victorious in 1918, Wilson determined to make his postwar vision a reality. He went personally to France in 1919 (becoming the first president to leave U.S. soil during his term of office) as head of the U.S. peace delegation. There he focused most of his energy on what he believed to be the most important element of his vision: the creation of a League of Nations. He personally wrote much of the League Covenant (constitution), the heart of which was Article X. This clause pledged united, mutual international support of the territorial integrity and political independence of its members. By pledging the united retaliation of all member states against any nation using war to threaten another country, Wilson believed, the League would hold the key to a peaceful world. Wilson not only successfully fought for the League of Nations, he had its creation incorporated into the Treaty of Versailles itself.

Wilson returned triumphantly home with the Treaty of Versailles, only to face an American public tired of war and opposition in the Republican-majority U.S. Senate, which had to ratify the treaty by a two-thirds majority. Senatorial opposition combined with Wilson's own stubborn refusal to compromise resulted in the Senate's rejection of the Treaty of Versailles—and the League of Nations.

Republican Warren G. Harding, pledging a "return to normalcy," easily defeated Democrat James M. Cox, who ran supporting the League of Nations, in the 1920 presidential race. Harding's election was interpreted by many as a sign that Americans were dubious of involvement in international affairs. The 1920s saw a resurgence of American isolationism and a backlash against the lofty ideal of "fighting for democracy" that had motivated Americans to fight in World War I but had not been realized. Moss writes:

> The war changed the public mood. Photographs and films revealed the brutal, deadly reality of trench warfare, dramatically different from the soaring rhetoric of President Wilson's speeches. Veterans cared only to return home and forget about their war experiences. Americans wearied of idealistic crusades; they became cynical about their international commitments. They turned inward, closing out the larger world.

The disillusionment following World War I and the Treaty of Versailles would continue to affect American foreign policy for the next two decades.

VIEWPOINT 1

"The United States must be neutral in fact as well as in name during these days that are to try men's souls."

The United States Should Be Neutral

Woodrow Wilson (1856-1924)

Woodrow Wilson was president of the United States from 1912 to 1920. A former college professor, president of Princeton University, and governor of New Jersey, Wilson had campaigned on a platform dedicated to domestic reform rather than foreign policy. "It would be the irony of fate," he remarked shortly before his inauguration, "if my administration had to deal chiefly with foreign affairs." Wilson did achieve an impressive record of domestic reforms during his term of office, but as fate would have it, foreign affairs—specifically World War I and its aftermath—were to provide Wilson his most momentous decisions and defining moments as president.

World War I erupted in Europe in August 1914, about eighteen months into Wilson's presidency. Triggered by the assassination of an obscure foreign prince in a remote European city few Americans had heard of, the war quickly developed into a protracted conflict between the Allies (primarily Great Britain, France, and Russia) and the Central Powers (primarily Germany and Austria-Hungary). Wilson's initial response was to issue a proclamation of neutrality on August 4, a position that maintained America's traditional refusal to take sides in European wars. In the following passage from a speech made to the American people on August 19, Wilson calls for all Americans to "act and speak in the

Woodrow Wilson, *Appeal for Neutrality*, 63rd Cong., 2nd sess., (1914) S. Doc. 566, pp. 3-4.

true spirit of neutrality," a position he asserted to be in the country's best interest. For the next thirty months, Wilson would struggle to maintain America's neutrality in what was fast becoming the largest and deadliest war up to that time.

My Fellow Countrymen:

I suppose that every thoughtful man in America has asked himself, during these last troubled weeks, what influence the European war may exert upon the United States, and I take the liberty of addressing a few words to you in order to point out that it is entirely within our own choice what its effects upon us will be and to urge very earnestly upon you the sort of speech and conduct which will best safeguard the Nation against distress and disaster.

The effect of the war upon the United States will depend upon what American citizens say and do. Every man who really loves America will act and speak in the true spirit of neutrality, which is the spirit of impartiality and fairness and friendliness to all concerned. The spirit of the Nation in this critical matter will be determined largely by what individuals and society and those gathered in public meetings do and say, upon what newspapers and magazines contain, upon what ministers utter in their pulpits, and men proclaim as their opinions on the street.

Americans from Many Nations

The people of the United States are drawn from many nations, and chiefly from the nations now at war. It is natural and inevitable that there should be the utmost variety of sympathy and desire among them with regard to the issues and circumstances of the conflict. Some will wish one nation, others another, to succeed in the momentous struggle. It will be easy to excite passion and difficult to allay it. Those responsible for exciting it will assume a heavy responsibility, responsibility for no less a thing than that the people of the United States, whose love of their country and whose loyalty to its Government should unite them as Americans all, bound in honor and affection to think first of her and her interests, may be divided in camps of hostile opinion, hot against each other, involved in the war itself in impulse and opinion if not in action.

Such divisions among us would be fatal to our peace of mind and might seriously stand in the way of the proper performance of our duty as the one great nation at peace, the one people holding itself ready to play a part of impartial mediation and speak the counsels of peace and accommodation, not as a partisan, but as a friend.

I venture, therefore, my fellow countrymen, to speak a solemn word of warning to you against that deepest, most subtle, most essential breach of neutrality which may spring out of partisanship, out of passionately taking sides. The United States must be neutral in fact as well as in name during these days that are to try men's souls. We must be impartial in thought as well as in action, must put a curb upon our sentiments as well as upon every transaction that might be construed as a preference of one party to the struggle before another.

My thought is of America. I am speaking, I feel sure, the earnest wish and purpose of every thoughtful American that this great country of ours, which is, of course, the first in our thoughts and in our hearts, should show herself in this time of peculiar trial a Nation fit beyond others to exhibit the fine poise of undisturbed judgment, the dignity of self-control, the efficiency of dispassionate action; a Nation that neither sits in judgment upon others nor is disturbed in her own counsels and which keeps herself fit and free to do what is honest and disinterested and truly serviceable for the peace of the world.

Shall we not resolve to put upon ourselves the restraints which will bring to our people the happiness and the great and lasting influence for peace we covet for them?

"In this cause . . . would not the people of the United States approve of the abandonment of Washington's advice that this country keep out of European complications?"

The United States Should Not Be Neutral

Charles W. Eliot (1834-1926)

When war broke out in Europe in August of 1914, the vast majority of Americans wanted nothing more than to stay out of the conflict. President Woodrow Wilson's appeal for Americans to be "impartial in thought as well as in action" struck a responsive chord in many who were shocked at the savagery of the war and uncertain about who was at fault.

One early dissent to Wilson's call for neutrality appears below in the form of a letter to Wilson from Charles W. Eliot. Eliot had much in common with the president of the United States. Both men were past presidents of Ivy League universities (Eliot at Harvard, Wilson at Princeton); both were noted advocates of educational and social reforms. In his letter to the president of August 6, 1914, Eliot urges a naval blockade against the Central Powers of Germany and Austria-Hungary. He argues that George Washington's 1796 advice to America to remain neutral in European politics was no longer relevant in the face of the threat the Central Powers posed to world peace and to the United States.

Excerpted from Charles W. Eliot's letter of August 6, 1914, to President Wilson. Reprinted in *The Intimate Papers of Colonel House*, Charles Seymour, ed., Houghton Mifflin, 1926-28.

DEAR PRESIDENT WILSON:

Has not the United States an opportunity at this moment to propose a combination of the British Empire, the United States, France, Japan, Italy, and Russia in offensive and defensive alliance to rebuke and punish Austria-Hungary and Germany for the outrages they are now committing, by enforcing against those two countries non-intercourse with the rest of the world by land and sea? These two Powers have now shown that they are utterly untrustworthy neighbors, and military bullies of the worst sort—Germany being far the worse of the two, because she has already violated neutral territory.

If they are allowed to succeed in their present enterprises, the fear of sudden invasion will constantly hang over all the other European peoples; and the increasing burdens of competitive armaments will have to be borne for another forty years. We shall inevitably share in these losses and miseries. The cost of maintaining immense armaments prevents all the great Powers from spending the money they ought to spend on improving the condition of the people, and promoting the progress of the world in health, human freedom, and industrial productiveness.

In this cause, and under the changed conditions, would not the people of the United States approve of the abandonment of Washington's advice that this country keep out of European complications?

A blockade of Germany and Austria-Hungary could not be enforced with completeness; but it could be enforced both by sea and by land to such a degree that the industries of both peoples would be seriously crippled in a short time by the stoppage of both their exports and their imports. Certain temporary commercial advantages would be gained by the blockading nations—a part of which might perhaps prove to be permanent.

This proposal would involve the taking part by our navy in the blockading process, and, therefore, might entail losses of both life and treasure; but the cause is worthy of heavy sacrifices; and I am inclined to believe that our people would support the Government in taking active part in such an effort to punish international crimes, and to promote future international peace.

In so doing this country would be serving the general cause of peace, liberty, and good will among men. . . .

I offer this suggestion in entire submission to your judgment as to its present feasibility and expediency. It seems to me an effective international police method, suited to the present crimes, and the probable issues of the future, and the more attractive because the European concert and the triple alliances have conspicuously

The End of Isolationism

The inaugural issue of the New Republic, *which appeared on November 7, 1914, featured an editorial stating that war in Europe meant an end to the American "delusion" about isolationism.*

The self-complacent isolation of a great people has never received a ruder shock than that which was dealt to the American nation by the outbreak of the European war. We have long been congratulating ourselves on something more than an official independence of Europe. We considered ourselves free in a finer and a deeper sense—free from the poison of inherited national antipathies, free from costly and distracting international entanglements, free from a more than incidental reliance on foreign markets for the sale of our products, free to make mistakes with impunity and to gather fruits by merely shaking the tree. We were more nearly self-contained, more completely the master of our own destiny, than any other nation of history. Yet this consummate example of political independence has been subjected to a visitation of fate almost as disconcerting as those which beset wandering Indian tribes. There broke over the country a European war which the American people individually and collectively were powerless to prevent or to mitigate, yet which may have consequences upon the future and policy of the country as profound and far-reaching as our self-made Civil War. Independence in the sense of isolation has proved to be a delusion. It was born of the same conditions and the same misunderstandings as our traditional optimistic fatalism; and it must be thrown into the same accumulating scrapheap of patriotic misconceptions.

failed. It, of course, involves the abandonment by all the European participants of every effort to extend national territory in Europe by force. The United States has recently abandoned that policy in America. It involves also the use of international force to overpower Austria-Hungary and Germany with all possible promptness and thoroughness; but this use of force is indispensable for the present protection of civilization against a savagery, and for the future establishment and maintenance of federal relations and peace among the nations of Europe.

I am, with highest regard,

Sincerely yours

CHARLES W. ELIOT

VIEWPOINT 3

"I know of nothing that would do more to prevent war than an international agreement that neutral nations would not loan to belligerents."

The United States Should Not Permit Loans to Any Warring Nations

William Jennings Bryan (1860-1925)

When the nations of Europe plunged into war in August 1914, President Woodrow Wilson resolved to keep the United States out of the fighting by maintaining a position of neutrality. But to determine just what neutrality meant in time of war was itself controversial. An example of such a controversy was the internal debate within the Wilson administration over whether the federal government should ban American loans to the Allied powers. Great Britain and France were purchasing massive amounts of food, munitions, and other goods from the United States, and needed loans to pay for them.

Favoring a governmental ban on loans was William Jennings Bryan. Bryan, a three-time unsuccessful Democratic candidate for president, was appointed secretary of state by President Wilson after providing him with crucial support in the 1912 election. A pacifist who abhorred war, Bryan advocated strict neutrality in U.S. dealings with both the Allies and Central Powers, unlike many others in the Wilson administration (including Wilson him-

From William Jennings Bryan's letter of August 10, 1914, to President Wilson, from the Bryan Papers, Library of Congress. Reprinted in *William Jennings Bryan: Selections*, Ray Ginger, ed., Bobbs-Merrill, n.d.

self) whose words and actions often favored Great Britain and France over Germany and Austria-Hungary.

In August 1914 the American financial firm J.P. Morgan and Company asked the Wilson administration's position on granting a war loan to France. Bryan feared that permitting such loans would inevitably draw the United States into the conflict on the side of the receivers of the loan, and make true neutrality impossible. His arguments against loans can be seen in the following letter, written to President Wilson on August 10, 1914. Bryan at first was successful in convincing the president of his position. On August 15, Bryan gave the following statement to the press: "There is no reason why loans should not be made to the governments of neutral nations, but in the judgment of this Government loans by American bankers to any foreign nation which is at war [are] inconsistent with the true spirit of neutrality."

Later Wilson relaxed his position on loans to the Allied powers. Bryan, convinced that the United States was drifting away from neutrality, resigned as secretary of state in June 1915.

I beg to communicate to you an important matter which has come before the Department. Morgan Company of New York have asked whether there would be any objection to their making a loan to the French Government. . . . I have conferred with Mr. [Robert] Lansing and he knows of no legal objection to financing this loan, but I have suggested to him the advisability of presenting to you an aspect of the case which is not legal but I believe to be consistent with our attitude in international matters. It is whether it would be advisable for this Government to take the position that it will not approve of any loan to a belligerent nation. The reasons that I would give in support of this proposition are:

First: Money is the worst of all contrabands because it commands everything else. The question of making loans contraband by international agreement has been discussed, but no action has been taken. I know of nothing that would do more to prevent war than an international agreement that neutral nations would not loan to belligerents. While such an agreement would be of great advantage, could we not by our example hasten the reaching of such an agreement? We are the one great nation which is not involved and our refusal to loan to any belligerent would naturally tend to hasten a conclusion of the war. We are responsible for the use of our influence through example and as we cannot tell what we can do until we try, the only way of testing our influence is to set the example and observe its effect. This is the fundamental reason in support of the suggestion submitted.

Second: There is a special and local reason, it seems to me, why this course would be advisable. Mr. Lansing observed in the discussion of the subject that a loan would be taken by those in sympathy with the country in whose behalf the loan was negotiated. If we approved of a loan to France we could not, of course, object to a loan to Great Britain, Germany, Russia, Austria or to any other country, and if loans were made to these countries our citizens would be divided into groups, each group loaning money to the country which it favors and this money could not be furnished without expressions of sympathy. These expressions of sympathy are disturbing enough when they do not rest upon pecuniary interests—they would be still more disturbing if each group was pecuniarily interested in the success of the nation to whom its members had loaned money.

Third: The powerful financial interests which would be connected with these loans would be tempted to use their influence through the newspapers to support the interests of the Government to which they had loaned because the value of the security would be directly affected by the result of the war. We would thus find our newspapers violently arrayed on one side or the other, each paper supporting a financial group and pecuniary interest. All of this influence would make it all the more difficult for us to maintain neutrality, as our action on various questions that would arise would affect one side or the other and powerful financial interests would be thrown into the balance. . . .

It grieves me to be compelled to intrude any question upon you at this time, but I am sure you will pardon me for submitting a matter of such great importance.

With assurances of high respect, I am, My dear Mr. President,

Yours very truly,
W J Bryan

P. S. Mr. Lansing calls attention to the fact that an American citizen who goes abroad and voluntarily enlists in the army of a belligerent nation loses the protection of his citizenship while so engaged, and asks why dollars, going abroad and enlisting in war, should be more protected. As we cannot prevent American citizens going abroad at their own risk, so we cannot prevent dollars going abroad at the risk of the owners, but the influence of the Government is used to prevent American citizens from doing this. Would the Government not be justified in using its influence against the enlistment of the nation's dollars in a foreign war?

"Our prosperity is dependent on our continued and enlarged foreign trade. To preserve that we must . . . assist our customers to buy."

The United States Should Permit Loans to the Allies

William Gibbs McAdoo (1863-1941)

When war broke out among the nations of Europe in August 1914, President Woodrow Wilson's immediate response was to declare the United States neutral. Upon the urging of his secretary of state, William Jennings Bryan, Wilson placed the national government on record as frowning on private loans to warring nations as being inconsistent with the spirit of neutrality. The policy left the Allied nations of Great Britain, France, and Russia, which had placed large orders for American supplies, unable to obtain loans from American banks to finance their purchases. (Loans to Germany and the Central Powers were not at issue because trade between them and the United States was negligible—in part because of American sympathies, but also because Great Britain's navy blocked most such trade.)

American bankers and those who supported an Allied victory in the war urged the repeal of the U.S. ban on loans. Among those who doubted the wisdom of the ban was Wilson's secretary of the treasury, William Gibbs McAdoo. A lawyer who had supported Wilson since the 1910 New Jersey gubernatorial campaign, McAdoo had married Wilson's daughter in 1914. His views on loans to the Allied powers can be found in the following letter to the president (whom he continued to address as governor), dated August 21, 1915. McAdoo argues that American economic prosperity would come to a halt if the Allies could not obtain American loans to pay for American goods already purchased or on

Excerpted from William Gibbs McAdoo's letter of August 21, 1915, to President Wilson. Reprinted in Charles Beard, *The Devil Theory of War*, Vanguard Press, 1936.

order. He asserts that American neutrality historically had preserved the right of American manufacturers to sell to warring nations, and that the same policy should hold for American bankers.

The arguments of McAdoo and others persuaded President
Wilson to relax the ban on loans. By early 1917, before the United
States entered the war, American banks loaned more than $1 bil-
lion to Great Britain and more than $300 million to France.

Dear Governor:

You know how loath I am always to burden you with Treasury
affairs, but matters of such great importance have arisen in connection with the financing of our export trade that you ought to
know the facts.

Great Britain is, and always has been, our best customer. Since
the war began, her purchases and those of her allies, France, Russia and Italy, have enormously increased. Food products constitute the greater part of these purchases, but war munitions,
which, as you know, embrace not only arms and ammunition, but
saddles, horses and mules and a variety of things, are a big item.

The high prices for food products have brought great prosperity to our farmers, while the purchases of war munitions have
stimulated industry and have set factories going to full capacity
throughout the great manufacturing districts, while the reduction
of imports and their actual cessation in some cases, have caused
new industries to spring up and others to be enlarged.

Great prosperity is coming. It is, in large measure, here already.
It will be tremendously increased if we can extend reasonable
credits to our customers. The balance of trade is so largely in our
favor and will grow even larger if trade continues that we cannot
demand payments in gold alone, without eventually exhausting
the gold reserves of our best customers which would ruin their
credit and stop their trade with us.

They must begin to cut their purchases from us to the lowest
limit, unless we extend to them reasonable credits. Our prosperity is dependent on our . . . foreign trade. To preserve that we
must do everything we can to assist our customers to buy.

We have repeatedly declared that it is lawful for our citizens to
manufacture and sell to belligerents munitions of war. It is lawful
commerce and being lawful is entitled to the same treatment at
the hands of our bankers, in financing it, as any other part of our
lawful commerce.

Acceptances based upon such exportations of goods are quite
as properly the subject of legitimate bank transactions as if based

Out of the Depths

American neutrality in World War I was severely tested by the sinking of the British passenger ship Lusitania *by a German submarine. The surprise attack killed 128 Americans and increased anti-German sentiment in the United States.*

on non-contraband. We have reaffirmed our position about munitions in our recent note to Austria, clearly and conclusively.

If our national banks are permitted to purchase such acceptances freely, it will greatly relieve the situation. They can do so without any danger of rendering "non-liquid" even a small part of our present extraordinarily large credit resources. But national banks will not buy such acceptances freely unless they know that they are eligible for rediscount at Federal Reserve Banks. . . .

It is imperative for England to establish a large credit in this country. She will need at least $500,000,000. She can't get this in any way, at the moment, that seems feasible, except by sale of short-time government notes. Here she encounters the obstacles presented by Mr. [William Jennings] Bryan's letter of Jan. 20, 1915, to Senator [William] Stone, in which it is stated that "war loans in this country were disapproved because inconsistent with the spirit of neutrality," &c., and "this government has not been advised that any general loans have been made by foreign governments in this country since the *President expressed his wish that loans of this character should not be made.*"

The underscored [italicized] part is the hardest hurdle of the entire letter. Large banking houses here which have the ability to finance a large loan will not do so or even attempt to do, in the face of this declaration. We have tied our hands so that we cannot help ourselves or help our best customers. France and Russia are in the same boat. Each, especially France, needs a large credit here.

The declaration seems to me most illogical and inconsistent. We approve and encourage sales of supplies to England and others, but we disapprove the creation for them of credit balances here to finance their lawful and welcome purchases. We must find some way to give them needed credits, but there is no way, I fear, unless this declaration can be modified. . . .

Notwithstanding Mr. Bryan's letter expressing disapproval of foreign loans, the German Government openly issued and sold last Spring through Chandler Brothers, bankers of Philadelphia and New York, $10,000,000 of its short-time bonds. England and her allies could sell a small amount of obligations, perhaps $25,000,000, in the face of your disapproval as expressed in this letter, but it would be fruitless. The problem is so huge that she must go "whole hog," and she can't do that unless our attitude can be modified.

Perhaps it could be done, if you decided that it should be done at all, by some hint to bankers, although I do not think that would do. In fact, England and her allies will have great difficulty in getting the amount of credit they need here even if our government is openly friendly. I wish you would think about this so we may discuss it when I see you. To maintain our prosperity, we must finance it. Otherwise it may stop and that would be disastrous.

I have not the slightest fear that we shall be embarrassed if we extend huge credits to foreign governments to enable them to buy our products. Our credit resources are simply marvelous now. They are easily five to six billion dollars. We could utilize one billion in financing our foreign trade without inconvenience and with benefit to the country.

VIEWPOINT 5

"The day has come when America is privileged to spend her blood and her might for the principles that gave her birth and happiness."

The United States Should Enter World War I

Woodrow Wilson (1856-1924)

President Woodrow Wilson waited until April 1917 to ask Congress for a declaration of war against Germany. For nearly three years Germany and Austria-Hungary had been at war with England, France, and Russia. Wilson had hoped that the United States would be able to remain neutral, despite the fact that both sides had been guilty of violating what America believed to be its neutral rights. England had mined the North Sea and intercepted American ships and American mail, and English ships had flown the American flag. Germany's actions were more deadly. It had thrown a blockade around England and turned loose the newly invented submarine. The "submarine warfare" tactics of sinking merchant ships without warning could—and did—mean death for Americans riding on ships of warring nations. Still, Wilson had been hesitant to take the United States to war.

In November 1916, Wilson stood for reelection as the peace candidate. Running on the slogan that "He Kept Us Out of War," the incumbent president secured a narrow victory over his Republican challenger, Supreme Court Justice Charles Evans Hughes. Within weeks of that victory Wilson tried one more time to offer American mediation to the warring parties. When no countries responded to his diplomatic overtures, Wilson delivered a speech to the Senate, in which he called for the warring nations to settle for a "peace without victory" that would not force any country to surrender.

Germany's answer to that speech was to embark on unre-

Excerpted from Woodrow Wilson's war message to Congress, April 2, 1917, 65th Cong., 1st sess., S. Doc. 5.

stricted submarine warfare—the sinking without warning of all vessels, American included, that approached England and France. Wilson responded by breaking diplomatic relations with Germany. He then asked Congress for permission to arm American merchant ships. The interception, decoding, and publication of the "Zimmermann Note" from the German foreign minister to his representative in Mexico, proposing a Mexican-German alliance against the United States, was another blow to peace. Worried that his domestic reforms would be neglected, concerned that military preparations would create an all-powerful central government, and anxious to preserve American neutrality, Wilson hesitated before asking Congress for a declaration of war. But in the end he could see no alternative.

In his speech before special joint session of Congress on April 2, 1917, Wilson tried to articulate his reasons for war. He asked his countrymen to embark on a crusade to end all wars by making the world safe for democracy. Only by spurning the nineteenth century tradition of isolationism could Wilson ask his fellow citizens to launch a crusade to bring American ideals of democracy and peace to the other side of the Atlantic. What follows are excerpts from one of the most critical and revealing documents in all of American history, Woodrow Wilson's war message to Congress.

I have called the Congress into extraordinary session because there are serious, very serious, choices of policy to be made, and made immediately, which it was neither right nor constitutionally permissible that I should assume the responsibility of making.

On the 3rd of February last, I officially laid before you the extraordinary announcement of the Imperial German government that on and after the 1st day of February it was its purpose to put aside all restraints of law or of humanity and use its submarines to sink every vessel that sought to approach either the ports of Great Britain and Ireland or the western coasts of Europe or any of the ports controlled by the enemies of Germany within the Mediterranean.

That had seemed to be the object of the German submarine warfare earlier in the war, but since April of last year the Imperial government had somewhat restrained the commanders of its undersea craft in conformity with its promise then given to us that passenger boats should not be sunk and that due warning would be given to all other vessels which its submarines might seek to destroy, when no resistance was offered or escape attempted, and care taken that their crews were given at least a fair chance to save their lives in their open boats. The precautions taken were meager and haphazard enough, as was proved in distressing instance after instance in the progress of the cruel and unmanly business, but a certain degree of restraint was observed.

The new policy has swept every restriction aside. Vessels of every kind, whatever their flag, their character, their cargo, their destination, their errand, have been ruthlessly sent to the bottom without warning and without thought of help or mercy for those on board, the vessels of friendly neutrals along with those of belligerents. Even hospital ships and ships carrying relief to the sorely bereaved and stricken people of Belgium, though the latter were provided with safe conduct through the proscribed areas by

Jay N. Darling. *The Des Moines Register*, 1917.

the German government itself and were distinguished by unmistakable marks of identity, have been sunk with the same reckless lack of compassion or of principle.

I was for a little while unable to believe that such things would in fact be done by any government that had hitherto subscribed to the humane practices of civilized nations. International law had its origin in the attempt to set up some law which would be respected and observed upon the seas, where no nation had right of dominion and where lay the free highways of the world. By painful stage after stage has that law been built up, with meager enough results, . . . but always with a clear view, at least, of what the heart and conscience of mankind demanded.

This minimum of right the German government has swept aside under the plea of retaliation and necessity and because it had no weapons which it could use at sea except these which it is impossible to employ as it is employing them without throwing to the winds all scruples of humanity or of respect for the understandings that were supposed to underlie the intercourse of the world. I am not now thinking of the loss of property involved, immense and serious as that is, but only of the wanton and wholesale destruction of the lives of noncombatants, men, women, and children, engaged in pursuits which have always, even in the darkest periods of modern history, been deemed innocent and legitimate. Property can be paid for; the lives of peaceful and innocent people cannot be.

Not Just America's War

The present German submarine warfare against commerce is a warfare against mankind. It is a war against all nations. American ships have been sunk, American lives taken in ways which it has stirred us very deeply to learn of; but the ships and people of other neutral and friendly nations have been sunk and overwhelmed in the waters in the same way. There has been no discrimination. The challenge is to all mankind.

Each nation must decide for itself how it will meet it. The choice we make for ourselves must be made with a moderation of counsel and a temperateness of judgment befitting our character and our motives as a nation. We must put excited feeling away. Our motive will not be revenge or the victorious assertion of the physical might of the nation, but only the vindication of right, of human right, of which we are only a single champion.

When I addressed the Congress on the 26th of February last, I thought that it would suffice to assert our neutral rights with arms, our right to use the seas against unlawful interference, our right to keep our people safe against unlawful violence. But armed neutrality, it now appears, is impracticable. Because submarines are in effect outlaws when used as the German submarines have been used against merchant shipping, it is impossible to defend ships against their attacks as the law of nations has assumed that merchantmen would defend themselves against privateers or cruisers, visible craft giving chase upon the open sea. . . .

There is one choice we cannot make, we are incapable of making: we will not choose the path of submission and suffer the most sacred rights of our nation and our people to be ignored or violated. The wrongs against which we now array ourselves are no common wrongs; they cut to the very roots of human life.

With a profound sense of the solemn and even tragical character of the step I am taking and of the grave responsibilities which it involves, but in unhesitating obedience to what I deem my constitutional duty, I advise that the Congress declare the recent course of the Imperial German government to be in fact nothing less than war against the government and people of the United States; that it formally accept the status of belligerent which has thus been thrust upon it; and that it take immediate steps, not only to put the country in a more thorough state of defense but also to exert all its power and employ all its resources to bring the government of the German Empire to terms and end the war.

What this will involve is clear. It will involve the utmost practicable cooperation in counsel and action with the governments now at war with Germany and, as incident to that, the extension to those governments of the most liberal financial credits, in order that our resources may so far as possible be added to theirs. It will involve the organization and mobilization of all the material resources of the country to supply the materials of war and serve the incidental needs of the nation in the most abundant and yet the most economical and efficient way possible. It will involve the immediate full equipment of the Navy in all respects but particularly in supplying it with the best means of dealing with the enemy's submarines. It will involve the immediate addition to the armed forces of the United States already provided for by law in case of war at least 500,000 men, who should, in my opinion, be chosen upon the principle of universal liability to service, and also the authorization of subsequent additional increments of equal force so soon as they may be needed and can be handled in training.

It will involve also, of course, the granting of adequate credits to the government, sustained, I hope, so far as they can equitably be sustained by the present generation, by well-conceived taxation. . . .

Our object now, as then, is to vindicate the principles of peace and justice in the life of the world as against selfish and autocratic power and to set up among the really free and self-governed peoples of the world such a concert of purpose and of action as will henceforth ensure the observance of those principles. Neutrality is no longer feasible or desirable where the peace of the world is involved and the freedom of its peoples, and the menace to that peace and freedom lies in the existence of autocratic governments backed by organized force which is controlled wholly by their will, not by the will of their people. We have seen the last of neutrality in such circumstances. We are at the beginning of an age in which it will be insisted that the same standards of conduct and of responsibility for wrong done shall be observed among nations and their governments that are observed among the individual citizens of civilized states.

No Enmity for the German People

We have no quarrel with the German people. We have no feeling toward them but one of sympathy and friendship. It was not upon their impulse that their government acted in entering this war. It was not with their previous knowledge or approval. It was a war determined upon as wars used to be determined upon in the old, unhappy days when peoples were nowhere consulted by their rulers and wars were provoked and waged in the interest of dynasties or of little groups of ambitious men who were accustomed to use their fellowmen as pawns and tools.

Self-governed nations do not fill their neighbor states with spies or set the course of intrigue to bring about some critical posture of affairs which will give them an opportunity to strike and make conquest. Such designs can be successfully worked out only under cover and where no one has the right to ask questions. Cunningly contrived plans of deception or aggression, carried, it may be, from generation to generation, can be worked out and kept from the light only within the privacy of courts or behind the carefully guarded confidences of a narrow and privileged class. They are happily impossible where public opinion commands and insists upon full information concerning all the nation's affairs.

A steadfast concert for peace can never be maintained except by a partnership of democratic nations. No autocratic government could be trusted to keep faith within it or observe its covenants. It must be a league of honor, a partnership of opinion. Intrigue would eat its vitals away; the plottings of inner circles who could plan what they would and render account to no one would be a corruption seated at its very heart. Only free peoples can hold their purpose and their honor steady to a common end and prefer the interests of mankind to any narrow interest of their own.

Does not every American feel that assurance has been added to our hope for the future peace of the world by the wonderful and heartening things that have been happening within the last few weeks in Russia? Russia was known by those who knew it best to have been always in fact democratic at heart, in all the vital habits

Profit Is Not U.S. Goal

James A. Reed was a Democratic senator from Missouri from 1911 to 1929. In this passage from the senatorial debate over President Wilson's call for declaration of war, he rejects the notion that U.S. entry into World War I is motivated by monetary concerns.

Sir, this war is not being waged over dollars. It is not being waged over commerce. It is not being waged over profits and losses. It is a war for the maintenance of the sovereign rights of the American Republic and for the preservation of American dignity in the councils of the nations of the earth.

There was a time when Great Britain sought to levy a little tax on tea. The tax amounted to nothing from the dollar-and-cent standpoint. . . . But there were patriots in that day who knew that a great principle was involved. They knew it was not a question of dollars. They knew that liberty was involved. They knew that back of the taxgatherer stood the power of a great country, that proposed to lay its heavy hand upon the liberties of this people; and so those Boston men went forth not to resist the tax, but to resist tyranny; not to save money, but to pour out their lifeblood that liberty might live on this side of the Atlantic.

And to-day, as the President of the United States calls our country to arms, he does not do so because of the loss of a few paltry dollars. He calls us to arms because the life of this Republic, its honor and its integrity, have been assailed. He calls us to arms in order that the rights of the American Nation upon the high seas shall not be sacrificed. He calls us to arms to the end that neutral nations, great and small, shall not be crushed beneath the iron heel of that military despotism which to-day threatens not alone the civilization of Europe but of the world at large.

of her thought, in all the intimate relationships of her people that spoke their natural instinct, their habitual attitude toward life. The autocracy that crowned the summit of her political structure, long as it had stood and terrible as was the reality of its power, was not in fact Russian in origin, character, or purpose; and now it has been shaken off and the great, generous Russian people have been added in all their naive majesty and might to the forces that are fighting for freedom in the world, for justice, and for peace. Here is a fit partner for a League of Honor.

One of the things that has served to convince us that the Prussian autocracy was not and could never be our friend is that from the very outset of the present war it has filled our unsuspecting communities and even our offices of government with spies and set criminal intrigues everywhere afoot against our national unity of counsel, our peace within and without, our industries and our commerce. Indeed, it is now evident that its spies were here even before the war began; and it is unhappily not a matter of conjecture but a fact proved in our courts of justice that the intrigues which have more than once come perilously near to disturbing the peace and dislocating the industries of the country have been carried on at the instigation, with the support, and even under the personal direction of official agents of the Imperial government accredited to the government of the United States.

Even in checking these things and trying to extirpate them, we have sought to put the most generous interpretation possible upon them because we knew that their source lay, not in any hostile feeling or purpose of the German people toward us (who were no doubt as ignorant of them as we ourselves were) but only in the selfish designs of a government that did what it pleased and told its people nothing. But they have played their part in serving to convince us at last that that government entertains no real friendship for us and means to act against our peace and security at its convenience. That it means to stir up enemies against us at our very doors the intercepted note to the German minister at Mexico City is eloquent evidence.

We are accepting this challenge of hostile purpose because we know that in such a government, following such methods, we can never have a friend; and that in the presence of its organized power, always lying in wait to accomplish we know not what purpose, there can be no assured security for the democratic governments of the world. We are now about to accept gage of battle with this natural foe to liberty and shall, if necessary, spend the whole force of the nation to check and nullify its pretensions and its power. We are glad, now that we see the facts with no veil of false pretense about them, to fight thus for the ultimate peace of the world and for the liberation of its peoples, the German peoples included: for the rights of nations great and small and the privilege of men everywhere to choose their way of life and of obedience.

The world must be made safe for democracy. Its peace must be planted upon the tested foundations of political liberty. We have no selfish ends to serve. We desire no conquest, no dominion. We seek no indemnities for ourselves, no material compensation for the sacrifices we shall freely make. We are but one of the champions of the rights of mankind. We shall be satisfied when those rights have been made as secure as the faith and the freedom of nations can make them.

Just because we fight without rancor and without selfish object, seeking nothing for ourselves but what we shall wish to share with all free peoples, we shall, I feel confident, conduct our operations as belligerents without passion and ourselves observe with proud punctilio the principles of right and of fair play we profess to be fighting for. . . .

It will be all the easier for us to conduct ourselves as belligerents in a high spirit of right and fairness because we act without animus, not in enmity toward a people or with the desire to bring any injury or disadvantage upon them, but only in armed opposition to an irresponsible government which has thrown aside all considerations of humanity and of right and is running amuck. We are, let me say again, the sincere friends of the German people, and shall desire nothing so much as the early reestablishment of intimate relations of mutual advantage between us—however hard it may be for them, for the time being, to believe that this is spoken from our hearts.

We have borne with their present government through all these bitter months because of that friendship—exercising a patience and forbearance which would otherwise have been impossible. We shall, happily, still have an opportunity to prove that friendship in our daily attitude and actions toward the millions of men and women of German birth and native sympathy who live among us and share our life, and we shall be proud to prove it toward all who are in fact loyal to their neighbors and to the government in the hour of test. They are, most of them, as true and loyal Americans as if they had never known any other fealty or allegiance. They will be prompt to stand with us in rebuking and restraining the few who may be of a different mind and purpose. If there should be disloyalty, it will be dealt with with a firm hand of stern repression; but, if it lifts its head at all, it will lift it only here and there and without countenance except from a lawless and malignant few.

It is a distressing and oppressive duty, gentlemen of the Congress, which I have performed in thus addressing you. There are, it may be, many months of fiery trial and sacrifice ahead of us. It is a fearful thing to lead this great peaceful people into war, into the most terrible and disastrous of all wars, civilization itself seeming to be in the balance. But the right is more precious than peace, and we shall fight for the things which we have always carried nearest our hearts—for democracy, for the right of those who submit to authority to have a voice in their own governments, for the rights and liberties of small nations, for a universal dominion of right by such a concert of free peoples as shall bring peace and safety to all nations and make the world itself at last free.

To such a task we can dedicate our lives and our fortunes, everything that we are and everything that we have, with the pride of those who know that the day has come when America is privileged to spend her blood and her might for the principles that gave her birth and happiness and the peace which she has treasured. God helping her, she can do no other.

VIEWPOINT 6

"The troubles of Europe ought to be settled by Europe, and . . . we ought to . . . permit them to settle their questions without our interference."

The United States Should Not Enter World War I

George W. Norris (1861-1944)

President Woodrow Wilson's April 2, 1917, address to Congress, in which he asked its members to declare war on Germany, was followed by four days of intense debate. On April 6 Congress voted for war, with only fifty representatives and six senators dissenting. One of the six opposing votes in the Senate was cast by Nebraska senator George W. Norris. Norris, a progressive Republican, had been elected to the U.S. Senate in 1912, having served in the House of Representatives since 1903. He would remain in the Senate until 1942.

Norris gained national attention with his speech against war given on April 4, 1917, excerpts of which are reprinted below. He argues that entering the war on the side of Great Britain against Germany because of German violations of American neutral rights is objectionable because both Great Britain and Germany violated international law by attacking American shipping. He accuses Wilson of showing favoritism toward Great Britain in his foreign policy.

In stark contrast to Wilson, who argued that war was necessary to preserve principles of democracy and international law and order, Norris asserts that the motive for an American declaration of war was profit—profit for arms manufacturers, profit for American banks who had loaned millions of dollars to the Allies, and

George W. Norris, *Congressional Record*, 65th Cong., 1st sess. (April 4, 1917), pp. 212-14.

profit for the stock market financiers on Wall Street. Norris concludes his speech with a call to heed George Washington's original warning against involvement in European conflicts, and argues that European problems must be solved by its people, much as America dealt with its own internal problems in the Civil War.

Mr. NORRIS. Mr. President,

The resolution now before the Senate is a declaration of war. Before taking this momentous step, and while standing on the brink of this terrible vortex, we ought to pause and calmly and judiciously consider the terrible consequences of the step we are about to take. We ought to consider likewise the route we have recently traveled and ascertain whether we have reached our present position in a way that is compatible with the neutral position which we claimed to occupy at the beginning and through the various stages of this unholy and unrighteous war.

No close student of recent history will deny that both Great Britain and Germany have, on numerous occasions since the beginning of the war, flagrantly violated in the most serious manner the rights of neutral vessels and neutral nations under existing international law as recognized up to the beginning of this war by the civilized world.

The reason given by the President in asking Congress to declare war against Germany is that the German Government has declared certain war zones, within which, by the use of submarines, she sinks, without notice, American ships and destroys American lives.

A Little History

Let us trace briefly the origin and history of these so-called war zones. The first war zone was declared by Great Britain. She gave us and the world notice of it on the 4th day of November, 1914. The zone became effective November 5, 1914, the next day after the notice was given. This zone so declared by Great Britain covered the whole of the North Sea. The order establishing it sought to close the north of Scotland route around the British Isles to Denmark, Holland, Norway, Sweden, and the Baltic Sea. The decree of establishment drew an arbitrary line from the Hebrides Islands along the Scottish coast to Iceland, and warned neutral shipping that it would cross those lines at its peril, and ordered that ships might go to Holland and other neutral nations by taking the English Channel route through the Strait of Dover.

The first German war zone was declared on the 4th day of

February, 1915, just three months after the British war zone was declared. Germany gave 15 days' notice of the establishment of her zone, which became effective on the 18th day of February, 1915. The German war zone covered the English Channel and the high sea waters around the British Isles. It sought to close the English Channel route around the British Isles to Holland, Norway, Sweden, Denmark, and the Baltic Sea. The German war zone decreed that neutral vessels would be exposed to danger in the English Channel route, but that the route around the north of Scotland and in the eastern part of the North Sea, in a strip 30 miles wide along the Dutch coast, would be free from danger.

Senator George W. Norris opposed U.S. involvement in both World War I and the League of Nations.

It will thus be seen that the British Government declared the north of Scotland route into the Baltic Sea as dangerous and the English Channel route into the Baltic Sea as safe.

The German Government in its order did exactly the reverse. It declared the north of Scotland route into the Baltic Sea as safe and the English Channel route into the Baltic Sea as dangerous. . . .

Thus we have the two declarations of the two Governments, each declaring a military zone and warning neutral shipping from going into the prohibited area. England sought to make her order effective by the use of submerged mines. Germany sought to make her order effective by the use of submarines. Both of these orders were illegal and contrary to all international law as well as the principles of humanity. Under international law no

69

belligerent Government has the right to place submerged mines in the high seas. Neither has it any right to take human life without notice by the use of submarines. If there is any difference on the ground of humanity between these two instrumentalities, it is certainly in favor of the submarines. The submarine can exercise some degree of discretion and judgment. The submerged mine always destroys without notice, friend and foe alike, guilty and innocent the same. In carrying out these two policies, both Great Britain and Germany have sunk American ships and destroyed American lives without provocation and without notice. There have been more ships sunk and more American lives lost from the action of submarines than from English mines in the North Sea: for the simple reason that we finally acquiesced in the British war zone and kept our ships out of it, while in the German war zone we have refused to recognize its legality and have not kept either our ships or our citizens out of its area. If American ships had gone into the British war zone in defiance of Great Britain's order, as they have gone into the German war zone in defiance of the German Government's order, there would have been many more American lives lost and many more American ships sunk by the instrumentality of the mines than the instrumentality of the submarines.

A Neutral America?

We have in the main complied with the demands made by Great Britain. Our ships have followed the instructions of the British Government in going not only to England but to the neutral nations of the world, and in thus complying with the British order American ships going to Holland, Denmark, Norway, and Sweden have been taken by British officials into British ports, and their cargoes inspected and examined. All the mails we have carried even to neutral countries have been opened and censored, and oftentimes the entire cargo confiscated by the Government. Nothing has been permitted to pass to even the most neutral nations except after examination and with the permission of the officials of the British Government.

I have outlined the beginning of the controversy. I have given in substance the orders of both of these great Governments that constituted the beginning of our controversy with each. . . .

The only difference is that in the case of Germany we have persisted in our protest, while in the case of England we have submitted. What was our duty as a Government and what were our rights when we were confronted with these extraordinary orders declaring these military zones? First, we could have defied both of them and could have gone to war against both of these nations for this violation of international law and interference with our

70

neutral rights. Second, we had the technical right to defy one and to acquiesce in the other. Third, we could, while denouncing them both as illegal, have acquiesced in them both and thus remained neutral with both sides, although not agreeing with either as to the righteousness of their respective orders. We could have said to American shipowners that, while these orders are both contrary to international law and are both unjust, we do not believe that the provocation is sufficient to cause us to go to war for the defense of our rights as a neutral nation, and, therefore, American ships and American citizens will go into these zones at their own peril and risk. Fourth, we might have declared an embargo against the shipping from American ports of any merchandise to either one of these Governments that persisted in maintaining its military zone. We might have refused to permit the sailing of any ship from any American port to either of these military zones. In my judgment, if we had pursued this course, the zones would have been of short duration. England would have been compelled to take her mines out of the North Sea in order to get any supplies from our country. When her mines were taken out of the North Sea then the German ports upon the North Sea would have been accessible to American shipping and Germany would have been compelled to cease her submarine warfare in order to get any supplies from our Nation into German North Sea ports.

There are a great many American citizens who feel that we owe it as a duty to humanity to take part in this war. Many instances of cruelty and inhumanity can be found on both sides. Men are often biased in their judgment on account of their sympathy and their interests. To my mind, what we ought to have maintained from the beginning was the strictest neutrality. If we had done this I do not believe we would have been on the verge of war at the present time. We had a right as a nation, if we desired, to cease at any time to be neutral. We had a technical right to respect the English war zone and to disregard the German war zone, but we could not do that and be neutral. I have no quarrel to find with the man who does not desire our country to remain neutral. While many such people are moved by selfish motives and hopes of gain, I have no doubt but that in a great many instances, through what I believe to be a misunderstanding of the real condition, there are many honest, patriotic citizens who think we ought to engage in this war and who are behind the President in his demand that we should declare war against Germany. I think such people err in judgment and to a great extent have been misled as to the real history and the true facts by the almost unanimous demand of the great combination of wealth that has a direct financial interest in our participation in the war. We have loaned many hundreds of millions of dollars to the allies in this controversy. While such action was legal and countenanced by international law, there is no doubt in my mind but the enormous amount of money loaned to the allies in this country has been instrumental in bringing about a public sentiment in favor of our country taking a course that would make every bond worth a hundred cents on the dollar and making the payment of every debt certain and sure. Through this instrumentality and also through the instrumentality of others who have not only made millions out of the war in the manufacture of munitions, etc., and who would expect to make millions more if our country can be drawn into the catastrophe, a large number of the great newspapers and news agencies of the country have been controlled and enlisted in the greatest propaganda that the world has ever known, to manufacture sentiment in favor of war. It is now demanded that the American citizens shall be used as insurance policies to guarantee the safe delivery of munitions of war to belligerent nations. The enormous profits of munition manufacturers, stockbrokers, and bond dealers must be still further increased by our entrance into the war. This has brought us to the present moment, when Congress, urged by the President and backed by the artificial sentiment, is about to declare war and engulf our country in the greatest holocaust that the world has ever known. . . .

American People Oppose War

Robert M. La Follette, a Wisconsin senator from 1906 to 1925, was the most famous of the six senators who voted against U.S. entry into World War I. In this excerpt from his speech on the Senate floor on April 4, 1917, he argues that the war lacks the support of the American people.

Will the President and the supporters of this war bill submit it to a vote of the people before the declaration of war goes into effect? Until we are willing to do that, it illy becomes us to offer as an excuse for our entry into the war the unsupported claim that this war was forced upon the German people by their government "without their previous knowledge or approval."

Who has registered the knowledge or approval of the American people of the course this Congress is called upon to take in declaring war upon Germany? Submit the question to the people, you who support it. You who support it dare not do it, for you know that by a vote of more than ten to one the American people as a body would register their declaration against it.

To whom does war bring prosperity? Not to the soldier who for the munificent compensation of $16 per month shoulders his musket and goes into the trench, there to shed his blood and to die if necessary; not to the broken-hearted widow who waits for the return of the mangled body of her husband; not to the mother who weeps at the death of her brave boy; not to the little children who shiver with cold; not to the babe who suffers from hunger; nor to the millions of mothers and daughters who carry broken hearts to their graves. War brings no prosperity to the great mass of common and patriotic citizens. It increases the cost of living of those who toil and those who already must strain every effort to keep soul and body together. War brings prosperity to the stock gambler on Wall Street—to those who are already in possession of more wealth than can be realized or enjoyed. . . .

Their object in having war and in preparing for war is to make money. Human suffering and the sacrifice of human life are necessary, but Wall Street considers only the dollars and the cents. . . . The stock brokers would not, of course, go to war, because the very object they have in bringing on the war is profit, and therefore they must remain in their Wall Street offices in order to share in that great prosperity which they say war will bring. The volunteer officer, even the drafting officer, will not find them. They will be concealed in their palatial offices on Wall Street, sitting behind mahogany desks, covered up with clipped coupons coupons soiled with the sweat of honest toil, coupons stained with mothers' tears, coupons dyed in the lifeblood of their fellow men.

We are taking a step to day that is fraught with untold danger. We are going into war upon the command of gold. We are going to run the risk of sacrificing millions of our countrymen's lives in order that other countrymen may coin their lifeblood into money. And even if we do not cross the Atlantic and go into the trenches, we are going to pile up a debt that the toiling masses that shall come many generations after us will have to pay. Unborn millions will bend their backs in toil in order to pay for the terrible step we are now about to take. We are about to do the bidding of wealth's terrible mandate. By our act we will make millions of our countrymen suffer, and the consequences of it may well be that millions of our brethren must shed their lifeblood, millions of broken-hearted women must weep, millions of children must suffer with cold, and millions of babes must die from hunger, and all because we want to preserve the commercial right of American citizens to deliver munitions of war to belligerent nations. . . .

A Final Plea

I know that I am powerless to stop it. I know that this war madness has taken possession of the financial and political powers of our country. I know that nothing I can say will stay the blow that is soon to fall. I feel that we are committing a sin against humanity and against our countrymen. I would like to say to this war god, You shall not coin into gold the lifeblood of my brethren. I would like to prevent this terrible catastrophe from falling upon my people. I would be willing to surrender my own life if I could cause this awful cup to pass. I charge no man here with a wrong motive, but it seems to me that this war craze has robbed us of our judgment. I wish we might delay our action until reason could again be enthroned in the brain of man. I feel that we are about to put the dollar sign upon the American flag.

I have no sympathy with the military spirit that dominates the Kaiser and his advisers. I do not believe that they represent the heart of the great German people. I have no more sympathy with the submarine policy of Germany than I have with the mine-laying policy of England. I have heard with rejoicing of the over-throw of the Czar of Russia and the movement in that great country toward the establishment of a government where the common people will have their rights, liberty, and freedom respected. I hope and pray that a similar revolution may take place in Germany, that the Kaiser may be overthrown, and that on the ruins of his military despotism may be established a German republic, where the great German people may work out their world destiny. The working out of that problem is not an American burden. We ought to remember the advice of the Father of our Country and keep out of entangling alliances. Let Europe solve her problems as we have solved ours. Let Europe bear her burdens as we have borne ours. In the greatest war of our history and at the time it occurred, the greatest war in the world's history, we were engaged in solving an American problem. We settled the question of human slavery and washed our flag clean by the sacrifice of human blood. It was a great problem and a great burden, but we solved it ourselves. Never once did we think of asking Europe to take part in its solution. Never once did any European nation undertake to settle the great question. We solved it, and history has rendered a unanimous verdict that we solved it right. The troubles of Europe ought to be settled by Europe, and wherever our sympathies may lie, disagreeing as we do, we ought to remain absolutely neutral and permit them to settle their questions without our interference. We are now the greatest neutral nation. Upon the passage of this resolution we will have joined Europe in the great catastrophe and taken America into entanglements that will not end with this war, but will live and bring their evil influences upon many generations yet unborn.

"We are disloyal to our ideals if we refuse to let our country enlist in this cause."

The United States Should Join the League of Nations

James D. Phelan (1861-1930)

President Woodrow Wilson viewed American participation in World War I as an opportunity to shape the subsequent peace. On January 8, 1918, he made a speech in which he listed what became known as the Fourteen Points that described his vision for a just and lasting peace. The Fourteen Points included a call for non-secretive peace treaties, freedom of the seas, self-government for European national groups, a reduction of armaments, and the removal of tariff barriers. Wilson's Fourteenth Point proposed that

> A general association of nations must be formed under specific covenants for the purpose of affording mutual guarantees of political independence and territorial integrity to great and small states alike.

Following Germany's surrender in November 1918, Wilson traveled to Paris, France, as head of the U.S. peace delegation (becoming the first president to leave the country while in office). Although Wilson made several compromises on his Fourteen Points in negotiating the Treaty of Versailles with the Allied nations and Germany, one point he held firm on was the creation of a League of Nations to prevent war. Wilson personally wrote much of the League Covenant (constitution) that created the international organization. The League of Nations was to consist of an Assembly to represent all member nations, a Council controlled by the leading powers including the United States, and a

James D. Phelan, *Congressional Record*, 66th Cong., 1st sess. (March 3, 1919), pp. 4870-71.

Permanent Court of International Justice. Member nations were pledged to arbitrate their differences, to seek disarmament, and to act together against aggressors that threatened the "territorial integrity" of countries.

Wilson's task was not over when he returned briefly to the United States in February 1919. He faced not only months of negotiating ahead in Paris, but also growing opposition in the U.S. Senate, where the Treaty of Versailles (which included the League of Nations) would have to be ratified by a two-thirds majority. For the next year the Senate was locked in a bitter debate over whether the United States should join the League.

The following viewpoint is taken from a speech by one of Wilson's backers, Democratic senator James D. Phelan of California. Phelan, a former mayor of San Francisco, served in the U.S. Senate from 1915 to 1921. On February 20, 1919, he delivered a speech in San Francisco before a meeting of the League to Enforce Peace, an organization of Republican internationalists. The meeting was chaired by the organization's leader, former U.S. president William Howard Taft, a supporter of the League of Nations. In his address, later entered in the *Congressional Record*, Phelan urges ratification of the Treaty of Versailles. He argues that the time has come for the United States to change its isolationist traditions, and that the views expressed in George Washington's famous Farewell Address are not applicable in an era when the United States is "the most powerful country in the world."

Now, I should think that all men of good will would support the principle of the league of nations. We may differ as to the details of the power which might be granted to the league. But as to the essential principle, to organize to avert the horrors of war, if possible, in this world, there can be no question. . . .

There is no partisanship involved in this. As President Taft said the other day, "In matters international, Woodrow Wilson and myself stand together." [Applause.] And the gentlemen who are so fond these days of quoting George Washington must have forgotten that in the Farewell Address there is a condemnation of partisan spirit. It was one of the things against which he warned his countrymen. And now they are suffering the partisan spirit to influence their sober judgment.

Woodrow Wilson declared long ago that the object of this war— and, I remember, he declared it at the tomb of Washington at Mount Vernon—was to establish "a reign of law with the consent

The League of Nations Argument in a Nutshell

Jay N. Darling, *The Des Moines Register*, 1919.

of the governed and sustained by the organized opinion of mankind." [Applause.] The organized opinion of mankind means nothing less than a league of nations, because it is only through the nations, unless you are ready to destroy all international barriers, that the opinion of mankind can be organized. And he has been busy ever since in making good his word.

But those Senators—and you see I am not in accord with their utterances, and they represent, I am glad to assure the league, a very small minority, I believe, of that body [applause]—are fond of quoting Washington, who warned us also against international entanglements. That sounds very good. But Washington also said in a letter to one of his contemporaries that we can not participate in European affairs for at least 20 years, because we have not the power to treat with them on terms of equality, and we might endanger our hard-won independence. But 120 years have passed, and the United States is the most powerful Nation in the world. [Applause.] So what Washington said at that time, modified by his own words in private correspondence, certainly does not apply to the United States today. And, as the object of this war was to give democracy to the small nations, and to the large ones as well, and to destroy autocracy and tyranny, George Washington, undoubtedly, if consulted, would say, "Those are the very purposes to which I have dedicated my word and my sword," and he would speed us on that road.

If we were acting contrary to the principles of Washington and the Fathers, it might be well to call a halt and say that we are traveling upon forbidden ground. But we have gone to Europe, and our boys have given the decisive blow to autocracy [applause], and this is merely a question in the organization of a league, of something to sustain them in their work. And I feel that there should be as much enthusiasm in this cause as there was in that other cause when we believed that our national rights at home and abroad, aye, our national existence, perhaps was involved in the issue of the conflict; because we can not sit down now and serenely regard Europe. On the contrary, the situation is full of misgivings. I will not enlarge upon the argument, which has been so elaborately set forth by our worthy President. But he has told you again and again that a large number of small countries have been set up and given democracy, and if they be abandoned to their fate we will have, within a very short time, the most horrible war in history in its ferocity, outclassing and distancing the conflict through which we have just passed. Because racial animosities would be aroused, and the old order, often sleeping but never dying, in clashes like this will reassert itself, and the little countries will make a futile resistance and be again amalgamated in the great nations over which tyrants will rule.

A Plea for the League

So, unless this league is established, there is absolutely no hope for democratic Europe; there will be no hope for the men, women, and children; there will be no hope for the workers, because their protection is in the establishment and in the maintenance of democracy, in which their voices are so tremendously potent. They are rudely expressing themselves in some of the countries today. But looking back upon history, we must not be alarmed, because it is only through revolution that order comes. That is the world's history. That must not discourage us. But when they return to reason and know that in this world there must be responsible government, without which there will be neither labor nor wages, then and in that event they will, I am convinced, yield to the arguments which have been advanced in their interests.

It has been said that a league of nations is impossible. When the American Engineers went to Europe, and when we shipped over two millions of men, with all the accessories of war, and built railroads and built great warehouses and provided the food not only

No Middle Course

In an attempt to gain public support for the League of Nations, President Woodrow Wilson went on a speaking tour of the United States. This passage is taken from a speech he made on September 25, 1919. Shortly afterward, Wilson collapsed and suffered a stroke, ending his leadership in the fight to pass the treaty.

We have got to do one or other of two things—we have got to adopt it or reject it. There is no middle course. You cannot go in on a special-privilege basis of our own. I take it that you are too proud to ask to be exempted from responsibilities which the other members of the League will carry. We go in upon equal terms or we do not go in at all; and if we do not go in, my fellow citizens, think of the tragedy of that result—the only sufficient guarantee to the peace of the world withheld! Ourselves drawn apart with that dangerous pride which means that we shall be ready to take care of ourselves, and that means that we shall maintain great standing armies and an irresistible navy; that means we shall have the organization of a military nation; that means we shall have a general staff, with the kind of power that the general staff of Germany had; to mobilize this great manhood of the Nation when it pleases, all the energy of our young men drawn into the thought and preparation for war. What of our pledges to the men that lie dead in France? We said that they went over there not to prove the prowess of America or her readiness for another war but to see to it that there never was such a war again. It always seems to make it difficult for me to say anything, my fellow citizens, when I think of my clients in this case. My clients are the children; my clients are the next generation. They do not know what promises and bonds I undertook when I ordered the armies of the United States to the soil of France, but I know, and I intend to redeem my pledges to the children; they shall not be sent upon a similar errand.

for our own men but for the men of other lands, it was an achievement of great magnitude. And somebody said, and I believe it has clung as a sentiment to the American Engineers, "It can not be done, but here it is!" A league can not be formed, but here it is. [Applause.] The President is on the ocean bearing the first draft, adopted unanimously, under pressure which I believe he exerted, as the one thing that he desired of all others to bring back to his countrymen as the reward of the war—not captives, not lands and territory, but peace for all the world. What greater ideal could there be? What greater achievement could he have won? And that is a thing accomplished by unanimous vote. The nations in conference having approved of the idea of the league, and their committee has drafted this measure, which will very soon, probably, be presented in an authoritative way by the President himself to the American people. And then he will go back, having consulted public sentiment—and, by the way, that is the work we are doing here, creating a public sentiment, without which there can be no government, and without which the President unsustained would be a mere pawn upon the European chessboard. He must have it, and he knows it, because his democracy is pure. He knows that without the people he can not succeed, and he always appeals over the heads of Senators and editors, even, to the great body of the people. [Applause.]

And I think, Mr. President, that it is more important for the audiences which you address throughout the land to respond to this call than it is for individual Senators, because the Senators, I must say in their defense, feel that after all they are representatives of the people. It is not the body that it was in the olden time—now your Senators come from the people, elected by popular vote, and not puppets set up by legislatures to serve private interests. They are amenable to your demands. They respond to your call. And I am glad to see here an audience so great tonight, because every man and woman of you must feel that you are rendering a substantial aid in the settlement of this question. If you show apathy, your representatives will show apathy. If you show interest, they will show interest. If you are for it, they are for it. [Applause.]

Individuals and Nations

One word more, Mr. President. I suppose the argument has often been made; but it seems to me that in its simplest form a league of nations bears a close analogy to civil society. Democracy is a league of men, banded together for mutual protection. And they yield certain of their natural rights for the purpose of establishing this democracy as ordered government. In a league of nations the nations must necessarily yield some of the exclusive rights which they now hold for the same purpose—their mutual protection. Is there anything wrong with that? Is the right of the individual more sacred than the right of the nation? But grant for the moment that it is. It is yielded willingly in the interest of organized government, organized democracies, where all have a voice and where all thrive; it is their self-determination, freely given, and all abide by the result of the expression of that voice, and the minorities are given protection. They are not destroyed, as in the old days of the Crusaders. And you may recall in this connection the story of the Crusader, who was told on his deathbed that he had to repent and forgive his enemies, and he naïvely responded, "Why, I have no enemies; I have killed them all." But a democracy respects the minority which does not quite agree with the majority government, and that is a little sacrifice they must make in order to preserve the peace of society.

Now, the United States, going into a compact of this kind will, let us concede to the objecting Senators, yield a part of what they regard as their exclusive rights about which they are very tender. But is not the prize worth the game? Is not the peace of the world worth the sacrifice? [Applause.] Is there anything more terrible than unleashed human beings destroying each other under circumstances of greatest cruelty? War, we are told, burdens a people with debt to go down from one generation to another, like the curse of original sin. It wipes the people from the earth as though Heaven had repented the making of man. Its evils can not be written, even in human blood. And our campaign is against war. And in that campaign every man is enlisted as a patriot, just as much as every man was enlisted in our recent campaign, where his loyalty was never questioned, to carry the Stars and Stripes, standing for equal rights and justice throughout the benighted countries of Europe and bringing hope and succor to those who for centuries have been the victims of oppression.

But we are disloyal to our ideals if we refuse to let our country enlist in this cause. We are all, by sacrifice and concession, working for a perfect State at home. The league is working for a more perfect world. And, my friends, just as the organization of society has abolished violence in the settlement of disputes and set up legislatures and courts, so this league of nations, if it carries its purpose through to the finish by creating international tribunals, will abolish war, which is only violence on a broader scale. Let us not dismiss this question by saying it belongs only to the sentimental. Sentiment is the best thing in the world, and the difficulty is in living up to it. Human nature is the meanest thing about us, and we are always trying to keep it down. That is the function of society; it is as well the function of the league.

VIEWPOINT 8

"The ... league of nations is a Pandora's box of evil to empty upon the American people the aggregated calamities of the world."

The United States Should Not Join the League of Nations

Lawrence Sherman (1858-1939)

When President Woodrow Wilson journeyed to Paris to negotiate the peace treaty following World War I, one of his major goals was the creation of an international organization to prevent future wars. Wilson succeeded in including the charter for the League of Nations in the Treaty of Versailles, but he ran into opposition in the U.S. Senate, which had to ratify the treaty by a two-thirds majority to complete his work.

One element of opposition centered around Henry Cabot Lodge, the new chairman of the Senate Foreign Relations Committee. The Massachusetts Republican circulated a letter, signed by thirty-nine senators and senators-elect (which was more than enough votes necessary to defeat the treaty), that stated that it was "the sense of the Senate that . . . the constitution of the league of nations in the form now proposed . . . should not be accepted by the United States." Lodge and his conservative Republican allies were not necessarily opposed to the concept of a league of nations, but they did want to embarrass the Democratic president and ensure that, if ratified, the League of Nations would not restrict American freedom of action.

A dozen other senators, dubbed the "irreconcilables," opposed the League in any form. One was Republican senator Lawrence

Lawrence Sherman, *Congressional Record*, 66th Cong., 1st sess. (March 3, 1919), pp. 4865-67.

Sherman of Illinois, a Springfield lawyer who served in the Senate from 1913 to 1921. Sherman was an outspoken opponent of the League, viewing it as an invitation to "become the knight-errant of the world." The League was a kind of world government, he believed, and no world government could or would pay attention to American interests.

Taking the floor to debate the issue on March 13, 1919 (when the president was making a brief return visit to the United States to drum up support for his treaty), Sherman, in his remarks excerpted in this viewpoint, stakes out a position of classic American isolationism, which highlights the differences between the Old World and the New, between a European heritage of "war" and an American heritage of "peace."

The combination of the opposition of the "irreconcilables," Lodge's delaying tactics and political stratagems, and Wilson's stubborn refusal to accept any compromises doomed Wilson's grand vision of a League of Nations to political defeat as the Senate refused to ratify the Treaty of Versailles.

Mr. President, the President and his appointees on the peace conference have no instructions from the American people to bind them in a perpetual alliance with the several nations of the earth. The Senate has no popular mandate to ratify such a proposed treaty. Neither the President nor the Senate nor both jointly has power to abrogate the Constitution that created them or transfer the sovereignty of the United States nor any of its essential attributes to any other human authority exercising or attempting to exercise that sovereignty over our Government or our citizens.

The qualified voters of this country and the indestructible States are the source of sovereignty. From them sprang the Federal Government, dual in nature and national in character. This mechanism so framed operates by the power transmitted through frequent elections and regulated by constitutional grants and limitations. Nowhere is the Government, its Congress, its Executive, or its courts given authority to surrender or transfer its powers to any alien creation. . . .

This peace conference will be a body of men from many nations, languages, customs, standards of conduct, races, habits, and religions. Their hopes, purposes, and national ideals develop under widely varying impulses. They may or may not excel ours and surpass us in the several fields of human achievement.

That is not the issue. What must be steadily seen is committing our country and our lives and our posterity irrevocably to an invisible and unknown power. If we cut the cables of constitutional government here we are caught in the irresistible tides that sweep us into the maelstrom of the Old World's bloody currents flowing from every shore. The feuds and spoliations of a thousand years become our daily chart of action. It is not do they threaten or menace us. All we can know is a few men in some hidden chamber, known as the executive council [of the League of Nations], wield over us powers of life and death.

An oligarchy is the worst possible form of government. The executive council is the worst possible form of an oligarchy. It orders Congress today to send half a million of our young men into central Asia to be hacked to pieces on the plateau of Tibet. Tomorrow Egypt is assailed by desert hordes and more levies are sent to slaughter in a struggle that does not remotely concern our peace.

We are not colonizers. We have not sought to sound our morning drumbeats around the world. From the day the first settler landed on the James River in the Old Dominion [Virginia] and the Pilgrim's prayer rose in the primeval forest of the old Bay State [Massachusetts] we have been content to cultivate and develop this our portion of the continent, and point the way for the industrious God-fearing immigrant to make a new home from across the sea. The great labor-saving machines, the communication of thought, the secrets of nature's processes seized and adapted to human use, the greatest of world discoveries have been our contribution to mankind.

The Old World

While nations fought for supremacy and territory around the globe, we labored with what we had to make the most of our blessings. They desolated the earth for glory and for gold. We tilled the earth and sailed the seas in peace. In turn the Dane, the Spaniard, the Briton, the Frank, and the Hun has stripped the confines of every land of its gold. The American has dug it from the mine and washed it from the sands. We created it from our fertile soil and inexhaustible resources. From commerce the calm pulse of nations showed no poison of ignoble conquest in our veins, no stains to sully an honorable ambition for bloodless gain.

While Europe, Asia, and Africa robbed and murdered, we farmed and manufactured, built railroads, and annexed nobody's territory. The Old World simply harvested the destruction she sowed. Her heritage has been war and ours peace. We are asked to abandon our own and adopt another's.

Now, having helped put the German where he belongs, and being willing in like circumstances to help do so again, we are asked to lend our lives and treasures to every feud that blazes out in three continents, whether it concerns or menaces our interests or safety or not. We are invited to become the knight-errant of the world. A nation's first duty is to its own people. Its government is for them.

John T. McCutcheon. *The Chicago Tribune*, 1918.

Nearly four months ago the belligerent nations signed the armistice that saved Germany from a destructive atonement for her crimes. In that time the responsible agents of the United States of America have not occupied themselves in ending the war and writing terms of peace upon which Germany shall pay the penalty of acknowledged defeat in her attempts against civilized mankind. They have busied themselves with an effort to create a superstate above the governments and peoples of nations to exercise supersovereignty over both nations and their individual citizens and subjects.

Advantage is taken of a wish for universal and permanent peace to present this device as a certain instrumentality to that desired end. . . .

[But] the constitution of the league of nations must be submitted to that scrutiny which will assay its service as a charter prescribing a rule of conduct among nations and whether obedience can be secured. It must be tested by the peoples grouped under sovereign governments to ascertain how it will affect them and what burdens are likely to be assumed; what measure of relief is practicable. Does this document give it, or if not, what can be written reasonably calculated to accomplish that measure of relief? These are inquiries which merit the highest effort of which this Senate and the American Nation are capable. Such a momentous issue seldom challenges free people for decision.

The nations now occupying the earth came from a remote past. Whatever others may think of history, I am compelled at times to have recourse to the history of the various governments and nations that have occupied the earth in order to obtain light on the present. Their governments descended from ancient thrones, sprang from revolution, or are the heritage of development and accumulated experience. Their customs, usages, and laws vary. They comprise many religions and ethics and standards of morals. Their ethnology embraces the entire human family with their several languages. History is the philosophic chain that binds the past with the living present and its deep, pulsating currents of action.

All nations with organic government sufficient to be dealt with as responsible powers can be assembled by their voluntary act under a code of international law. Twenty-six nations so obligated themselves in 1899 in the first Hague convention. Forty-four nations were signatory in 1907 to the second Hague convention. When the armistice was signed November 11, 1918, all the warring nations were contracting parties agreeing in 1907 to arbitrate differences as a substitute for war. Every outrage perpetrated by Germany she had bound herself not to commit. Her deliberate policy of frightfulness she had solemnly covenanted should never be pursued. The indispensable end to be sought, therefore, is not to multiply international agreements, but to discover means of compelling or persuading nations to keep them when made.

I am skeptical on moral suasion as a coercive agency on some governments. It is idle to appeal to the people ruled by such governments for an improved or higher sense of right or wrong. Independent nations having their own governments generally have as good ones as they are capable of operating. Not as good as they desire often, but as good as they can get and keep in the long run. It is a considerable journey from despotism to free government. It is a ceaseless task to prevent free government from degenerating into a dissolution of just restraints. At one extreme is arbitrary power to a king; at the other, arbitrary power in a class or multitude, and there is no difference in the intrinsic evils of either.

What Germany or Russia may develop lies in the realm of conjecture. What their established relations may be with the rest of the world is uncharted diplomacy. Who knows whether they will emerge from their civil chaos and bloody tumults with a sense of national honor and obligation that will make them keep their faith when pledged or be merely predatory freebooters, to be restrained only by armies and navies?

Europe contains many independent sovereign nations. Some submerged nationalities, overwhelmed by wars reaching back some centuries, will undoubtedly rise to reassumed sovereignty. With the latter we may be concerned. They might be converted into warlike forces against us if subject to a dominant government, our enemy. Much European bloodshed has had its origin in commercial rivalry resulting in territorial aggression. It may be repeated. Most wars of modern times have begun in Europe. Kings have fought to gain thrones for their kin and subordinates. Ancient feuds of reigning families have sent armies into many a disastrous field. Ambitious men have risen to shake continents with their struggles for power.

That is all to end, however, because we now hear that kings are no more and the people will administer all future governments. We fervently pray it may be so. Yet some of the people we are asked by this league to invest with sovereign power over us may well engage our concern.

Russia is the fountainhead of bloody chaos and the attempted dissolution of every civil and domestic tie dear to the Anglo-Saxon race. Germany may be passing from despotic rule to class government founded on Marxian socialism.

The restless elements of Europe, inured to violence and disliking the monotony of private industry, are always explosive material. Erecting them into states does not insure tranquillity. To all such people, if they have not wisdom and virtue, self-restraint and justice to the minority, liberty is the greatest of all possible evils, not only to them but to the world.

If we ratify this league in its present form, we invest such people with equal power over us. Their vices and misfortunes react upon us. Their follies and crimes become in turn a menace, because we have given them an equal vote in the league with our own country. It may become not a means of removing a menace but of creating one beyond our power either to abate or to remove.

The constitution of the league of nations is a Pandora's box of evil to empty upon the American people the aggregated calamities of the world, and only time is the infallible test even of our own institutions.

What is our internal strength, and what burdens can we safely carry from the Old World? Are we the governmental Ajax upon whose shoulders rest the calamities and the burdens of the earth? This document assumes it. It was this wholesome solicitude that woke the wise counsels of those who hewed with sturdy stroke and laid deep and strong the great foundation stones of civil liberty and self-government.

Not doctrinaires nor dreamers floating serenely in the cloud-lands of speculative philosophy were the men who wrote our charters and forged the mighty instruments of freedom in the Western Hemisphere. They were not novices. They had fought battles. They had felt the depression of defeat. Victory had not relaxed their unceasing vigilance. With peace they returned to their homes and families and the cares of private life. They assumed the task of framing a Government to save in peace what they had gained in war. We are asked to ratify and create something that will lose in peace what we won in war. . . .

Our forefathers warred . . . with their lives and fortunes at stake. They left us the heritage of their sacrifices and their solemn admonitions summed up in the Farewell Address [of George Washington] read annually in this Chamber. Against their wisdom and experience now rise the dreamer and the bookman, the Socialist, and the mere haberdasher in phrases which intoxicate and mislead; sincere men some whose zeal for the millenium made by human hands blinds them to mere human faults and limitations. . . .

The founders of this Government had a working knowledge of the great headlands of civil liberty. They had known the elemental struggles to safeguard human rights, to curb the great and raise the low. They knew Europe, its quicksands, its bloody pitfalls in which their ancestors had died for a thousand years. They hated its kings, its nobles, its mobs, its revolutions, its heartless caste, its cruelty, and its crimes. They left their solemn warning to posterity to let Europe settle her own quarrels. . . .

World War I

When the United States by joint resolution of Congress entered the war April 6, 1917, we signed no pact with the Governments arrayed against the central powers. The American felt in his heart Germany was a menace to the free governments of the world. There was an instinctive horror at Germany's methods of making war and her avowed policy of frightfulness. It was known she aimed at world dominion. Those in authority at this Capitol knew we must fight the danger alone or jointly with the allies.

We chose to make common cause against a common danger. To do so we abdicated no sovereign power. We bound ourselves in no perpetual alliance to draw the sword whenever and so long as a majority of European governments voted it upon us. Our practical expression in this crisis was to reserve for ourselves the power to decide when and how long a controversy between two or more nations in some quarter of the globe was of such magnitude as to warrant our interference even to the extremity of war.

A working status was in fact established between our Government and the allies. Under it the war was fought successfully to the armistice of November 11, 1918. No nation surrendered its sovereignty. They voluntarily combined their strength against the common peril. It was a union of equals, and each was in an equally common self-defense bound to give all it had if the struggle demanded it. This is the key to any league of nations that will survive the ephemeral theories and impossible yearnings of the alleged friends of humanity who are more fertile in phrase making than successful in the practical affairs of men. . . .

The actual working alliance between our Government and Germany's European enemies . . . implies no loss of sovereignty and no violence to national sentiment. It is a cooperative expression of the law of self-defense, an American doctrine on which every patriot can join his fellow man. It impairs no constitutional power of Congress. It invades no executive domain, and it leaves our Government the responsible instrumentality to direct the will of our people. We escape the perils of surrendering our country to the mandates of a majority of the Governments of the Old World by this course.

The same public opinion in a free government that would unite our people under the proposed league would lead to concerted action under a treaty whose obligation rests in good faith. If public opinion does not support the league, it can not send armies into the field. America will not sacrifice her lives and her treasure unless her heart is in the war. No mere language written on parchment can in practice make any compact between sovereign nations more binding than a treaty unless some supersovereign force be contemplated as a coercive agent upon the American Government and its people. Force converts such a league into a tyranny and international oppressor. Such a compact becomes the source of universal war, not the means of permanent peace. . . .

Article 10

In article 10 [of the Covenant (constitution) of the League of Nations] the members of the league bind themselves to preserve each other, and the executive council is required to advise upon the means by which all the league members shall be protected against external aggression which will impair their territorial integrity and political independence. If this article avails anything it binds our Government, its Army, its Navy, its people, and its Treasury to defend Great Britain's colonial dependencies any place in the world. A like obligation attends us for France, Italy, and every other league member. England's territorial possessions are in every part of the globe. Russia is a vast area with 180,000,000 people, and Germany with 70,000,000. The United Kingdom of Great Britain has in Europe fewer than 50,000,000 population. More than 300,000,000 souls acknowledge the supremacy of England's flag in Asia. Great Britain feels, as seldom before, the need of help to maintain her territorial integrity. . . .

I decline to vote to bind the American people to maintain the boundary lines and political independence of every nation that may be a league member. It ought to be done only when the question menaces our peace and safety. It must be a treaty uniting our associated nations in the mutual and common bonds of self-defense. It becomes, then a league of sovereigns acting with the common purpose of self-preservation. The law of nations is like the law of individuals. Self-defense is the first law and is justified before every tribunal known to civilized man. . . .

This league, Mr. President, sends the angel of death to every American home. In every voice to ratify it we can hear the beating of his wing. There will be none to help; no decrees from omniscience will direct us to sprinkle with blood the lintel of every American home. If this supersovereignty be created, conscription will take from all, and we will bear the white man's burden in every quarter of the world.

On this issue I challenge the President and his administration and the sympathizers with this constitution to appeal to the great jury of the American people. I will be content with no less, whatever the Senate may do. I am willing to take that responsibility. I invite the President to remove the limitations upon a censored press and censored free speech that we may combat with him in an open forum and on equal terms. If he is not a political and governmental coward, he will give us that right. An honorable antagonist would do no less.

CHAPTER 3

The 1930s and the Height of Isolationism

Chapter Preface

The 1930s were a time of economic depression, not only for America, but for the world. Different nations responded to the economic crisis in different ways. The United States, under President Franklin D. Roosevelt, experimented with a wide variety of government and social programs. Both the president and the people of the United States focused their energies on Roosevelt's New Deal and their own economic welfare. At the same time, however, other nations were seeking to solve their economic problems by intimidating and/or invading weaker countries. Japan invaded China in 1931. Italy invaded Ethiopia in 1935. Germany under Adolf Hitler broke the Treaty of Versailles in making moves toward rearmament. The League of Nations, without the United States, proved ineffectual in preventing these actions. Americans were not unaware of these foreign events, but they were ambivalent, wishing to help the victims but not wanting to become involved in foreign wars.

Part of this ambivalence is attributable to renewed questions concerning World War I. A special Senate committee chaired by Senator Gerald P. Nye of North Dakota held hearings from 1934 to 1936 to investigate why the United States went to war. Historian Robert E. Kelley writes in *The Shaping of the American Past:*

> A sensational show featuring accusations against war industries was put on. Stretching out over two years, it never actually proved anything, but nevertheless firmly planted in the public mind the belief that bankers and arms manufacturers had dragged the country into war.

This belief was reinforced by the writings of journalists and historians. Books such as Walter Millis's *Road to War* and Charles A. Beard's *The Devil Theory of War* argued that U.S. involvement in World War I was an unnecessary and unwise decision promoted by arms manufacturers and wealthy interests. The books were widely read and contributed to American isolationist sentiment in the 1930s.

The view that America should shun involvement in foreign affairs (especially European affairs) united many people who otherwise had little in common. Manfred Jonas writes in his study *Isolationism in America:*

> Isolationism transcended socioeconomic divisions and was supported by Americans of widely divergent status. On the subject

of America's relationship to the conflicts in Europe and Asia, Socialist intellectuals shared the views of the American Legion. The Chicago Federation of Labor agreed with Henry Ford. Midwestern Progressives who had spent their lives fighting against Eastern banking interests espoused ideas on neutrality legislation first expounded by [Wall Street financier] Bernard Baruch. Herbert Hoover's arguments were supported in the pages of the *New Republic*.

Jonas goes on to examine how isolationists in the 1930s, while sharing a common antipathy toward foreign entanglements, differed in their underlying goals and rationales.

Belligerent isolationists believed in vigorous defense of American rights, reliance on international law, and strict adherence to the unilateral foreign policy of the nineteenth century. Timid isolationists were prepared to surrender some traditional rights in order to minimize direct contact with foreign nations at war and thus avoid entanglements. Radical isolationists sought to keep out of war at all costs in order to facilitate the establishment of a new social order in America. Conservative isolationists saw war as the final blow to the old order whose institutions and traditions they were desperately attempting to save. Acting from different motives and advocating varying methods, all . . . shared certain ideas and assumptions. This common ground was the basis for American isolationism in the years before the Second World War.

Isolationists of all kinds were united enough in the 1930s to pass a series of important Neutrality Acts. These laws prohibited the shipment of arms to any belligerent nation, authorized the president to forbid American travel on foreign ships, and denied bankers the right to extend credit to warring powers. They were designed to prevent the repetition of what their sponsors believed were the causes of U.S. involvement in World War I.

Whether President Roosevelt himself could be considered an isolationist during the 1930s was and is a matter of debate. Roosevelt's record included service for eight years as assistant secretary of the navy under Woodrow Wilson. As the Democratic candidate for vice president in 1920, he had campaigned for Wilson's internationalist agenda. However, his primary concern when he was elected president in 1932 was the American economy. Acutely aware of the popularity of isolationism in both Congress and the public, he did not stress foreign policy matters in his speeches to the American people, and chose to sign the Neutrality Acts passed by Congress. Historian George Moss writes in *America in the Twentieth Century:*

Although he remained a Wilsonian internationalist at heart, President Roosevelt expressed isolationist attitudes during the mid-1930s, as did most senators and congressmen. It was not until the late 1930s that Roosevelt and many other Americans, at last perceiving the danger of Axis aggression, cautiously distanced themselves from the noninterventionists.

Following Roosevelt's reelection in 1936 the president began to make a few small overtures in the direction of breaking free from a foreign policy of political isolation. In a dramatic speech in Chicago in 1937, Roosevelt called for an international "quarantine" against international aggressors. The fact that Roosevelt's subsequent actions did not live up to such rhetoric is attributed by most historians to the enduring hold isolationism had on the United States.

VIEWPOINT 1

"We propose that American citizens who want to profit from other people's wars shall not be allowed again to entangle the United States."

Congress Should Legislate a Mandatory Arms Embargo Against All Belligerents

Bennett Clark (1890-1954)

In the 1930s Congress enacted a series of legislative measures designed to keep the United States out of war. The impetus for these laws stemmed in part from the activities of the Senate Munitions Investigating Committee. From 1934 to 1936 the committee, chaired by Senator Gerald P. Nye of North Dakota, held a series of hearings investigating the origins of World War I, which revealed that many American banks and munitions manufacturers had made large profits from lending money and selling arms to the Allied nations. In part because of the hearings, much of the American public became convinced that U.S. entry into World War I was a mistake that had been encouraged by those seeking to capitalize from war.

The way to avoid entanglement in a future foreign war, many people believed, was to stop the economic activity that profited from it. The series of Neutrality Acts passed in the 1930s was designed to do just that. The first Neutrality Act was passed in August 1935 and charged the president to declare an embargo on arms shipments to any nations at war. The Neutrality Act of 1936, which was passed on February 29, added a ban on extending

Abridged from Bennett Clark, *Congressional Digest*, vol. 15, January 1936, pp. 18-20.

loans or credits to belligerents. The Neutrality Act of 1937, passed on May 1, added strategic materials such as steel, oil, and copper to the embargo list, and made it illegal for U.S. citizens to travel on ships of nations at war. None of these acts distinguished between aggressor and victim nations in applying these restrictions.

A strong supporter of the Neutrality Acts was Bennett Clark, a Democratic senator from Missouri from 1933 to 1945. A veteran of World War I who had risen to the rank of army colonel, Clark later became convinced that U.S. involvement in that war had been a dreadful mistake. The following viewpoint is taken from the January 1936 issue of *Congressional Digest*, in which he argues that the first Neutrality Act of 1935 should be expanded to prevent all American economic involvement with warring nations. To insist on American neutral rights to trade with all belligerents, he argues, would simply entangle America in foreign wars. An embargo should be automatic and include all nations at war, he concludes, for it to achieve its desired goal of American noninvolvement.

The desire to keep the United States from involvement in any war between foreign nations is very strong today—well-nigh universal. But there was an almost equally strong demand to keep out of the last war. In August, 1914, no one could have conceived that America would be dragged into a European conflict in which we had no part and the origin and ramifications of which we did not even understand. Even as late as November, 1916—after 2 years of carnage in Europe—the American people reelected Woodrow Wilson "because he kept us out of war." And yet 5 months later we were fighting to "save the world for democracy" in the "war to end war."

In the light of that experience it is high time that we gave some thought to the hard, practical question of just how we propose to avoid war if it comes again. No one who has made an honest attempt to face the issue will assert that there is any easy answer. No one who has studied the history of our participation in the World War will tell you that there is a simple way out. There is none—no simple panacea, no magic formula. But if we have learned anything at all we know the inevitable and tragic end to a policy of drifting and trusting to luck. We know that however strong is the will of the American people to refrain from mixing in other people's quarrels, that will can only be made effective if we have a sound, definite policy from the beginning. No lesson of the last war is more clear than that such a policy cannot be improvised after war breaks out. It must be worked out in advance, before it is too late to apply reason. I say with all possible earnestness that if we want to avoid another war we must begin at once to formulate a policy based upon an understanding of the problem confronting us.

I frankly confess that I make no pretension to knowing of a policy which can provide an absolute and infallible guaranty against involvement in war. Certainly there is no such policy which can be written into the law or enacted as legislation. The only sure way to avoid another war is to prevent that war from breaking out. I have advocated preventive measures and I have supported disarmament and settlement of disputes by peaceful means. But if these fail or if nations insist on preparing for armed conflict and that conflict comes, then I insist that we must do everything in our power to stay out. And I believe that the United States can stay out of the next war if it wants to, and if it understands what is necessary to preserve neutrality.

The best way to reach such an understanding is to examine the forces which are likely to involve us in war. In 1914 we knew very little about these forces. President Wilson issued his proclamation of neutrality and we went on with business as usual, in the happy belief that 3,000 miles of ocean would keep us out of the mess. Our professional diplomats were not much more astute. . . . They took the position that "the existence of war between foreign governments does not suspend trade or commerce between this country and those at war." They told American merchants that there was nothing in international law to prevent them from trading with the warring nations. They told munitions makers that they were free to sell their war materials to either or both sides. They took no steps to warn American citizens of the dangers of travel on vessels of the warring nations, even after passenger ships had been sunk without warning. This attitude, strange as it may seem today, was in full accord with the rules of international law as generally understood at that time.

We are wiser today. We know more about war and much more about neutrality. And yet it is remarkable how much we seem to have forgotten. In the course of the Senate investigation of the munitions industry this winter Senator Nye and I have had occasion to go rather deeply into the activities of our arms merchants and other traders in war material during the early years of the conflict. We have examined again the tortuous record of our diplomatic correspondence. From this survey four broad conclusions stand out:

1. That a policy based on defense of our so-called "neutral rights" led us into serious diplomatic controversy with both the Allies and the Central Powers, and in the end brought us to a

point where we were compelled to choose between surrendering these rights or fighting to defend them. In 1917 we chose to fight.

2. The "national honor" and "prestige" of the nation are inevitably involved when American ships are sunk on the high seas—even though the owners of these ships and their cargoes are private citizens seeking to profit from other nations' wars. . . .

3. That the economic forces, set in motion by our huge war trade with the Allies, made it impossible to maintain that "true spirit of neutrality" which President Wilson urged upon his fellow citizens at the outbreak of the conflict.

4. That among these economic forces, those which involved us most deeply were the huge trade in arms and ammunition and other war materials with the Allies.

The Lessons of 1917

Arthur H. Vandenberg, who represented Michigan in the United States Senate from 1928 to 1951, was one of America's leading isolationists. In a 1936 speech he argues that America's experiences leading up to World War I demonstrate the wisdom of avoiding economic ties with warring nations.

We learned in 1914-17 that neutrality is calculated to be counterfeit if it masks loan and credits or the shipment of war supplies to belligerents. We learned that this commerce—plus the travel of Americans on belligerent ships—releases an inevitable controversy and a controlling impulse which can sweep us to the ultimate battle line ourselves. Therefore the old conception of "neutral rights" must give way to a new conception of "neutral duties." We should make no loans; grant no credits; ship no arms, ammunition or implements of war to *any* belligerent. We should prohibit American travel on belligerent ships. Thus we would endeavor to quarantine war as an institution instead of piously condemning it in the abstract while exploiting it in the concrete.

And just a word about the futility of trying to defend our neutral rights and freedom of the seas. As a neutral we claimed the right to trade in war materials and all other goods with the warring nations. This right—with two main exceptions—had been recognized under the rules of international law which had grown up over more than a hundred years. The exceptions were important: A warring nation, or belligerent, had a right which we recognized, to capture goods called "contraband." Originally "contraband" consisted of guns and explosives and other munitions intended for the use of the armed forces. Great Britain, for example, had a legal right to stop an American ship on the high seas if it could prove that the vessel carried munitions bound for Germany. In 1909 the leading sea powers drew up a list of contraband in a famous statement of maritime law which came to be known as the "Declaration of London."

World War I and Neutral Rights

When the World War broke out, however, this declaration had not been put into force by any of the governments. When our State Department asked the British Government whether it would accept the list of contraband articles in the declaration of London the British declined. They argued, with some logic, that under modern conditions of war, food and raw materials, and almost everything except ostrich feathers, which were sent to the enemy were just as important as guns and explosives for the army. Modern war is not merely a contest between armies on the field of battle. It involves the entire population of nations and becomes a death struggle in which the warring country tries to overcome the will of the enemy to resist. Anything which helps the enemy to carry on the war is of vital importance. By the end of 1916, therefore, Great Britain had placed almost every article exported by the United States on the lists of contraband. Our State Department protested that the British had no right to change the old rules of international law. We sent a stream of indignant notes to London. But Great Britain was engaged in a death struggle, and we knew that one way to win the war was to starve the enemy. . . .

Our Government protested even more violently to Germany. While British ships were seizing contraband and taking American vessels into port, German submarines were sinking merchant ships on sight. The Imperial German Government argued that their submarine campaign was the only effective means of combatting the allied blockade which was starving the German people. They complained bitterly against the blockade and they protested our huge trade in munitions and war materials with the Allies.

Public opinion in the United States became inflamed at the ruthless destruction of unarmed merchant ships and passenger vessels. When the *Lusitania* was sunk in May, 1915, with the loss of 124 American lives, our patriots began to shout for a strong policy. President Wilson parried with diplomatic notes and for a time Germany offered to compromise. No one, it seems, thought of asking whether private American citizens in pursuit of fat profits had a right to involve us in war. In the end we were led to the point where we had to choose: We could try to defend our neutral rights by force of arms or we could give up those rights and stay out. On April 6, 1917, Congress declared that a state of war existed between the United States and Germany.

The only logical result of attempting to enforce these neutral "rights," as they are described, is to get us into war with both sides or to force us to join hands with one violator of our rights against another. It is logical and it is crazy. . . .

Let us not claim as a right what is an impossibility.

The only way we can maintain our neutral rights is to fight the whole world.

Failing that, we only pretend to enforce our neutral rights against one side and go to war to defend them against the other side.

But defense of our neutral rights was not the only cause of our being dragged into the World War. There were many factors, including the vast campaign of propaganda which began with the manufactured atrocity stories in the invasion of Belgium. The American people ceased to be neutral almost on the outbreak of hostilities. Our newspapers became violently partisan, and even our best citizens were soon shouting for preservation of the national honor. But among all these forces the economic entanglement of our one-sided but profitable war trade stands out in bold relief.

One point which stands out sharply in this record is that we cannot improvise a policy of neutrality after a war breaks out. From our first shipment of munitions our feet were irrevocably committed to the path which led to war, and the only question was as to whether the war could be ended before we were forced in. In the Congress of the United States during the early war years many resolutions were introduced for the purpose of stopping this trade in war materials. As early as August 28, 1914, Representative Towner, of Iowa, saw that even the trade in food and clothing would "invite our own entanglement." At the other end of the Capital Senator Hitchcock, of Nebraska, introduced a bill calling for an embargo on munitions and war material; but it was already too late. Our State Department took the position that it would be an unneutral act to place an embargo after war had come. It would be like changing the rules in the middle of the game, and would favor one side to the disadvantage of the other. The Allies and their American sympathizers echoed this view, and Hitchcock's bill was quickly pigeon-holed.

In the light of this record, what are the possibilities for the future? I say with all sincerity that I believe there is still time to formulate a policy to keep the United States out of the next war. I believe that the American people want to stay out, and I believe that the American people are willing to support such a new policy to insure their neutrality, even though the price may be high. . . .

We propose that American citizens who want to profit from other people's wars shall not be allowed again to entangle the United States. We learned in our munitions inquiry that some of

our American armament firms have been making money by helping Germany rearm with airplanes. We deny that this obliges us
to put our own boys on the receiving line when those airplanes
start dropping their bombs. We propose to take the American flag
off the munition ships.

Specifically, this new neutrality legislation contains four vital
provisions:

1. A complete embargo on the shipment of all arms and ammunition and other war materials to all belligerents in time of war.

2. A similar automatic embargo on all loans and credits to the
warring nations for the purchase of war materials or other contraband.

3. A law forbidding the granting of passports to American citizens traveling in war zones or on belligerent ships.

4. A law requiring that anyone who exports any article declared
to be contraband of war by any belligerent country shall do so at his
risk or at the risk of the foreign government or foreign purchaser.

This legislation, we frankly admit, cannot safeguard us against
poisonous propaganda or the inflaming of people's minds which
may follow in the wake of another war. It is not an automatic
safeguard of our neutrality. But it does, we believe, lessen some of
the most important dangers as revealed by our World War experience. It involves a cost, and it may mean the loss of lucrative profits. It may mean a loss to some of our vested interests and may
demand a sacrifice from those who might otherwise profit.

Let the man seeking profits from the war-time countries do so
at his own risk. Every man profit-bent or impelled by idle curios-
ity in the war-torn areas of the world carries in his body the death
of a hundred thousand American boys. He can be made the cause
for war. His profits from the warring countries are his own business; let his risk be his own business, too.

If there are those so brave as to risk getting us into war by traveling the war zones—if there are those so valiant that they do not
care how many people are killed as a result of their traveling, let
us tell them and let us tell the world, that from now on their
deaths will be a misfortune to their own families alone, not to the
whole nation.

Let us not fool ourselves. After a war has been started all the
public opinion in the world cannot change by one jot or tittle the
manner in which the most desperate of the belligerents chooses to
carry it on. If one side uses gas on the civilian populations of the
enemy, the other side will use gas the next day. The chemical industries of all nations stand ready to produce it.

Our only hope for keeping out of war, from keeping away from
using gas, and from being on the receiving end of it, is to lay
plans to keep out of war now, before the war has started.

VIEWPOINT 2

"To assume that by placing an embargo on arms we are making ourselves secure from dangers of conflict with belligerent countries is to close our eyes to manifold dangers in other directions."

Congress Should Not Legislate a Mandatory Arms Embargo Against All Belligerents

Cordell Hull (1871-1955)

The 1930s marked a high point for isolationism in Congress and among the U.S. public. Isolationists in Congress, convinced U.S. entry into World War I had been a mistake, pushed through several legislative measures they believed would help keep America out of future foreign wars. In August 1935 Congress passed the first of what would be a series of Neutrality Acts. This law charged the president to impose an arms embargo on nations participating in an international war, and to warn Americans traveling on vessels of warring nations that they did so at their own risk. President Franklin D. Roosevelt signed the 1935 legislation, but only after failing to persuade Congress to include a clause that would give the president discretionary power to determine if there was an aggressor nation and target an embargo for it alone. Isolationists in Congress rejected such arrangements as threatening to American neutrality.

Cordell Hull, *Congressional Digest*, vol. 15, January 15, 1936, pp. 24-25.

The first test of this policy came when Italy invaded Ethiopia in October 1935. Roosevelt declared that a state of war existed, thus triggering the mandatory arms embargo and travel warning.

The 1935 Neutrality Act was written to expire six months after its passage, but isolationist members of Congress soon called for its provisions to be extended or made permanent. The Roosevelt administration again called for changes giving the president greater discretion. An argument for such changes is found in the following passage from a speech by Cordell Hull, which was printed in the January 15, 1936, issue of *Congressional Digest*. Hull was Roosevelt's secretary of state from 1933 to 1944. Prior to his appointment Hull had been a longtime member of Congress, and had supported America's entry into World War I and the League of Nations. He argues here that mandatory embargoes on all warring nations would not have the desired effect of keeping the United States out of foreign wars. He asserts that such actions force the president to conduct U.S. foreign policy from a position of weakness.

The views of Hull and Roosevelt failed to sway Congress, which continued to support mandatory embargoes with no presidential discretion in the Neutrality Acts of 1936 and 1937.

Because of the generally unsettled world conditions, and the existence of hostilities between two powers with which we are on terms of friendship, the one phase of our "foreign policy" uppermost in the minds of our people today is that of neutrality. It is being discussed from the platforms, in the press, and in the streets. It is of concern to our people in every walk of life. They have not forgotten the bitter experiences of the World War, the calamitous effects of which will not be erased from their memories during our present generation. Is it, therefore, any wonder that they should be concerned rewarding our policy of neutrality and the steps that their Government is taking to avoid a repetition of those experiences?

Modern neutrality dates from the latter part of the Middle Ages. Prior to that time neutrality was unknown for the reason that belligerents did not recognize an attitude of impartiality on the part of other powers; under the laws of war observed by the most civilized nations of antiquity the right of one nation to remain at peace while neighboring nations were at war was not admitted to exist. Efforts made by nations from time to time to adopt an attitude of impartiality were successfully resisted by the belligerents, who proceeded on the theory that any country not an ally was an enemy. No intermediate relation was known to the pagan nations of those earlier times, and hence the term neutrality did not exist.

Neutrality and Public Opinion

Frederic R. Coudert, a lawyer specializing in international law, writes in the January 15, 1936, issue of Congressional Digest *that the widespread public belief that America can keep out of war by avoiding all economic and political ties with foreign countries is misguided.*

The theory of the man in the street, voiced largely by the newspapers of the land, is that America should refrain, as far as possible, from all dealings with foreign nations, even to the lending of money; and that it should rely for its peace and prosperity solely on its own efforts and its own internal trade; and that, above all, no responsibility must be assumed which might call for American armed intervention. . . .

Now, that state of mind, however unfortunate, and however erroneous we may deem it, is a brute fact with which we must deal. That state of mind necessarily assumes, however, that peace may be maintained by America's refraining from all cooperative efforts with European countries directed toward assuring peace, and that the traditional policy of neutrality will, in the event of a future general conflict, keep the nation clear of war. It is that basic assumption that I challenge.

Neutrality is not that perfectly safe, foolproof policy which American public opinion apparently seems to think today that it is.

During the 16th century, however, neutrality as a concept in international law began to be recognized. In 1625 Hugo Grotius, sometimes referred to as the father of international law, published his celebrated treatise on the laws of peace and war. While his treatment of the subject of neutrality is brief and necessarily so because of the undeveloped status of the law of his time, he nevertheless recognized the possibility of third parties' remaining neutral. He did not, however, have that conception of neutrality to which we have been accustomed in more recent times. He stated that it was the duty of those not engaged in a war "to do nothing whereby he who supports a wicked cause may be rendered more powerful, or whereby the movements of him who wages a just war may be hampered."

Since the days of Grotius, neutrality has passed through several stages of evolution. No nation has done more toward its development than has the United States. In 1794 Congress passed our first neutrality act, temporary in character, covering a variety of subjects. In 1818 permanent legislation on these subjects was passed. This legislation formed the basis of the British act of a similar character of 1819, known as the British Foreign Enlistment Act. Other legislation has been passed by Congress from time to time, including that enacted during the World War . . . and that enacted as recently as the last session of Congress—the Joint Resolution approved August 31, 1935. This last mentioned Resolution, intended to supplement prior legislation, is designed primarily *to keep the United States out of foreign wars.*

Pursuant to this Resolution the President has issued two proclamations regarding the war now unhappily existing between Ethiopia and Italy. One of these declared the existence of a state of war within the meaning and intent of Section 1 of the Resolution, thus bringing into operation the embargo on the shipment of arms, ammunition and implements of war from the United States to either belligerent, and the other declared that American citizens who travel on vessels of the belligerents shall do so at their own risk.

The effect of issuing the proclamation bringing into operation the embargo on the shipment of arms was automatically to bring into operation the provisions of Section 3 of the Resolution prohibiting American vessels from carrying arms, ammunition or implements of war to any port of a belligerent country named in the proclamation, or to any neutral port for transshipment to or for the use of the belligerent country.

Any discussion of the avoidance of war, or of the observance of neutrality in the event of war, would be wholly incomplete if too much stress were laid on the part played in the one or the other by the shipment, or the embargoing of the shipment, of arms, ammunition, and implements of war. The shipment of arms is not the only way and, in fact, is not the principal way by which our commerce with foreign nations may lead to serious international difficulties. To assume that by placing an embargo on arms we are making ourselves secure from dangers of conflict with belligerent countries is to close our eyes to manifold dangers in other directions. The imposition of an arms embargo is not a complete panacea and we cannot assume that when provision has been made to stop the shipment of arms, which as absolute contraband have always been regarded as subject to seizure by a belligerent, we may complacently sit back with the feeling that we are secure from all danger. Attempts by a belligerent to exercise jurisdiction on the high seas over trade with its enemy, or with other neutral countries on the theory that the latter are supplying the enemy, may give rise to difficulties no less serious than those resulting from the exportation of arms and implements of war. So also transactions of any kind between American nationals and a belligerent may conceivably lead to difficulties of one kind or another between the nationals and that belligerent. Efforts of this Government to extend protection to these nationals might lead to difficulties between the United States and the belligerent. It was with these thoughts in mind that the President issued his timely warning that citizens of the United States who engage in transactions of any character with either belligerent would do so at their own risk.

Every war presents different circumstances and conditions which might have to be dealt with differently both as to time and manner. For these reasons, difficulties inherent in any effort to lay down by legislative enactment inelastic rules or regulations to be applied to every situation that may arise will at once be apparent. The Executive should not be unduly or unreasonably handicapped. There are a number of ways in which discretion could wisely be given the President which are not and could not be seriously controversial. These might well include discretion as to the time of imposing an embargo. Moreover, we should not concentrate entirely on means for remaining neutral and lose sight of other constructive methods of avoiding involvement in wars between other countries. Our foreign policy would indeed be a weak one if it began or ended with the announcement of a neutral position on the outbreak of a foreign war. I conceive it to be our duty and in the interest of our country and of humanity, not only to remain aloof from disputes and conflicts with which we have no direct concern, but also to use our influence in any appropriate way to bring about the peaceful settlement of international differences. Our own interest and our duty as a great power forbid that we shall sit idly by and watch the development of hostilities with a feeling of self-sufficiency and complacency when by the use of our influence, short of becoming involved in the dispute itself, we might prevent or lessen the scourge of war. In short, our policy as a member of the community of nations should be twofold—first, to avoid being brought into a war and second, to promote as far as possible the interests of international peace and good will. A virile policy tempered with prudent caution is necessary if we are to retain the respect of other nations, and at the same time hold our position of influence for peace and international stability in the family of nations.

In summary, while our primary aim should be to avoid involvement in other people's difficulties and hence to lessen our chances of being drawn into a war, we should, on appropriate occasions and within reasonable bounds, use our influence toward the prevention of war and the miseries that attend and follow in its wake. For after all, if peace obtains, problems regarding neutrality will not arise.

VIEWPOINT 3

"Under the proposed plan the question of war or peace will be decided exactly as it should be decided, with every citizen casting his vote in the privacy of the ballot booth."

A War Referendum Should Be Added to the Constitution

Louis Ludlow (1873-1950)

The U.S. Constitution names the president "commander in chief" of the U.S. armed forces, and reserves to Congress the power to declare war. In January 1938 members of the House of Representatives debated a proposed constitutional amendment that would have fundamentally affected both of these provisions. The amendment, proposed by Representative Louis Ludlow of Indiana, called for a national referendum before American troops could be committed to a foreign war. (Under the amendment no such vote would be required before American troops could be deployed to repel a foreign attack.) The amendment drew considerable support from isolationists in Congress, who believed that the American people would never vote to participate in a foreign war.

The following passage is taken from Ludlow's speech before Congress in favor of his amendment. Ludlow, who served in Congress from 1929 to 1949, argues here that under the existing system a small minority of special interests could involve the United States in a war most people would not want—a scenario many Americans believed may have happened in 1917. Ludlow contends that the decision to go to war is of such importance that the American people should be given the greatest direct say, and

Louis Ludlow, remarks to the House of Representatives, January 14, 1938. Reprinted in *Congressional Digest*, vol. 17, February 1938.

that recent improvements in technology enable the people themselves, rather than their elected representatives, to vote and decide whether to go to war.

Strongly opposed by the Roosevelt administration, the Ludlow Amendment was defeated in the House by a vote of 209-188. The level of support for such a major change in the Constitution, however, is illustrative of the depth of isolationist sentiment of the time.

At the outset I want to say that I hold the Constitution in the highest reverence as the sheet anchor of our liberties and the arch stone of our public welfare, and I will never be a party to amending it for any light and inconsequential causes. When I propose an amendment to the Constitution, particularly one dealing with so important a matter as the exercise of the war power, I realize that the burden of proof is on me to show that the Constitution should be so amended.

What, then, are some of the defects of the present constitutional method of declaring war? What is there about the existing constitutional method of declaring war that makes it a menace to peace? Let us analyze the situation. Under the existing constitutional mechanism war is declared by Congress; that is to say, by a majority of each branch. There are 435 members of the House and 96 Senators, and war may be declared by 218 Representatives and 49 Senators, a total of 267 individuals, while about 127,000,000 other people have nothing to say about it. Thus we find the war power vested in a very little group in Washington, a group that is singularly influenced and dominated by one other individual, the other individual being whoever may happen at any given time to occupy the office of President of the United States.

I would be the last person in the world to cast aspersions on Members of Congress. For 36 years as a newspaper correspondent and a representative I have lived among them and I have a good opinion of their average patriotism and capacity. It is a high average. But when the war pressure from a thousand directions is on and the heat is applied and the propaganda is in full swing, Members of Congress are likely to crack under the strain and vote for war when they would not want to do so. Members of Congress are, after all, human. No Member wants to be called "yellow" and no Member wants to be seared and burned by the opprobrious epithet of "traitor." It is not fair to Members of Congress to ask them or to expect them to vote on a declaration of war. This most vital of all questions should be decided not by the agent but by the principal, and in this case the principal is the 127,000,000 people who comprise the American Nation. In the way provided in my resolution the agent will advise the principal, but the principal will act. As war is now declared, the agent acts and the principal has nothing to say about it. Under the proposed plan the question of war or peace will be decided exactly as it should be decided, with every citizen casting his vote in the privacy of the ballot booth, alone with his Maker, and the majority of all ballots will be the verdict of the combined judgment and conscience of America. With the millions upon millions of God-fearing citizens deciding this great question by the ballot the wiles of the Machiavellian schemers will be of no avail and the shafts of the wicked will break and fall. Ulterior influences cannot reach and tamper with that jury.

The Pressures of War

Let us try to visualize just a few of the myriad of influences and pressures that may now be brought to bear on Congress to force a declaration of war—influences and pressures which might be effective on Congress but which would be wholly ineffective if applied to the Nation under the war referendum system.

Illustration No. 1: Senator John Smith has a brother who is president of a large munitions company. The brother has visions of enormous bonuses certain to come to him if war is declared. If Senator Smith were a judge assigned to try a case under such circumstances he would be expected to disqualify himself, but as a Senator he is under no such compulsion and he will have a vote on the declaration of war.

Illustration No. 2: Representative John Brown owes a large sum of money to the home bank at Smithville, his loan being subject to call. The Smithville bank is affiliated with a great big bank in New York which belongs to a ring of international financiers. The New York bank and its associates are promoting the war movement. It says to its Smithville correspondent: "Take care of Congressman Brown and see that he votes right on the declaration of war."

Illustration No. 3: War-clouds are gathering over America and, let us say, Japan. A break appears imminent. During the week immediately following the time set for a vote in Congress on a war resolution the congressional convention will be held in Congressman John Jones' district, and Congressman Jones is a candidate to succeed himself. Without the support of the Sharpsville *Bugle*, the leading newspaper of his political faith in the district, John Jones could not get within a thousand miles of the nomination. The *Bugle* is violently anti-Japanese, and is demanding that Representative Jones vote for war.

Illustration No. 4: With the war declaration pending in Congress the Legislature of the State of New York meets, and in its assumed capacity to speak for the people of that sovereign State, it adopts a resolution in the form of a memorial demanding that the New York delegation in Congress, two Senators and forty-five Representatives, shall vote for war. The action of the legislature is unanimous. The vote of the New York delegation in Congress is numerically equal to the combined votes of many other States. If it is cast as directed from Albany it will tip the scales in favor of war. It is known that ulterior influences were very busy around Albany before the legislature took action.

Democratic representative Louis Ludlow's isolationist beliefs are evidenced by his sponsorship of a constitutional amendment to guarantee a popular vote before the United States could commit troops to a foreign war.

UPI/Bettmann

These are but instances of many forms of pressure to which Congress may be subjected in war times. A thousand other illustrations could be given of special pressures that might be brought to bear on Congress to force a declaration of war, influences which could not possibly be brought to bear on the country at large in a referendum on war. If the decision of war or peace were left to all of the people of the country the action of the New York Legislature would not have an effect altogether out of proportion to its actual importance. It might have a little influence on the great national jury but it assuredly would not be a determining factor in the result. The Sharpsville *Bugle* might bugle to its heart's content but its raucous calls would hardly swing a nation.

There is no desire or intent in this recital of just a few of the ulterior influences that may now operate to defeat the popular will, to speculate on how John Smith, John Brown, John Jones, and the New York delegation would vote on a declaration of war. Giving to all of them the credit of being honest, sincere, and patriotic men who will see their duty and do it, nevertheless it must be obvious to everybody that such a system of declaring war is all wrong.

An Existing Defect

Now let me call your attention to another defect in our existing constitutional war-making mechanism which I believe is far more serious than anything I have mentioned and that is the opportunity it would give to a tyrant in the White House to plunge the Nation into war at any time to pursue his selfish aims or for his own aggrandizement.

The tendency of governments all around the world is to go centripetal at an amazing rate, [and] 19 democracies have died since the World War and with them have died the hopes and aspirations of the common people of those countries. Centralization is the order of governmental development everywhere. Too often all power is being centralized in tyrants who play with the lives of their subjects as they would with so many toys, moving them here, there and yonder on war's checkerboard, using them as cannon-fodder without the slightest regard for humane considerations.

In our own country we have not escaped the trend toward centralization of authority. I hold before me a list of 77 major laws that were passed by the Seventy-second and Seventy-third Congresses. Of these, 18 originated in Congress and 59 originated in the Executive departments. I mention this trend of Executive influence over Congress not in criticism, because Executive leadership was necessary to bring our country out of the darkest night of economic distress and despair it ever has known, and an all-wise Providence was kind to America in furnishing one who was capable of that leadership, but if the man who happens at any given time to be President has so much influence over Congress in an economic emergency, less serious than war, to what lengths might not a tyrannical President go in usurping the war power and plunging America into war to satisfy his own whims. If we are to stabilize peace in America and do our part toward stabilizing the peace of the world we should decentralize the war power and vest it with the people themselves. That is where it ought to be. That is where sovereignty abides, and we should do this before it is everlastingly too late, before some tyrant makes his appearance in the White House. No stauncher friend of peace ever occupied the Executive Office than President Roosevelt, but, after all, the period of one President's service is but a second in the life of a nation and I shudder to think what might happen to our beloved country some time in the future if a tyrant of Napoleonic stripe should appear in the White House, grab the war power and run amuck.

As matters now stand, with the war power lodged where it is, such a tyrant would find the situation exactly to his liking. There would be nothing to prevent him from plunging America into war with half of the world.

President Woodrow Wilson well said that he had heard of governments making war on governments, but that in all the range of his observation he never knew "of peoples making war on peoples," and our present great Executive, Franklin D. Roosevelt, uttered a sentiment of cheer and inspiration to the human race around the world when he said that "war by governments" must give way to "peace by peoples." If in every country on the globe the war power could be democratized and vested with the people, war probably would almost vanish from the earth, for the people do not want war. They are sick of its heartaches, of its grief and suffering; of the pain it puts in the hearts of mothers. America has always been noted for its primacy as an exponent of righteousness and high ideals; and I ask to what greater cause could we dedicate ourselves than to assume the leadership in trying by precept and example to emancipate the human race from the curse of war.

There are two ways, as I conceive it, to prevent war or at least to minimize the possibility of our involvement in foreign wars. My proposed "Peace Amendment" covers both ways. One way is to give all the people—women as well as men—the right to vote on a declaration of war. And why should not women have that right? Women go down into the valley of the shadow of death to bring our boys into the world. Why should they not have something to say as to whether their flesh and blood shall be hurled into the hell of a foreign conflict? Of the 531 Members of Congress at the present time, only 6 are women, so you see how utterly negligible is the prospect of giving expression to whatever may be women's viewpoint on any particular war proposal. The other way to prevent war is to take the profit out of war. Take the profit out of war and there will be fewer wars. My proposed Peace Amendment is based on the philosophy that those who have to suffer, and if need be to die, and to bear the awful burdens and heartaches of war, should have something to say as to whether war should be declared. What could be more elementally just than that?

Now, you may ask, if the existing method of declaring war is so imperfect and undependable as a means of registering the Nation's will in regard to war, why did the founding fathers adopt it at the beginning? Why was such a mechanism ever written into the Constitution? Why did not George Washington favor a war referendum? Why did not Thomas Jefferson, who wrote into the great Declaration the immortal doctrine that "all men are created

Church Leaders Support Ludlow Amendment

On January 9, 1938, fourteen prominent religious leaders joined in signing the following statement in support of the Ludlow Amendment.

As Christian ministers committed to the service of the Prince of Peace, we are impelled to make public our support of the proposal introduced in Congress by Representative Louis I. Ludlow, of Indiana, known as the war referendum, which provides that excepting invasion a majority of the American people must approve in a national plebiscite before Congress may declare war.

We believe that the people who will be called on in war to sacrifice their sons and their own lives, and who will be expected to pay for and to suffer the demoralizing consequences of armed violence, have an inalienable moral and religious right to participate in any decision as momentous as that by which war is determined. . . .

The signers of this letter are men of peace. We consider war the greatest evil of our time. We believe that the war referendum would make it unlikely that this Nation would ever again become involved in a war which would take American soldiers to fight on foreign soil. We therefore say, let the people vote on war.

equal" see to it that a provision for a popular vote on war was included in his cherished Bill of Rights? Pertinent and proper questions, all of these. Certainly no one doubts the breadth and depths of the altruism of the seers who founded this Republic. But far-seeing as they were, they could not foresee the development in the means of communication that has made a war referendum practicable. Acting in the light of their times they lodged the war-making power the nearest to the people it could be put under the conditions then existing—and that was in the Congress. There was great rejoicing among the friends of the people in the Constitutional Convention when they were able to defeat a movement to lodge the war power with the President, which was the aim of the monarchists of that time; and Thomas Jefferson in one of his letters spoke exultantly of that victory for the people. The only kind of representative government the founding fathers knew was representative government at its best, and when they got the war power vested in Congress they consoled themselves with the thought that it was lodged nearest to the people.

A New World

In those times the railroad, the telegraph, the telephone, the radio were in the bosom of the unknown future. Even the pony express was as yet undreamed of. A letter mailed on the eastern seaboard was 6 months reaching the uttermost frontiers of the

113

country, if indeed it ever got there, and traveling was so tedious, long-drawn-out and precarious that Members of Congress were allowed mileage at the rate of 20 cents a mile to cover tavern bills, etc., on the long journey to Washington and return to their homes.

Now the fast train roars across the country in 100 hours; the airplane in 24; the telegraph, telephone, and radio have annihilated time and space. The two great broadcasting systems gave me time over their networks to explain my Peace Amendment to the people of the country, and sitting before a microphone in Washington I talked to the entire Nation. The only tenable argument ever made against a war referendum, namely, that it would consume too much time, thus giving an enemy nation the advantage, has been completely nullified by modern perfection in the means of communication. . . .

Now if any one has jumped to the conclusion that the constitutional amendment I am advocating is a pacifist proposition, as the word pacifist is generally understood, I want to correct that impression. This proposition has nothing whatever to do with the size of our national defense. It goes only to the one point of deciding how the war-making power shall be exercised, whether by a little group or oligarchy in Washington or by the people who have to do the suffering and dying and who pay the bills. I believe it should be vested with the people. Personally I believe that with conditions in the world as they are today we must have strong and adequate national defense. The Constitution enjoins upon the Government the duty of protecting the national welfare. How can the national welfare be protected without an adequate Army and Navy to do it with?

The Peace Amendment I have introduced will appeal to the sound judgment of my colleagues as they analyze it in the light of reason. It would not interfere in any way with the exercise of our right of self-defense but it would tend to lift us out of the miasmas and quicksands of war and the unholy concomitants of war. It would be a great and helpful factor in keeping us out of all foreign wars and out of all wars we should not enter.

As far as finite vision can discern, some wars appear to be foreordained and inescapable, as for instance the War of the American Revolution, which forged into our social structure great principles of right and justice. But some wars, and I think most wars, are not unavoidable. Most wars are caused by greed and ambition, and hate and selfishness and are initiated by plots and machinations that are in the highest degree antisocial and antipathetic to every principle of humanity. It is to protect our children and our children's children and the America of posterity from such ungodly wars that the Peace Amendment is directed.

"Under our form of government, the President is in charge of foreign relations. Under the Ludlow Referendum, his leadership . . . would be considerably curtailed."

A War Referendum Should Not Be Added to the Constitution

Millard Tydings (1890-1961)

In 1938 Congress debated a proposed constitutional amendment that would have required a national referendum of the American people before the United States could send soldiers to foreign wars. The Ludlow Amendment, named for Representative Louis Ludlow of Indiana, who originated it, was strongly supported by congressional isolationists who thought it would prevent American involvement in such wars. It was strongly opposed by President Franklin D. Roosevelt and members of his administration, who spoke out and acted against it with much more dedication than they had shown in opposing other congressional anti-war measures such as the Neutrality Acts. In part because of the president's criticisms, the proposed amendment was defeated.

One opponent of the Ludlow Amendment was Senator Millard Tydings of Maryland. A lieutenant colonel in World War I, Tydings was elected as a Democrat to the House of Representatives in 1922. Four years later he was elevated to the U.S. Senate, where he remained until his defeat in 1950. The following viewpoint is taken from a speech he gave on January 2, 1938, detailing his reasons for opposing the Ludlow Amendment. He begins by stating that he and the amendment's supporters share the common goals of

Millard Tydings, a speech before the Town Hall of Washington, D.C., January 2, 1938. Reprinted in *Congressional Digest*, February 1938.

avoiding future war, but that they disagree over whether the amendment provides the best means toward that goal. He argues that the president and his cabinet, as well as Congress, can make a more informed decision over war than can the American people. He also makes the argument that aggressor nations, believing that a national referendum would keep the United States from responding, might be more willing to attack countries close to the United States or otherwise threaten America's interests in the world.

With the huge cost of life and treasure of the last war still fresh in our minds, the people of the United States are searching as never before for a means to avoid future wars.

We wish very fervently for peace in all the world. It is a commonplace to hear people in all walks of life say, when referring to the struggles taking place in other countries, "I certainly hope we can keep out of it." If wishing could accomplish peace, we would never again hear the tread of martial feet.

Yet the longing for peace drives us in our search for the best ways and means of preserving it at home and abroad. While we cannot know the future, we do know the past, and in our thinking we must look to the past, to the lessons of history, in order to find from the pages of grim experience the course best calculated to keep our country on the highway of peace.

Popular opinion runs the whole gamut of proposals. Some favor the largest navy in the world as a means of peace. Others advocate building no ships at all. There are those who want a large army, and still other groups who want no army at all. There are proponents and opponents of the League of Nations and the World Court. . . . Many men and women favor various neutrality policies for our country. Still others would make a condition to a foreign war the approval of our people to it, through a national referendum.

These proposals do not differ as to objective. They differ widely as to the method of attaining it.

In my opinion, there is no royal road to peace. History supports this view. On the contrary, it is a hard, long, difficult road. Those who would walk it must be prepared for great sacrifices, for co-operation, for the utmost tolerance, and for a wide understanding of all the elements that make for peace or war.

The Ludlow Amendment

One of these so-called peace proposals is pending now before the House of Representatives—a proposition known as the Ludlow Constitutional Amendment. What does it mean? Exactly what it says—that under no circumstances whatsoever shall there be a declaration of war against any nation of the earth (unless a foreign nation invades our own country) until a majority of the voters of the nation shall declare in favor of such war.

In short, the Ludlow referendum would deprive the Congress of the prerogative of declaring war, and leave it up to the people. It presupposes that the people will be less inclined to vote for war than would be the Congress.

A Dangerous Idea

Not all isolationists supported the Ludlow Amendment. One who did not was Senator Arthur H. Vandenberg of Michigan, whose views appeared in the January 1, 1938, issue of the Literary Digest.

In my view it would be as sensible to require a town meeting before permitting the fire department to face a blaze. To the last possible degree America should mind her own business and keep out of other people's wars. I favor every effectual insulation. But, with the greatest respect for the earnestness of those who promote the referendum idea, I believe it highly dangerous rather than protective.

Whether this conclusion is true, no one knows. It is possible to conceive of a situation where the President and the Congress might oppose war, and the majority of the people might vote for it.

On the other hand, it is equally possible to conceive that the people might be opposed to a war and the Congress declare war nevertheless.

It cannot be denied that the President, his Cabinet and the Congress are in a better position to act than are the people, for the simple reason that they are in possession of more complete, better and more accurate information than are the masses scattered from the Atlantic to the Pacific. The State Department, through its representatives abroad, knows of the secret treaties existing between groups of nations and what the terms of these treaties are, and in case war is declared against a single nation, what other nations may come to her defense. This information is available to the President and to some extent to Congress, but not to the people at large.

Under our form of government, the President is in charge of foreign relations. Under the Ludlow Referendum, his leadership in this field would be seriously curtailed. . . .

Even with the Ludlow Resolution, the President, as commander-in-chief, can send the entire fleet to the Orient and our whole

117

army to the Philippines and Hawaii. Indeed, he could so handle our foreign affairs as to create an incident which would invite attack by a foreign government and we would be at war anyhow, if such an incident were created, but still we would be under a constitutional prohibition against an actual declaration of war until the people ratified the declaration. In this event the hostilities would be going on anyhow.

It is also probable that the President might want to declare war and that Congress would oppose him. As the Constitution now stands, that would end the matter—there would be no war. But, after the Ludlow Resolution was adopted, the President could appeal over the heads of a Congress—which did not desire to declare war—to the people for ratification of the war declaration. . . .

At least this much can be said, that the President and Congress, even though the Ludlow Referendum were adopted, could pass embargo and neutrality laws which might lead to war, then as now, so that the referendum as a check on war would in that case be more of a theoretical check than an actual one.

The resolution also says in effect that if Japan declares war on Mexico and lands troops just below the southern border of the United States, and seems to have the intention of using Mexico as a base for an attack upon the United States, that Congress could do nothing until all the people of America voted on the course to be pursued. In the period of thirty or sixty days while we were waiting for the people to vote, a situation might arise where twice as much life and treasure would have to be sacrificed to repel the invader than if action were taken early.

A Troubling Scenario

Now let us assume that Japan did land troops in Mexico and in foreign countries adjoining the Panama Canal, but did not attack us. Suppose there was a referendum on whether or not we should declare war on Japan, and suppose that the people voted against war. In the meantime, Japan kept on transporting troops and supplies, and establishing naval, military and aeroplane bases throughout Mexico after the referendum against war had been taken. I suppose that as the situation became more serious we would have to have another referendum. We will suppose that our people voted the second time against war with Japan, until finally Japan had an army of 600,000 men, 1,000 bombing planes, and her entire fleet based in Lower California, close to the Mexican oil fields, and finally did attack the United States. Would it not cost more in life and treasure to wait until that situation developed, than would have been the case if the President and Congress had had a free hand to deal with such an emergency at the start?

If during that emergency the President told the Japanese Gov-

118

ernment he looked with displeasure upon the landing of troops in Mexico, the Japanese Government would know, with the Ludlow Amendment in force, that the United States could do nothing until after the people had voted on the question some thirty or sixty days thereafter.

"But," you may say, "the Mexico-Japanese illustration is a fantastic supposition." So was the thought of a million Japanese soldiers in China a year ago. So was the thought of civil war in Spain two years ago. So was the thought of our entire world at war in 1913.

We are told there is a secret alliance between Germany, Italy and Japan. Who knows what Japan will do in the event of another world war?

Already to the south of us, Fascism is taking root. Indeed, there are only four or five countries south of the Rio Grande that are real democracies. Most of them have dictatorships.

Lest I be misunderstood, I must explain I do not intend to convey the impression that if Japan should land troops in Mexico, Congress would instantly declare war. Maybe that would not be wise. Maybe Congress would not want to. But the fact that it could legally declare war instantly without an interval of thirty to sixty days transpiring after the landing of the troops is of transcendental importance. The right of Congress to declare war instantly is a powerful deterrent, in my opinion, to the development of such a situation as I have imagined.

Again, if our ships trading between the United States and neutral countries are sunk upon the high seas, the President can negotiate with the aggressor nation, and always there is the threat of force behind his notes. If the Ludlow Referendum were adopted, this threat would be largely minimized, and the President's notes might be so disregarded by the aggressor nation as to provoke a situation of insult or humiliation tantamount to war, which might have otherwise been avoided.

An Eager Congress

On the other hand, we might have a Congress too eager to declare war, and the referendum might be a wholesome deterrent. The answer to these things is in the lap of the gods. If we could know the future, we could know the answer. It is perfectly possible to conceive that in a given case the Ludlow Referendum would be a good thing for our own country and for civilization, while in another given case it might be the end of our country, and of civilization. . . .

The Ludlow Resolution . . . springs, no doubt, from a worthy and wholesome desire for peace. Yet many members of Congress who will support it will do so with a question in their minds as to whether or not what they are doing is going to be for the ultimate best interests of the United States. They can only guess. They cannot know. We will be giving hostages to fortune, in our attempt to be certain that we guess the future accurately.

There is a phase of the Ludlow Referendum which should give us deep concern. Suppose that Congress and the country, in some international emergency, did not want war. But suppose a strong minority in the country wanted war, because of some harrowing incident, the loss of world trade causing a depression, or some other reason. So much pressure might be put on Congress by this minority that Congress, in order to pass the buck, might ask the people to express themselves in accordance with the Ludlow Referendum. I suppose that the air and the press would be full of war news and that paid propagandists would stir our citizenship to a high pitch.

No Conception of Modern War

President Franklin D. Roosevelt strongly opposed the Ludlow Amendment. He explains some of his reasons in a memorandum dated January 20, 1938, to James Roosevelt, his son and presidential assistant.

National defense is a current, day to day problem of administration in the hands of the President under our Constitution, and it has been on the whole wisely administered. The safeguard is that war shall not be entered into except by Congressional sanction.

National defense represents too serious a danger, especially in these modern times where distance has been annihilated, to permit delay and our danger lies in things like the Ludlow Amendment which appeal to people who, frankly, have no conception of what modern war, with or without a declaration of war, involves.

On the Pacific Coast especially, the defense of the Coast lies not on the Coast, but between three and four thousand miles from the Coast.

Once the defense of the Coast is withdrawn to the Coast itself, no government can give adequate security to Portland or any other city within two hundred miles of the Pacific Ocean.

Then, when the vote was taken, if it was against war, it might serve notice to aggressor nations that they could attack weaker nations, such as the countries of South America, with impunity, because our people had declared against war. In other words, so long as foreign nations are uncertain as to what course we would pursue, aggressors would be reluctant to take action in this hemisphere, particularly, against our weaker neighbors. But after one referendum against war, they certainly would feel more secure in attacking our southern neighbors, and eventually the first referendum might result in a war which, without the referendum vote, might never have happened.

Bear in mind, that should the Ludlow Resolution fail in Congress, it does not necessarily mean that we are going to war any more quickly than we would with the resolution in force.

The proposition can be argued either way: with the Ludlow Resolution, we may not go to war as quickly as we would without it; with the Ludlow Resolution we may go to war more quickly than we would without it. With the resolution, there might be no war; with the resolution there might be a war, which might never have taken place, had the resolution not been adopted.

Of course, the time element is a primary factor. Wars come quickly and suddenly. Perhaps a cooling period of thirty to sixty days with the referendum in force might avert a serious war, but on the other hand, the waiting period might be equally disastrous, as in the case I have visualized with Mexico. I think it is fairly reasonable to assume that once the people have voted against war in a referendum, the aggressor nations would be encouraged to new excesses, and our own country brought nearer to new dangers. Also, a small minority in the country might force a referendum showing where the country stood when uncertainty of our course toward the aggressors would be our best deterrent against war.

So we cannot be too certain that the Ludlow Resolution will keep us out of war. While undoubtedly conceived as a measure to insure peace, like the neutrality legislation, it may fail to achieve its purpose. Indeed, it may work out in a given case just oppositely to its declared objective.

Wars and Economics

It has always been a belief of mine that economics play a larger part in the causing and winning of wars than almost any other factor. Let me illustrate. In our own country, in the year 1935, we produced 52 billion dollars' worth of goods. That same year we exported two billion, three hundred million dollars' worth of goods or around five per cent. of our total production.

Now, according to the last census, there were 48 million persons over ten years of age, male and female, gainfully employed in the United States. Therefore, if we sold to outside countries five per cent. of all the goods we produced, it stands to reason that five per cent. of those working—one out of every twenty—or roughly, two million five hundred thousand workers, were employed in manufacturing products for consumption outside of the United States. If our world trade is to be surrendered, then two million, five hundred thousand people who worked in the rather dull year of 1935 would find themselves unemployed, in addition to the other millions who were without work.

Now let's see what the further consequences might be of the adoption of the Ludlow Referendum. Suppose there is a war between England and Japan in the Far East. Suppose the Japanese sink three American ships enroute to China, on the ground that the cargo would ultimately go to the English. The President asks for indemnities, apologies and assurances. Suppose the Japs stand their ground and refuse the indemnities, assurances and apologies. Then suppose the Japs sink two more of our ships, although bound for China, a neutral country? Well, it's no use for the President to send a second sharp note again, and he must either content himself with allowing our commerce with neutral nations to be sent to the bottom willy-nilly, or he must ask for a referendum vote on a declaration of war against Japan.

But, as the ships were sunk far away near China, the people of the United States vote against war. All right! What of our commerce after that? It's gone. Ship-owners and crews know the United States does not stand behind its flag on the high seas even when our ships are trading with neutral nations.

If America is not going to maintain her trade on the sea with the police power of her Government behind it, then it seems to me the logical thing would be, first, to have no merchant marine at all, with the exception of that part required in naval operations, and notify Americans all over the world to sell their property and bring their families back home.

If this is done, we will have an army of three million extra unemployed, to say nothing of their dependents, through the loss of our foreign trade. We will then have to rearrange our entire mode of living and tax those who are working very heavily in order to support those who are thrown out of work through the loss of our foreign trade which is now about five per cent. of our total production of goods, cut down agricultural production and seriously lower our entire standard of living to a point from ten to twenty-five per cent. less than we enjoy today.

In such a contingency, I estimate that there will be from ten to fifteen million persons annually looking to the Government for work, and subsistence, while those who are working must give up a very large portion of their earnings to furnish the Government with revenue. Yet the Ludlow Resolution, to some extent at least, paves the way for such a course, for it tinges our entire international relations with the foreign consciousness that America is not interested in anything outside of its own borders and is not likely to fight a war under any circumstances unless it is attacked at home.

"The peace-loving nations must make a concerted effort in opposition to those . . . creating a state of international anarchy . . . from which there is no escape through mere isolation or neutrality."

The Quarantine of Aggressor Nations Will Prevent Greater Wars

Franklin D. Roosevelt (1882-1945)

Franklin D. Roosevelt's presidency during his first term could arguably be characterized as isolationist, despite his past personal record of internationalism. He had served as an assistant secretary of the navy under President Woodrow Wilson during World War I, and as the Democratic vice presidential candidate in 1920 he ran (unsuccessfully) on a platform supporting Wilson's League of Nations. But after his election as president in 1932, a time when the nation was suffering from the Great Depression, Roosevelt concentrated almost all his attention on domestic affairs. In many cases he needed the support of isolationists in Congress (both Republican and Democrat) to help pass his New Deal agenda, and was thus unwilling to antagonize them in foreign affairs.

These priorities began to change after Roosevelt entered his second term, following his resounding reelection victory in 1936. By that point much of his New Deal was in place and, perhaps more importantly, the world was changing dramatically. In 1935 Italy under fascist dictator Benito Mussolini attacked and conquered Ethiopia. In 1936 Germany under Adolf Hitler marched troops into the demilitarized Rhineland in violation of the 1919 Treaty of Versailles. In 1937 Japan invaded China. Roosevelt and his for-

Abridged from Franklin D. Roosevelt's "Quarantine Speech," *Development of United States Foreign Policy: Addresses and Messages of Franklin D. Roosevelt*, 77th Cong., 2nd sess., Senate Doc. no. 188, #10676, pp. 21-24.

eign policy advisers believed that the United States had to take some sort of action to stem the rising tide of world aggression. But American opinion, as revealed in polls, was overwhelmingly against any action that could be construed as entanglement in other countries' affairs and wars. Roosevelt's advisers, including Secretary of State Cordell Hull, urged Roosevelt to make a public address describing the world situation and the need for international cooperation to preserve world peace.

Roosevelt agreed, and the result was the "Quarantine" speech given on October 5, 1937, in Chicago, Illinois—a site deliberately chosen as a place where isolationism was entrenched. In his speech, excerpted here, Roosevelt argues that isolationism is neither a sufficient nor a desirable basis for U.S. foreign policy in an increasingly dangerous world. He asserts that the majority of nations who desire peace are being threatened by the small minority of aggressor nations—aggressors that need to be "quarantined."

Commentators of the time and historians today disagree over just what Roosevelt meant by the "quarantine" analogy. Did Roosevelt mean the imposition of sanctions on or other specific actions against aggressor nations, or perhaps a general desire for greater U.S. involvement in collective security schemes? Few specifics were given in the speech itself, and Roosevelt's actions in the following months did little to answer the question. But despite the absence of specifics, this famous address can be seen as the beginning of the end of the isolationist years of the Roosevelt presidency, and as the start of a national debate over how America should respond to aggressor nations.

I am glad to come once again to Chicago. . . . And yet, as I have seen with my own eyes, the prosperous farms, the thriving factories and the busy railroads, as I have seen the happiness and security and peace which covers our wide land, almost inevitably I have been compelled to contrast our peace with very different scenes being enacted in other parts of the world.

It is because the people of the United States under modern conditions must, for the sake of their own future, give thought to the rest of the world, that I, as the responsible executive head of the Nation, have chosen this great inland city and this gala occasion to speak to you on a subject of definite national importance.

The political situation in the world, which of late has been growing progressively worse, is such as to cause grave concern and anxiety to all the peoples and nations who wish to live in peace and amity with their neighbors.

Some fifteen years ago the hopes of mankind for a continuing era of international peace were raised to great heights when more than sixty nations solemnly pledged themselves not to resort to arms in furtherance of their national aims and policies. The high aspirations expressed in the Briand-Kellogg Peace Pact and the hopes for peace thus raised have of late given way to a haunting fear of calamity. The present reign of terror and international lawlessness began a few years ago.

The Isolationist

Albert Hirschfield. *New Masses*, 1938.

It began through unjustified interference in the internal affairs of other nations or the invasion of alien territory in violation of treaties; and has now reached a stage where the very foundations of civilization are seriously threatened. The landmarks and traditions which have marked the progress of civilization toward a condition of law, order and justice are being wiped away.

Without a declaration of war and without warning or justification of any kind, civilians, including vast numbers of women and children, are being ruthlessly murdered with bombs from the air.

In times of so-called peace, ships are being attacked and sunk by submarines without cause or notice. Nations are fomenting and taking sides in civil warfare in nations that have never done them any harm. Nations claiming freedom for themselves deny it to others.

Innocent peoples, innocent nations, are being cruelly sacrificed to a greed for power and supremacy which is devoid of all sense of justice and humane considerations.

To paraphrase a recent author, "perhaps we foresee a time when men, exultant in the technique of homicide, will rage so hotly over the world that every precious thing will be in danger, every book and picture and harmony, every treasure garnered through two millenniums, the small, the delicate, the defenseless—all will be lost or wrecked or utterly destroyed."

America Cannot Escape

If those things come to pass in other parts of the world, let no one imagine that America will escape, that America may expect mercy, that this Western Hemisphere will not be attacked and that it will continue tranquilly and peacefully to carry on the ethics and the arts of civilization.

If those days come "there will be no safety by arms, no help from authority, no answer in science. The storm will rage till every flower of culture is trampled and all human beings are leveled in a vast chaos."

If those days are not to come to pass—if we are to have a world in which we can breathe freely and live in amity without fear—the peace-loving nations must make a concerted effort to uphold laws and principles on which alone peace can rest secure.

The peace-loving nations must make a concerted effort in opposition to those violations of treaties and those ignorings of humane instincts which today are creating a state of international anarchy and instability from which there is no escape through mere isolation or neutrality.

Those who cherish their freedom and recognize and respect the equal right of their neighbors to be free and live in peace, must work together for the triumph of law and moral principles in order that peace, justice and confidence may prevail in the world. There must be a return to a belief in the pledged word, in the value of a signed treaty. There must be recognition of the fact that national morality is as vital as private morality. . . .

There is a solidarity and interdependence about the modern world, both technically and morally, which makes it impossible for any nation completely to isolate itself from economic and political upheavals in the rest of the world, especially when such upheavals appear to be spreading and not declining. There can be no stability or peace either within nations or between nations except under laws and moral standards adhered to by all. International anarchy destroys every foundation for peace. It jeopardizes either the immediate or the future security of every nation, large or small. It is, therefore, a matter of vital interest and concern to the people of the United States that the sanctity of international treaties and the maintenance of international morality be restored.

The Peaceful Majority

The overwhelming majority of the peoples and nations of the world today want to live in peace. They seek the removal of barriers against trade. They want to exert themselves in industry, in agriculture and in business, that they may increase their wealth through the production of wealth-producing goods rather than striving to produce military planes and bombs and machine guns and cannon for the destruction of human lives and useful property.

In those nations of the world which seem to be piling armament on armament for purposes of aggression, and those other nations which fear acts of aggression against them and their security, a very high proportion of their national income is being spent directly for armaments. It runs from thirty to as high as fifty percent. We are fortunate. The proportion that we in the United States spend is far less—eleven or twelve percent.

How happy we are that the circumstances of the moment permit us to put our money into bridges and boulevards, dams and reforestation, the conservation of our soil and many other kinds of useful works rather than into huge standing armies and vast supplies of implements of war.

I am compelled and you are compelled, nevertheless, to look ahead. The peace, the freedom and the security of ninety percent of the population of the world is being jeopardized by the remaining ten percent who are threatening a breakdown of all international order and law. Surely the ninety percent who want to live in peace under law and in accordance with moral standards that have received almost universal acceptance through the centuries, can and must find some way to make their will prevail.

The situation is definitely of universal concern. The questions involved relate not merely to violations of specific provisions of particular treaties; they are questions of war and of peace, of international law and especially of principles of humanity. It is true that they involve definite violations of agreements, and especially of the Covenant of the League of Nations, the Briand-Kellogg Pact and the Nine Power Treaty. But they also involve problems of world economy, world security and world humanity.

It is true that the moral consciousness of the world must recognize the importance of removing injustices and well-founded grievances; but at the same time it must be aroused to the cardinal necessity of honoring sanctity of treaties, of respecting the rights and liberties of others and of putting an end to acts of international aggression.

The Call to Quarantine

It seems to be unfortunately true that the epidemic of world lawlessness is spreading.

When an epidemic of physical disease starts to spread, the community approves and joins in a quarantine of the patients in order to protect the health of the community against the spread of the disease.

It is my determination to pursue a policy of peace. It is my determination to adopt every practicable measure to avoid involvement in war. It ought to be inconceivable that in this modern era, and in the face of experience, any nation could be so foolish and ruthless as to run the risk of plunging the whole world into war by invading and violating, in contravention of solemn treaties, the territory of other nations that have done them no real harm and are too weak to protect themselves adequately. Yet the peace of the world and the welfare and security of every nation, including our own, is today being threatened by that very thing.

No nation which refuses to exercise forbearance and to respect the freedom and rights of others can long remain strong and retain the confidence and respect of other nations. No nation ever loses its dignity or its good standing by conciliating its differences, and by exercising great patience with, and consideration for, the rights of other nations.

War is a contagion, whether it be declared or undeclared. It can engulf states and peoples remote from the original scene of hostilities. We are determined to keep out of war, yet we cannot insure ourselves against the disastrous effects of war and the dangers of involvement. We are adopting such measures as will minimize our risk of involvement, but we cannot have complete protection in a world of disorder in which confidence and security have broken down.

If civilization is to survive, the principles of the Prince of Peace must be restored. Trust between nations must be revived.

Most important of all, the will for peace on the part of peace-loving nations must express itself to the end that nations that may be tempted to violate their agreements and the rights of others will desist from such a course. There must be positive endeavors to preserve peace.

America hates war. America hopes for peace. Therefore, America actively engages in the search for peace.

Viewpoint 6

"In spite of Mr. Roosevelt's alarm, this country is in little danger of attack within its continental borders."

The Quarantine of Aggressor Nations Will Not Prevent Greater Wars

The New Republic

President Franklin D. Roosevelt made an address in Chicago on October 5, 1937, that was meant to educate the American people on the increasing global dangers posed by aggressor nations such as Germany and Japan, and to suggest, if somewhat vaguely, American cooperation with other nations to "quarantine" aggressors. His address received national attention, and was both praised and criticized. Many isolationists were disturbed by the implications of his address. Senator Gerald P. Nye of North Dakota, a leading isolationist, responded, "Once again we are baited to thrill to a call to save the world."

Isolationists of the 1930s came from all points of the political spectrum, and criticisms of Roosevelt's speech came from both liberal and conservative isolationists. Liberal isolationists worried that foreign entanglements would cause the country to neglect domestic reform, while conservative isolationists feared entanglements would inevitably enhance the power of the national government, something they strongly opposed.

One of the main forums of liberal isolationist thought during the 1930s was the *New Republic*, a weekly journal of opinion founded in 1914. Ironically the magazine was at first a strong supporter of U.S. involvement in World War I and Woodrow Wilson's conception of a League of Nations. But by the 1930s its editors had become disillusioned with the League's ineffectiveness,

"Forcible-Feeble Diplomacy," *The New Republic*, October 20, 1937.

and the magazine, under editor Bruce Bliven, evolved into a strong voice against any international obligations that might involve the United States in foreign wars. The following viewpoint is taken from an editorial criticizing Roosevelt's 1937 address. The editors review what they consider the failures of the League of Nations, and argue that, short of war, the United States could and should do little outside its borders.

When President Roosevelt made his eloquent speech at Chicago denouncing international aggressors, he used a language made familiar by Woodrow Wilson twenty years ago, and one which has been the stock-in-trade of adherents of the League of Nations, of "collective security," of the doctrine that "peace is indivisible" ever since. The speech of course gained poignancy from the fact that aggression is rampant and that war against women and children is being waged by bombing planes in China and Spain. But the philosophy behind it is the same. Treaties must be respected. All nations are threatened when any one of them is unjustly invaded. Even the United States is not safe from attack if international anarchy is unchecked. Neutrality and isolation offer no escape. Ninety percent of the people of the world are peaceably inclined; it is the wicked ten percent who cause the trouble. The peace-loving nations must take concerted action to stop the war-makers; the militarist nations must be "quarantined."

The Philosophy of Neutrality

This is the exact opposite of the idea which gave rise to the neutrality legislation passed by Congress, which the President has declined to call into force in the present crisis. The philosophy behind the neutrality law is that threats against aggressors are unlikely to stop war, and greatly increase the danger of our involvement if it occurs. We may not be able to stay out in any case, but our chance of doing so is larger if we so limit our commercial relations with all belligerents as to minimize the incidents that cause trouble. Such measures may injure the victim of aggression as well as the aggressor, but at least they help to preserve an area of peace in the world. We shall have more chance of success in the attempt to stay out of war if we go about it correctly than in the more ambitious project of keeping the whole world at peace.

If Mr. Roosevelt means anything by his words, he means that he has abandoned the neutrality course laid out for him by Congress. *The New Republic*, which has supported this course from the beginning, believes he has made a dangerous and tragic choice. But if the United States is to follow the line that he seems to have chosen, it will be fatal to pursue it with anything less than whole-hearted vigor. Let us think back over the history of the past twenty years to see why this is so.

The Versailles Treaty, which ended the last war, was an expression of two contrary purposes. One was to punish and weaken the defeated nations, so that they would never be able to fight again, carving up Europe into a congeries of states which it was hoped would block any more imperialist ambitions on the part of the Central Powers. The other was to establish a regime of international justice and coöperation through the League of Nations, which would furnish a means for peaceful settlement of grievances, would effect disarmament, and also would bring the whole force of the world to bear upon any power or group of powers which failed to respect international order. It threatened aggressors with diplomatic, economic and, if necessary, military sanctions. To those who objected that the terms of the treaty were unjust, would cause profound economic dislocation, would breed new wars, it was replied that in due course the League would remedy all that. The League, of course, failed to make any substantial modification of the terms of the treaty, as those who opposed American participation in it feared would be the case. Disarmament was a fraud. Capitalist nationalism went ahead as usual, to cause disputes and economic disorders. New potential aggressors arose out of the turmoil, as realists all along had foreseen. The sole hope of the League, as a machinery for peace preservation, came to lie not in its ability to heal but in the menace of its threats.

A Fatal Delusion

Among the weaknesses of the idealistic pacifism which relied upon the League, the most fatal was the delusion that the mere threats of sanctions expressed in the League Covenant would make it unnecessary to apply them. You did not need to worry about the cost or effectiveness of economic embargoes, because no nation would be foolhardy enough to risk incurring them. Still more, if you threatened to use armies and navies as an "international police" you would never have war—that is, you would never need to use the armies and navies. Consequently you could be morally and physically unprepared to fight just because you had threatened to do so.

The trouble was that certain powers were shrewd enough, and reckless or desperate enough, to gamble on the hollowness of threats uttered by people who did not want to fight. Japan was the first to do so, when she seized Manchuria. The League duly

131

condemned her aggression, but when the nations—and particularly Great Britain—actually had to count the cost of sanctions, economic or military, the job of stopping Japan seemed too quixotic. Germany challenged the League, first by rearmament, then by reoccupation of the Rhineland. The League Powers saw at once that they could not do anything to prevent Germany from accomplishing these things without a war, and for war neither the governments nor the peoples were prepared. Of course the Ethiopian affair is fresh in our minds. Mussolini, encouraged by the collapse of the League in other instances, went out frankly for conquest of a League member nation, and got away with it. The League, mustering all its resolution for a now-or-never attempt, did obtain the application of economic sanctions against Italy—but they did not cover enough products or materials, and were not vigorously enough applied, to stop her. When it came to denying her oil, or using warships to blockade her coasts, or keeping her transports from passing through the Suez Canal, nobody had the nerve to do it because these things could not be done without taking a very big risk that Mussolini would start a war in the Mediterranean—and that meant in all of Europe. Finally, the failure of the sanctions which sought to quarantine the Spanish war is a world scandal.

Dangerous Nonsense

The inescapable lesson from all this is—when a nation is bent upon military aggression, there is no way to stop her save ability and readiness to defeat her by force of arms. There is a slight chance of preserving peace by "concerted action of peace-loving nations" if these nations can surely enforce their will and are known by the trouble-makers to be willing to do so. Otherwise all the talk of collective security is dangerous nonsense. Unless we are prepared to fight Japan, Italy and Germany before things get any worse and are willing convincingly to say so, we had much better adopt a firm policy of abstention in the first place. Tall talk about international morality has no effect when coupled with a declaration that we do not intend to go to war. It merely provides the agitation necessary to excite us to a fighting pitch after the damage is done and our potential enemies have gone too far to withdraw. We become convinced of our peaceable righteousness and of the wickedness of the aggressors. In the end we succumb to the argument that as devoted lovers of peace we must go to war to preserve it.

What sort of "quarantine" can Mr. Roosevelt have in mind as a means of causing Japan to cease in her attempt to conquer China? A refusal to sell arms, ammunition and implements of war would have no more effect on Japan than upon Italy, if as much. Japan is equipped to make all she needs of these things. She has bought airplanes from us, but only to the extent of $1,500,000 in the eighteen months preceding July, 1937. Japan is nearly self-sustaining in food; she cannot be starved out. She does, however, need raw materials for her industries; her principal imports consist of cotton, wool, iron ore, pig iron, scrap metal, copper and oil. A complete and effective embargo would cause serious injury to her economic life, and would eventually—though probably not for many months—diminish her ability to fight. It would also deprive our Southern states of about one-quarter of the foreign market for their cotton, and Australia of a large outlet for her wool. Meanwhile Japan would be compelled to push her conquests in Asia, perhaps extending them to the Dutch East Indies or possi-

The President Turns His Back on Neutrality

Immediately following President Franklin D. Roosevelt's "Quarantine" speech, the New Republic *of October 13, 1937, offered an editorial rebuttal. The editors of the magazine find a disturbing parallel between Presidents Woodrow Wilson and Roosevelt, and predict that Roosevelt's policy ideals will involve the United States in another world war.*

In one of the most important speeches of his career, President Roosevelt at Chicago definitely turned his back on the neutrality policy prescribed for him by Congress, a policy which he has so far refused to execute in relation to the Chinese war. The rationale of the new neutrality is that the principal national aim should be to stay out of war when it comes. Mr. Roosevelt on the contrary accepts the thesis of those who believe in "collective security"—that it is impossible to stay out; that in fact if international anarchy and aggression continue, we shall be attacked. Therefore it is necessary for the "peace-loving" nations to take positive measures against the aggressors and check them before it is too late. These aggressors, whom he roundly denounces, are easily identifiable from his language as Italy, Germany and Japan. The speech is interpreted by the diplomatic world as giving the clear signal to the League of Nations or to Great Britain and France for any policy of sanctions they may wish to adopt in Europe and Asia. We should say it not merely opened the way for such measures, but actually made them more likely. The moralistic fervor of the speech, its tone of anger against treaty-breakers and disturbers of the peace, are reminiscent of Woodrow Wilson at his most effective. Much depends upon what concrete meaning may be put into the "quarantine" which Mr. Roosevelt wants to establish against the guilty nations, but the inescapable conclusion is that if things go very far along this line, the United States is likely to be involved in a new world war.

bly to British India, in order to obtain the cotton, oil and iron that Western nations denied her. Furthermore, such embargoes could not be enforced without naval operations and clashes with Japanese warships. We should be faced with precisely the same dilemma that bedeviled the League against Italy—either the sanctions would be so weak as to be ineffectual, or they would be so drastic as to involve us in war.

War against Japan carried on at long distance, principally by British and American navies, would be a futile and exhausting affair. And of course either the diversion of British naval resources to this arena or the participation of Soviet Russia would give Italy and Germany their long awaited chance in Europe.

New Fears

There is little doubt that an alliance of the peace-loving powers could in the end defeat the new aggressors, after a long and bloody war. But there is a great deal of doubt that any policy of threats short of expression of a resolute intention to use extreme measures would give them pause at the present juncture. There is no use going in for collective security and then doing nothing about it except to give Japan a tap on the wrist, or lecturing Il Duce and Der Führer about Humanity. . . . There is no warrant for believing that international action to check Japanese imperialism will be any more effective than previous international action on the same model. After all, none of the peace-loving nations wants to fight or even to sacrifice trade. If we follow this lead, we shall bluster and work ourselves up into a state of hot indignation, until we find that we shall either have to stop bluffing or make good. And then the very world war that the President fears will be on.

There are just two chances of keeping this country at peace. One is to resolve firmly not to fight, whatever happens, and apply the measures necessary to implement that resolution. This means, at the least, invoking the present neutrality act. Congress, when it meets in special session, has the power to make this mandatory on the President, and should do so if he has not already accepted its will. In spite of Mr. Roosevelt's alarm, this country is in little danger of attack within its continental borders, and might well reserve its military power to repel such an unlikely assault. The other chance is to unite with France, Great Britain and the Soviet Union in a firm warning that further aggression anywhere will be resisted to the utmost, by force of arms. Such a warning is certainly not warranted by the temper of the American people, and is unlikely to be favored by the British. But it is the only expression of the policy of "concerted action" that amounts to more than deceptive and dangerous fog.

CHAPTER 4

Isolationism and the Road to World War II

Chapter Preface

As the 1930s came to an end, Americans watched nervously as tensions mounted in Europe and Japan continued its aggressive war against China. Then on September 1, 1939, Germany invaded Poland. Soon France and Great Britain declared war on Germany (which had just signed a nonaggression pact with the Soviet Union), and World War II—featuring most of the same European antagonists as World War I—was on.

On September 5, 1939, President Franklin D. Roosevelt, as President Woodrow Wilson had done before him in World War I, declared the United States neutral in the conflict. However, there were two significant differences between the two proclamations. First, President Roosevelt, unlike President Wilson, did not ask Americans to be personally neutral toward the conflict. Instead he expressed the desire that the Allied nations of Great Britain and France would win. Roosevelt, who in private conversations referred to the three Axis Powers of Germany, Italy, and Japan as "bandit nations," did not hesitate to share his desire for their defeat with the American public.

The second major difference between Wilson's and Roosevelt's respective neutrality proclamations was that Roosevelt's put into force legislation that had not existed in 1914—neutrality legislation passed in the 1930s that sought to limit American involvement in foreign conflicts. The United States in 1939 was forbidden by that legislation to sell or provide arms to any warring nations, including Great Britain and France. Three days after his neutrality proclamation, Roosevelt announced plans to call Congress into a special session, where he asked that the ban be lifted. In the first major legislative defeat for the isolationists in Roosevelt's presidency, he got his wish.

The controversy over revising U.S. neutrality laws began a national debate that would engage Americans for the next two years while war raged in Europe and Asia. While worsening U.S.-Japan relations were a concern, most of the public debate focused on the situation in Europe. Following the sudden fall of France in June 1940, Great Britain was for several crucial months the only barrier standing against German domination of Europe. New British prime minister Winston Churchill appealed to Roosevelt for greater aid; Roosevelt responded in September 1940 by signing an executive agreement loaning the British navy fifty "surplus" destroyers in return for long-term leases on British overseas bases. Many isolationists criticized the agreement as compromising American neutrality.

Isolationists were also critical of Roosevelt's calls for billions of dollars in new defense spending, peacetime compulsory military service, and "lend-lease" aid to Great Britain, which was running out of cash to pay for American arms. All of these steps, unlike the destroyers-for-bases agreement, had to be passed by Congress, where isolationists during the 1930s had been able to dictate U.S. foreign policy. These proposals and others were intensely debated within Congress and by the public at large. On one side were Franklin D. Roosevelt and those who wanted to ensure Allied victory. A Gallup poll in the fall of 1940 found a majority of voters willing to help England "even at the risk of getting into war." On the other side were isolationists opposing American involvement in the war. In September 1940 a group of businessmen, college students, and other isolationists formed the America First Committee, which within a year had 450 chapters with hundreds of thousands of members. However, despite the efforts of the organization and of other isolationists, Roosevelt was able to get all of his major foreign policy initiatives and proposals passed by Congress in 1940 and 1941.

Isolationists charged that Roosevelt's actions in aiding the Allies would directly lead to American military involvement in the war. Roosevelt, however, consistently defended his actions as necessary for keeping America out of war and American soldiers at home. While campaigning in Boston for a third term as president in 1940, Roosevelt stated,

> I have said this before, but I shall say it again and again and again: Your boys are not going to be sent into any foreign wars.

Historians have differed over whether Roosevelt himself believed those words or was guilty of deception or at least of a lack of candor with the American public.

The national debate ended quite suddenly on December 7, 1941, when Japan launched a surprise attack on Pearl Harbor in Hawaii. The next day Roosevelt called for Congress to declare war on Japan. The decision whether to formally declare war on Germany became moot when Germany declared war on the United States. The America First Committee disbanded shortly thereafter, and most of its members and other former isolationists pledged themselves to support America's effort in World War II.

VIEWPOINT 1

"Too many Americans have been brought up to think that in case of trouble in the world it wouldn't be necessary for us to do anything but sit still and let nature take its course."

The United States Must Reject Its Isolationist Past

Henry Stimson (1867-1950)

Events in Asia and Europe in the late 1930s convinced an increasing number of Americans that remaining isolated from world conflicts was a luxury the country could no longer afford. Japan's invasion of China, Italy's conquest of Ethiopia and subsequent invasion of Albania, and Nazi Germany's annexation of Austria were viewed as part of a larger pattern that threatened global peace. The threat seemed to increase after these three nations signed a mutual assistance pact and formed what came to be called the Axis alliance.

This string of disturbing world events continued in March 1939 when Adolf Hitler's Germany forcibly absorbed what was left of Czechoslovakia. Germany's act of aggression was in direct violation of Hitler's promises to England and France in the September 1938 Munich Agreement, which was supposed to, in the words of British leader Neville Chamberlain, assure "peace in our time." The United States condemned this act "of wanton lawlessness" but could do little else, in part because of the strict neutrality legislation passed in 1935 and subsequent years.

One person who advocated a rethinking of American foreign policy was Henry Stimson. Stimson had served as secretary of war and as secretary of state under Republican presidents William Howard Taft and Herbert Hoover respectively. His advo-

Henry Stimson, "We Must Drop Our Isolation," a speech to the Senate Foreign Relations Committee, April 5, 1939. Reprinted in *Vital Speeches of the Day*, April 15, 1939.

cacy of a bipartisan foreign policy was underscored when he became secretary of war in July 1940 under Democratic president Franklin D. Roosevelt.

On April 5, 1939, Stimson, then a lawyer in private practice, was asked by the Senate Foreign Relations Committee to provide his views on the world scene and on whether the Neutrality Acts of the 1930s needed to be revised or repealed. In his testimony, excerpted here, Stimson argues that the growing threat posed by Germany, Italy, and Japan mean that an isolationist foreign policy is no longer a realistic alternative for America. America must use its wealth and power to ensure not only its own safety, he asserts, but the safety of other nations as well.

For nearly four centuries mankind has been trying to build up a code of behavior within what is called the family of nations. That code has been based upon the foundation stone that every State in the family recognizes and respects the independent sovereignty of every other State. That has been the foundation of what we call international law. That has been deemed to be the principle upon which the world had the best chance of living in peace.

And it is in our Western Hemisphere that that principle and practice has reached its fullest flower of consummation. In every Pan-American conference from the beginning of their relations over a century ago the smallest and most insignificant State in size and power has been accorded an equal vote with the largest, and the disapproval of any such State is sufficient to protect it from the corporate action of all the rest.

Of course throughout the world controversies have periodically arisen which have caused nations to fight with one another. But the underlying principle of their conduct in the absence of war has been this principle of mutual respect. And the code of behavior for carrying out their relations one with another in normal times has been aptly likened to the code of mutual respect and courtesy which prevails among gentlemen in ordinary life.

Aggressor Nations

I have only to describe this long existing theory and standard to indicate how it has been shattered by present events. Today three of the seven most powerful nations of the world have rejected this code of behavior with open scorn and contempt. They have adopted as their most conspicuous foreign policy a system of aggressive action against their neighbors. To that end they have developed a very skillful technique which during the past few years they have been practicing with great success.

Under the name of unilateral action they have also proceeded to tear up all the net of promises, treaties and codes which had been adopted under the old system of mutual respect and which stood in the way of their own aggrandizement and purposes. Threats, aggression and treaty violation have gone hand in hand as the interlocking elements of this, their system.

A Stake in Europe

Max Lerner, a former editor of the Nation *magazine and a noted educator and columnist, argues in a symposium on foreign affairs in the March 1939 issue of* Common Sense *that the United States has an enormous stake in the rise of fascism in Europe—a stake that might justify future military involvement.*

I believe that America has an enormous stake in the European conflict, whether she likes it or not. It is even incorrect to speak of it as a European conflict. We are part of it, whether we go to war or not, because our fate depends on the outcome. To speak of America stepping in after the European contestants have exhausted themselves, and imposing a benevolent Carthaginian peace, is to indulge in one of those fantastic dreams that [Neville] Chamberlain has had, of Britain acting as a delighted arbiter after Russia and Germany have fought each other to exhaustion. The fact is that if the fascist powers win, the issue of fascism will have been decided once and for all, not only for the contestants but also for the rest of the world. The fascists will not even have to strike a blow at us. We will anticipate them by our ready acquiescence. If, on the other hand, the capitalist democracies win, we shall be in a position to take up again our task of solving our internal problems.

My own preference, like the preference of every American, is for America to stay out of the war just as long as it possibly can consistently with its own ultimate survival. At what point the limits of tolerance will be reached cannot possibly be foretold now. But it would be a man arrogant of his prescience and blind to the pervasive effects of a fascist victory, who would assert with complete certitude that those limits will never be reached.

In succession the attacks, all in violation of former treaties and of international law, upon Manchuria, North China, South China, Ethiopia, Spain, Austria, Czecho-Slovakia and Lithuania, have made clear the revolutionary and widespread nature of the change with which we are now confronted. They have shown to even the most reluctant critic that this new system is not a matter of domestic government among the States which practice it, or ideology, as we now call it, but is a reversal of the whole system of international practice in the world. . . .

The problem is further complicated by the fact that these three powerful nations occupy strategically very favorable positions for their attacks upon most of their peace-loving neighbors. If there were only one of them, the problem for the whole world would not be so serious. But the three are acting skillfully together, and geography has placed them with such relation to the lines of communication and the consequent national defense of the other nations as to make common action in such defense practically imperative if it is to be successful.

This is the novel situation which confronts the world today and I think the mere statement of it will indicate how it has affected some of our former customs and traditions. For example, take our old attitude toward the question aggression in war which has been the basis of our attitude toward neutrality.

In the former world we had a doctrine that in considering the controversies of our neighbors across the Atlantic or the Pacific we could entirely disregard the question of aggression and treat both sides with perfect impartiality without trying to make any inquiry into the rights and wrongs of the origin of their conflict. But today the fact of systematized aggression stares us in the face and we know only too well who the aggressors are. We pick up our newspapers every morning with apprehension to read the most recent evidence of their policy. They boast of it. It is the life and breath of their principal policy to which they have applied the appropriate name of an axis. We also know only too well who their victims are, both present and potential. We only have to read about some of the occurrences to the south of us to realize that even we are within the zone of their orbit.

A Shopworn Tradition

All this suggests another former tradition which begins to look a little shopworn in the present situation—the isolation, so-called, of the United States. Too many Americans have been brought up to think that in case of trouble in the world it wouldn't be necessary for us to do anything but sit still and let nature take its course. It looks a little differently now. The axis is moving much too rapidly and the world has become far too small and interconnected and interdependent. I have had official occasion to study the protected position of our country; its superb natural resources; its unmatched opportunity for self-containment in the maintenance of its defense. No one is more keenly alive than I am to this great advantage or to the comparative security of this country.

But the real question before us today is one of method. How shall these great advantages be most effectively used not only

141

with regard to our own safety for this present year of our Lord, 1939, but for the future, for the protection not only of ourselves but of our children and our children's children and of the institutions of our country. Shall we be content to sit idly in this present security, which may be only momentary, or shall we use these great advantages carefully, moderately, but firmly and above all intelligently to help protect the world, which includes ourselves, from its imminent and continuing danger?

By reason of our present security we can do this more safely than can any other nation. And the fact that we are known to be ready to do so will not only tend to slow down the axis, the members of which know very well that language, but—what is even more important—will at the same time encourage their intended victims not to make surrenders which will ultimately endanger us.

For myself I agree with the President that there are methods which are "short of war but stronger and more effective than mere words." I have taken occasion to study and ponder over such possible methods.

This country is said to supply about one-third of the known raw materials of the world and to account for more than one-third of the known economic and industrial life of the globe. For the past two years we have allowed these matchless resources to be used in very large part to stimulate the activities and aggressions of our potential enemies. That, I am bound to say, does not strike me as a very intelligent behavior.

I know that it is sometimes said that an economic weapon is a dangerous one. In the case of ourselves, I have been rather inclined to doubt its truth. If it is, we are certainly in a safer position to use it than any other country in the world. And when it comes to the danger of irritating aggressor nations, why the very fact that we are a democracy irritates the axis. Economic action would do no more and it has the possibility of most effective restraint for, after all the chief hope of today lies in the fact that each of the three members of the axis are in a notoriously vulnerable economic condition.

The foregoing is a very cursory statement of the conditions of today bearing upon our neutrality law and in the light of which it must be considered. The first act was drawn nearly four years ago, and events have traveled more rapidly during those four years than ever since the Great War. Their rapidity today is greater than ever. On its face that statute was evidently drawn under the influence and traditions of the past rather than to face conditions as they exist at present.

On its face it assumed that it would never be in our own peremptory interest to distinguish between an aggressor and its victim. On its face it assumed that it would never be in our own peremptory interest that an ill-prepared foreign nation should be able to defend its liberties by purchasing arms from us after it had been aggressively attacked. By this assumption the act violated one of the oldest traditions of the United States. On its face it was evidently designed to curb narrowly the discretionary power of the Executive in dealing with foreign conditions by making the operations of some of its chief provisions automatic and inflexible.

In all these respects it apparently assumed that the Congress in 1935 and 1937 was able to know exactly the course which the people of the United States would wish their government to follow under the conditions of 1939. Too meticulous foresight is often perilous, particularly in the drafting of unchangeable commitments. Every lawyer is familiar with the fate of a client who insists on having his will drawn as if the Lord Almighty had vested him with exact information as to what the condition of the world and his estate would be at the time of his death. And we all know that the Lord Almighty has an embarrassing habit of bringing to confusion such rigid efforts.

It is this rigidity of the act which seems to me its chief danger. I believe that in all such laws the President should have more discretion. I am a Republican and the present Administration is Democratic, but I have always tried to limit my partisanship in the zone of foreign affairs. I am a strong believer in the system of representative government, and from my observation I have come to the belief that in no sphere of government action is representative action so essential, so effective or so safe from abuse as in the conduct of foreign relations.

I am not impressed with the fear that in that zone Presidential discretion is likely to be abused. It is my observation that in no sphere of political action is the sobering effect of terrific responsibility upon one man so marked as in the sphere of our country's relations with the outside world Certainly, in the case of the two wars in which we have been involved within my lifetime the Presidency was the most cautious and conservative element in the country, clinging to every effort for peace until it was clear either that the people were determined upon war or that no other course than war would preserve our safety.

Today we find in the light of hindsight that this act has automatically placed in the hands of foreign nations, some of them possibly our future enemies, the decision as to with whom this country shall carry on some of its trade and commerce. Today we find that it compels us to treat alike the peaceful and suffering people of China and the militaristic enemies who by conquest are trying to turn China into a reservoir of potential future aggression against the rest of the world. We find that it compels us to be an effective party to this aggression on the pain of otherwise depriving China of the means for her own defense.

Recently we found that by depriving the Loyalist government of Spain of the right to buy arms for defense against the Rebels who were being supported by Mussolini and Hitler it made us a strong factor in the overthrow of the very government which the United States had recognized as legitimate. It seems entirely likely that should a general war come in Europe this Spring this Neutrality Act might put us in the position of facilitating a result of that war which would make the United States the next victim of attack.

The American People

Finally the psychological effects of such a statute may be even more widespread and disastrous than the physical results. The American people are not insensible to cruelty and aggression. Nor are they so unintelligent that under the conditions of today they cannot distinguish an aggressor nation from its victim. On the contrary, being served with the most free and enterprising press in the world, they are probably better informed of the facts necessary for such a determination than any other people. Moreover, they are not a constitutionally timid people, nor are they smitten with such an inferiority complex as to make them wish their government to avoid decisions which are really necessary to their own future interests.

Yet the form of this statute today tends to make the outside world believe each one of these fantastic falsehoods and to guide their own policy in that belief. Without going into the details of any new legislation, I believe that the greatest step to be taken and the one which would do more than anything else to give the American Government a helpful influence in preventing the threatened general war would be to make it clear beyond peradventure that these misconceptions do not represent the real present views of the American people.

VIEWPOINT 2

"The man who says that America must go out to protect all those in the world who seem to us to need protection . . . is no true American."

The United States Must Not Reject Its Isolationist Past

William R. Castle (1878-1963)

Isolationists were not confined to Congress or the media—some were veterans of international affairs. Among them was William R. Castle, a longtime U.S. ambassador and diplomat. Castle had been chief of the Division of Western European Affairs in the U.S. State Department between 1921 and 1927. He later served as assistant secretary of state, as ambassador to Japan, and finally as undersecretary of state under President Herbert Hoover, working under Hoover's secretary of state, Henry Stimson. Retiring from the State Department in 1933, he established a reputation in the 1930s as a firm advocate of neutrality legislation as a means of keeping the United States out of European wars.

The following is taken from a speech made by Castle to the Bar Association of Canton, Ohio, on March 18, 1939. In it, he calls for a strong American defense and, citing the Monroe Doctrine, for keeping the Western hemisphere under American influence. But he questions the concept, which he attributes to President Woodrow Wilson, that the United States should go to war in Europe or elsewhere to promote the cause of democracy. Criticizing his "missionary frame of mind," he argues that while the spread of democracy is desirable, U.S. exhortations and actions (especially war) are not the way such a desirable goal is achieved.

Abridged from "Let's Mind Our Own Business," a speech by William R. Castle to the Bar Association of Canton, Ohio, March 18, 1939. Reprinted in *Vital Speeches of the Day*, April 1, 1939.

Castle's thoughts on Europe and Asia expressed in this speech are consistent with his view that America should remain neutral in foreign conflicts. He claims that the Soviet Union is a worse dictatorship than Nazi Germany, and that Germany, Italy, and Japan may have legitimate grievances and do not pose a significant threat to the United States. He argues that the tense situation in Europe was the product of the ineptitude of Great Britain and France following World War I, and that those two nations should not feel they can rely on the United States to help them again.

We Americans believe that a republican form of government, a representative democracy, is the best ever devised. We believe that the world has progressed as it has become more democratic, . . . we are sure that the more democracy there is in the world the less is the danger of war. Disagreement on policy arises only when we begin to argue as to the best way to carry out our mission.

I might just as well admit at the start that I am a firm believer in some of the traditions of diplomacy.

I am certain, for example, that more can be accomplished through courtesy than through arrogance; that one of the most dangerous and therefore indefensible positions in international relations is bluff. If you make a threat—and this should never be done except in extremity—be sure that you have the determination and the ability and popular backing to be able to carry through, even though war is the final result. I saw the other day an account of a new kind of elevator so sensitive that it could be stopped at a touch. The paper said that to prove the machine could really be stopped by a mere touch an egg was placed at the bottom of the shaft. When the elevator, in descending, reached the egg it stopped without breaking the shell. (This must be true because it was printed in a newspaper.) The action of a threat is not so easily brought to an end. Diplomatic eggs have thin shells and once broken it is very difficult to put them together again. The trouble with being brutally outspoken in dealing with other nations is that irritation results, and calm thought never goes hand in hand with irritation. In all too many instances there have been temperamental explosions which a little calm thought and a little more courtesy would have prevented. And in international matters the stakes are so large that no precaution is too great in guarding against possible misunderstanding. The eggs absolutely must not be broken.

It is necessary to say all this because, in my belief, we can do

146

our duty in safeguarding democracy only by helping to prevent war. Every ill-considered word, every insult, no matter how much it may be deserved, is a step along the road to war. The so-called [1938] Peace of Munich, some will say, marked the retreat and the definite weakening of democracy. I should agree to the retreat, if it is admitted as something temporary, but not to the weakening. It takes a lot of courage and is sometimes much more a builder of character to hold back, to admit that the action your every instinct urges you to take must not be taken, than recklessly to plunge ahead into disaster. If there had been war instead of a truce democracy might have been destroyed then and there. Most of you remember that the great war was preached in 1917 as the "war to make the world safe for democracy." The democratic nations were then relatively stronger than they are today but even with their victory it is difficult to see that the world has been made safe for democracies. Would there be any better chance now? I am afraid that, instead of saving democracy, a new world war would result in just a series of dictatorships—of which we should be one. . . .

When I use the word "promote" in the phrase "promote the principle of democracy" I do not mean we must go to war to destroy dictatorships and in their place to establish democracies in the world; or even that we must do so to save other democracies. Our "promotion" must be in accord with international law and with our traditions. It does not mean any departure from our determination not to interfere with others, to dictate the form of government others must have. We should never tolerate interference from abroad with our own way of life and what we should not tolerate ourselves we must not try to impose on others. There is a world of difference between the purpose of the missionary and of the diplomat. The one is sent abroad to convert; the other to report and to maintain good international relations. But the two purposes are all too often confused in these days. There are too many American diplomats who ignore their real field in order to become preachers. They are no longer objective but tend to become violently the protagonists of one side or the other. . . . Our representatives abroad can fulfill their duty to promote democracy by proving to others the virtues of our own democracy. They do not fulfill their duty when they attack others, because then they become missionaries and endanger their own country. Yet if they fail to do what they should not do many Americans accuse them of neglect of duty. In a well known magazine the other day I saw a sentence which pretty well summed up this point of view. The article was on the Far East and the writer said of our career diplomats there, "They act as though they had been sent to the Orient *merely* to protect and forward American interests." But that is exactly why they are there and as soon as they go outside this duty they are bad public servants.

Put Our Own House in Order

The question before this nation at the present day which is most important in our foreign policy is how best we may fulfill our obligation to civilization, first to our fellow citizens of America and then to the rest of the world. I have already said that it must be in the maintenance and the promotion of the Democratic principle. I believe that this can most effectively be done by putting our own house in order, by showing the world that a democratic government is the most efficient and the most beneficent, altogether the best form of Government that exists. We must make ourselves the beacon light of the nations. We must also hold fast to the principles of foreign policy which have served us so well in the past. One of these has been the ability to get along in a world made up of all kinds of governments, if we do not like them to leave them alone, because what others do is not our business, and always to insist that they shall not molest us. But those who cry for an active defense of the democracies decry this stand as lack of principle or timidity because, they say, we are afraid to go to war. . . .

The argument of those who advocate an active policy is based on the idea that the fascist governments are in alliance for the sake of destroying the democracies. This cannot be proved and I do not believe that it is the case. I think that Germany and Italy and Japan were honest in calling their understanding a front against communism. They are all afraid of Soviet methods. I think that the reason they hold together now is that they are the have-not nations and that they seek relief from those who have, nations which just happen to be democracies. Germany and Italy and Japan want colonies as an outlet for their surplus population. They want raw materials. It is, therefore, a natural and perhaps an inevitable alliance but it is not aimed at democracy as a system. True, it may conceivably lead to war if nothing is done to satisfy at least some of the legitimate desires of these have-not nations. But verbally to attack them day by day as is done by too many officials of the American Government is only to make the possibility of peaceful solution more remote. You are just beginning to read in their papers that America is evidently determined to destroy all governments which do not admit the virtue of democracy.

We all want to build up armament in this country sufficient to give us as nearly as possible impregnable defense, and that defense under the Monroe Doctrine must be of the hemisphere. But we do not want to build at such a rate that all the world will suspect that we are preparing to go into Europe as soon as trouble arises. The proponents of an active policy say that it will prevent

America Cannot Save Europe

American historian and social critic Charles A. Beard had supported American entry into World War I, but later came to view that support as a huge mistake. Participating in a symposium in the isolationist magazine Common Sense *in March 1939, Beard makes a case for staying out of the next European war and for limiting America's ambitions for reforming the world.*

Although it is my firm conviction that the United States should stay out of the next war in Europe and all the wars that will follow the next war, I do not rest my case upon the assumption that by staying out we shall "do more good" than by getting into the fray. I rest my case solely on two grounds: (1) that by no process can the United States "settle" European affairs, make the peoples of Europe prosperous, happy, and good, make human nature in Europe anything else than it is and will be, and close the long and bloody history of Europe by the beatitudes; and (2) that by getting into the next war and the following wars the United States will suffer incalculable damages, material, intellectual, and moral.

If Great Britain, France, Russia, and the Balkan countries so immediately threatened by the fascist menace cannot make use of the preponderant power which they undoubtedly have, or will not make use of it, why should the United States try to make up the deficiency? I see no reason under the sun. Nor do I think that it is within the power or the intention of the Government of the United States to effect that combination of European interests necessary to save Europe from its own history. Surely it is no mean and contemptible undertaking to seek the maintenance of peace in this hemisphere and it will take all the talents we can command to do that much, perhaps more talents. As for myself, I am not impressed by the rattle and clatter of those who feel sure that they know Europe and that the United States can, if it would, "save Europe." And I deem it no crime against mankind to have smaller ambitions.

war to notify the dictatorships that we are prepared to defend the democracies by force of arms. But are we? And is not this a notification to the democracies that, with the United States back of them they need not make any compromises nor even try to satisfy any of the legitimate needs of the have-not countries? We cannot assert that the sum of wisdom and fairness is with Great Britain and France. They too have had their moments of imperialism. The people in this country who should have and do have the final voice when it is a question of war are not Government officials but the American people themselves. And I am dead certain that the American people have no desire to get into another European war. On the contrary I am sure that they are determined to keep out. It is not, therefore, playing fair with the American people to lure them along a path which, although it is bordered with pious phrases, leads inevitably toward war. This seems to me not a council of timidity but rather one in the interests of fair play.

If members of our Government are going to say to France, for example, "You can depend on our support in case of war," I should infinitely rather have the Government propose publicly an alliance of the democracies against the dictatorships, an alliance to be ratified by Congress. This would be contrary to all our traditions but it would be open and above board, fairer both to the American people and to our friends in Europe. As it stands now I am afraid that France would feel that we were traitors to our word if, in case of war, we did not immediately join in—and with the American people thinking as they are thinking now on the subject I do not believe that it would be possible to persuade Congress to make a declaration of war. As a declared ally we could speak our mind, but as it stands now we have no say at all about the various policies of the European countries, have no check on their actions. If a war should start because France seized a few square miles of desert from Italy or if Italy seized a few square miles from France, I cannot see America rushing to arms. It would not, in such a case, be even a question of principle but only one more example of the European quarrels which kept our colonies always in hot water with someone, a condition which caused George Washington to warn us to keep out of Europe's troubles. Let us avoid, above all, any secret commitments, just as we should avoid all incitement to war.

Greatest Dictatorship

Another weakness in all these arguments against certain dictatorships seems to me to be that they ignore the greatest dictatorship of them all, Soviet Russia. When we sorrow over German oppression of religion, particularly the Jewish religion, we should not forget that probably the greatest organized anti-religious drive that has ever been seen is the drive against Christianity in Russia. There you see wholesale murder of priests, wholesale persecution of those who dare to hold to their religion, wanton destruction of churches. People who were in Russia at this time last year said that the crowds of people kneeling in the streets on Easter in Moscow was an utterly tragic sight. They could not get into the churches because only the smallest had been left standing. But of all this we are told nothing. The American Government, speaking through the mouth of the President, says that we shall not endure persecution of religion—yet this persecution seems to be all right so long as it does not occur in Germany or in Italy. The answer to this distinction between dictatorships would be that Russia has no plans for military adventure and therefore can be ignored. It is probably true that the Soviet has no plans for military adventure abroad, although it prides itself in having the largest army in the world and although it has just announced that it is building a navy inferior to none. But does this make persecution of religion any less bad? Furthermore, there can be conquests in other than a military sense. Communism is essentially internationalist. The true communist considers it his duty to create communist states and to make communism supersede the democratic or other government which it tries to displace. Fascism on the other hand is essentially nationalistic. It has no desire to create other fascist states except in so far as the spread of fascism seems to create a more sympathetic world in which to try to get the space and the raw materials which it needs. Let us at least be wholly honest with ourselves and if we are attacking dictatorship include all dictatorships which are opposed to democracy. Certainly at the present time communism is better organized in this country and is a far greater menace to our system of free and democratic government than is fascism. . . .

The Mistreatment of Germany

Let us glance in passing at one more reason why we should keep out of the European mess. Much of the trouble is due to the ineptitude of the Allied nations after the war. I believe that here in America the general feeling was, "The war is over and Germany is thoroughly licked. It has adopted a democratic form of government and ought to be taken back into the family of nations. Let's all get together and help." If this idea could have been carried out I think Germany would be a democratic nation today. Instead of this the German frontiers were kept closed after the armistice and the suffering of the people for want of food and clothes was terrific. Germany was disarmed by the treaty and was made to understand that the Allies were shortly going to reduce their own armament. Nothing was done, however, in the way of disarmament through the League of Nations although the United States always took the lead in urging it. The League finally admitted Germany to membership, but coldly, making the Germans feel that they were pariahs. France occupied the Ruhr. The Saar was held for years although it was obvious that a vast majority of the population was eager to go back to the Reich. Nothing was done to help Germany financially and the country went through horrible deflation which ruined the middle classes and caused a bitterness which will not be wiped out entirely until a new generation has grown up. The result of this was that the German people lost all faith in their democratic government which seemed unable either to improve conditions at home or to put up a defense against aggression from abroad. When this happened Hitler's day had come. Europe should never have played with the idea of making Germany a slave nation. . . .

I speak of all these things only for the purpose of pointing out that in taking any part in the present antagonisms of Europe we run into the serious danger of supporting arrangements which we did not make and of which we seriously disapproved at the time they were made. Thank God that we, at least, were very little responsible for Hitler's accession to power. We dislike him because we dislike everything for which he stands in the science of government. But we must recognize that the move which made him the Fuehrer was a purely German move, happening because of economic and moral despair. We must recognize also that he has kept the movement purely German, that his seizures of territory have been a territory inhabited by Germans. . . . The thing to note is that whenever Germany, under Hitler, has moved out it has been to include Germans in the Reich. There has so far been no attempt to include other races. And does not this in itself a little destroy the force of the argument of the direct-actionists that the democracies are in danger of military attack by the dictatorships? Again I assert there is no proof that this is true. . . .

Internationalists Are Wrong

And now we get back to the assertion of the internationalist group that we must not be afraid to fight on the side of the democracies against the dictatorships. I doubt if any of us here would be afraid to make the fight if we believed it would do any good. The reason we are struggling to avoid that particular fight is that we feel that it would issue only in disaster. . . . Another world war would be a disaster to civilization, as we know it. Another world war would probably leave all participating nations in the hands of dictators either of the right or of the left. It would wipe democracy from the face of the earth, even if the nations which we now know as democracies were the nominal winners. I do not think that these assertions can be denied.

What then? Are we to drift, without policy or principles? By no means. We must work calmly toward one definite purpose, the prevention of war and the promotion of justice The man who says that justice can be attained only through war is a man of little vision. The man who says that America must go out to protect all those in the world who seem to us to need protection from their own governments is no true American. He is on the lookout for trouble. I remember that many years ago the Department of State was persuaded to instruct our minister in Poland to protest the reported pogroms of Jews in that country. The prime minister listened politely and then said, "I am glad you brought me this message because it shows the kindly heart of America. I am glad also because it enables me to protest against the lynchings of negroes in your own South. We have wanted to do it for a long time but have not felt that we had a right to as they are your citizens, not ours."

This seems to be a time when the United States is again getting into a missionary frame of mind. We make up our minds what form of government is the best form and then want to force it on others, whether they want it or not. We have gone through those phases, and they have almost always coincided with strong drives for trade. . . .

Of one thing we can be absolutely sure and that is that increase of hatred in the world inevitably increases the danger of war. We must hate that which is evil and fight with all the strength in us to keep the poison from our own country but we cannot hate a nation as wholly evil because every nation is always a compound of good and bad. It is always propaganda that paints for us the half true and wholly one-sided picture that is all black or all white. Believe it or not there is good as well as bad in Germany and Italy and Japan, and there is bad as well as good in Russia and France and England—and even in the United States, although I like to think of our own picture as most filled with sunshine of all of them.

I am quite aware that in daring to speak in this fashion I shall be called pro-Nazi. This is, of course, nonsense. I am merely trying to be objective and pro-American. A friend of mine said the other day that when he was called pro-anything it made him angry because he felt that it denied his intelligence, that it cut off possibility of debate. . . . I believe we shall be better able to combat the principles of the dictator countries if we try to understand them. Only if we understand shall we be saved from tilting at windmills. . . . What I hope profoundly is that you may follow me in the belief that the greatest thing we have to do now, the safest thing for us and eventually the best for the world, is to build up our own nation along peaceful lines, to make it once more prosperous and a power for good, to prove, by demonstrating it in our own case, that a representative democracy is not only ideally the best form of government but that it is the only government which can raise a nation to the heights, which can best bring happiness and prosperity to the people, which can make us most capable of assisting others who need help. Let's mind our own business—and keep our powder dry—avoid all the ideologies which are contrary to our own good system. Let us so live our own lives in a world of neighbors that we shall be a power for good because we have the respect of all.

VIEWPOINT 3

"To those who say that this program would involve a step toward war on our part, I reply that it offers far greater safeguards than we now possess . . . to protect American lives and property from danger."

The Arms Embargo Should Be Repealed

Franklin D. Roosevelt (1882-1945)

War broke out in Europe on September 1, 1939, when Germany invaded Poland, and Great Britain and France declared war on Germany. On September 5, President Franklin D. Roosevelt proclaimed United States neutrality, which under the 1937 Neutrality Act prohibited the export of arms and supplies to the countries at war. On September 21, he addressed a special session of Congress he had called to urge repeal of the arms embargo provisions of the Neutrality Act. Excerpts from his speech, outlining reasons for the change in law, are reprinted here.

To Roosevelt, neutrality did not have to mean impartiality. In an earlier "fireside chat" to Americans on September 3, he had insisted that the United States should and would stay out of the conflict, but, unlike President Woodrow Wilson in 1914, he did not ask Americans to be personally neutral toward the war. Roosevelt wished Great Britain and France to emerge victorious, and in his speech he proposes that Congress allow the United States to sell to these countries arms and needed supplies, provided they do not borrow money from American banks and do not use American ships to transport their purchases to the war zone. Such a "cash-and-carry" policy, Roosevelt argues, will make direct American military intervention in the conflict unnecessary. It would also uphold the traditional American policy of insisting on

Abridged from "Repeal the Arms Embargo," a speech to Congress by Franklin D. Roosevelt, September 21, 1939. Reprinted in *Vital Speeches of the Day*, October 1, 1939.

its traditional neutral rights to sell whatever goods to whatever country it chooses.

Both the Senate and house passed legislation repealing the embargo, on October 27 and November 2 respectively. It was Roosevelt's first significant legislative victory over the isolationists in Congress.

I have asked the Congress to reassemble in extraordinary session in order that it may consider and act on the amendment of certain legislation, which, in my best judgment, so alters the historic foreign policy of the United States that it impairs the peaceful relations of the United States with foreign nations.

At the outset I proceed on the assumption that every member of the Senate and of the House of Representatives, and every member of the executive branch of the government, including the President and his associates, personally and officially, are equally and without reservation in favor of such measures as will protect the neutrality, the safety and the integrity of our country and at the same time keep us out of war.

Because I am wholly willing to ascribe an honorable desire for peace to those who hold different views from my own as to what those measures should be, I trust that these gentlemen will be sufficiently generous to ascribe equally lofty purposes to those with whom they disagree.

Let no man or group in any walk of life assume exclusive protectorate over the future well-being of America—because I conceive that regardless of party or section the mantle of peace and of patriotism is wide enough to cover us all.

Let no group assume the exclusive label of the peace "bloc." We all belong to it.

I have at all times kept the Congress and the American people informed of events and trends in foreign affairs. I now review them in a spirit of understatement.

Since 1931 the use of force instead of the council table has constantly increased in the settlement of disputes between nations, except in the Western Hemisphere. . . .

America Opposes War

During these years also the building up of vast armies, navies and storehouses of war has proceeded abroad with growing speed and intensity. But during these years, and extending back even to the days of the [1928] Kellogg-Briand pact, the United

Democracies Threatened

President Franklin D. Roosevelt's proposal to arm Great Britain and France was attacked by American hero Charles A. Lindbergh in an October 13, 1939, radio speech. The following day Key Pittman, the Democratic senator from Florida who chaired the Senate Foreign Relations Committee, took the Senate floor to dispute some of Lindbergh's arguments. He argued that there are democracies in Europe defending themselves against a totalitarian Germany who deserve American help.

Colonel Lindbergh says: "I do not believe that repealing the embargo would assist democracies in Europe, because I do not believe this is a war for democracy."

I don't know what definition Mr. Lindbergh gives to democracies or what definition he gives to totalitarian powers. There are certainly totalitarian powers in Europe and there are other powers that are not totalitarian, which are based upon principles of democracy as we understand such principles.

Was Czecho-Slovakia a democracy? Was Czecho-Slovakia attempting to defend her democracy or was Czecho-Slovakia engaged in power politics?

Was poor Poland mobilizing her forces and attempting to obtain arms, ammunition and implements of war for the purpose of power politics or for the purpose of defending her democracy?

Were Esthonia, Latvia and Lithuania, through the mobilization of their forces, preparing to defend their form of government, or were such mobilizations for the purpose of power politics?

Germany, before she brought about war against Czecho-Slovakia and Poland, purchased arms, ammunition and implements of war from the United States. Was it right to permit a country preparing for war to obtain arms, ammunition and implements of war, and when she was prepared, start war, and then to prevent her peaceful neighbors from obtaining the same materials for defense?

Are Finland, Norway and Sweden mobilizing their forces by reason of power politics and a desire for conquest?

Isn't it evident that they are threatened by conquest and are seeking to defend their democracies? . . .

The most unfortunate part of Colonel Lindbergh's statement is that it encourages the ideology of the totalitarian governments and is subject to the construction that he approves of their brutal conquest of democratic countries through war or threat of destruction through war.

States has constantly, consistently and conscientiously done all in its power to encourage peaceful settlements, to bring about reduction of armaments and to avert threatened wars.

We have done this not only because any war anywhere necessarily hurts American security and American prosperity, but because of the more important fact that any war anywhere retards the progress of morality and religion and impairs the security of civilization itself.

For many years the primary purpose of our foreign policy has been that this nation and this government should strive to the utmost to aid in avoiding war among other nations. But if and when war unhappily comes, the government and the nation must exert every possible effort to avoid being drawn into the war.

The executive branch of the government did its utmost, within our traditional policy of non-involvement, to aid in averting the present appalling war. Having thus striven and failed, this government must lose no time or effort to keep the nation from being drawn into the war. In my candid judgment we shall succeed in these efforts.

We are proud of the historical record of the United States and of all the Americas during all these years because we have thrown every ounce of our influence for peace into the scale of peace. . . .

Last January I told the Congress that "A war which threatened to envelop the world in flames has been averted, but it has become increasingly clear that peace is not assured." By April new tension had developed; a new crisis was in the making. Several nations with whom we had friendly, diplomatic and commercial relations had lost, or were in the process of losing, their independent identity and sovereignty.

During the Spring and Summer the trend was definitely toward further acts of military conquest and away from peace. As late as the end of July I spoke to members of the Congress about the definite possibility of war. I should have called it the probability of war.

Last January, also, I spoke to this Congress of the need for further warning of new threats of conquest, military and economic; of challenge to religion, to democracy and to international good faith. I said:

> An ordering of society which relegates religion, democracy and good faith among nations to the background can find no place within it for the ideals of the Prince of Peace. The United States rejects an ordering and retains its ancient faith.
>
> We know what might happen to us of the United States if the new philosophies of force were to encompass the other continents and invade our own. We, no more than other nations, can afford to be surrounded by the enemies of our faith and our humanity. Fortunate it is, therefore, that in this Western Hemisphere we have, under a common ideal of democratic government, a rich diversity of resources and of peoples functioning together in mutual respect and peace.

Last January, in the same message, I also said:

157

We have learned that when we deliberately try to legislate neutrality our neutrality laws may operate unevenly and unfairly—may actually give aid to an aggressor and deny it to the victim. The instinct of self-preservation should warn us that we ought not to let that happen any more.

It was because of what I foresaw last January from watching the trend of foreign affairs and their probable effect upon us that I recommended to the Congress in July of this year that changes be enacted in our Neutrality Law. The essentials for American peace in the world have not changed since January. That is why I ask you again to re-examine our own legislation.

Beginning with the foundation of our constitutional government in the year 1789, the American policy in respect to belligerent nations, with one notable exception, has been based on international law. Be it remembered that what we call international law has had as its primary objectives the avoidance of causes of war and the prevention of the extension of war.

A History Lesson

The single exception was the policy adopted by this nation during the Napoleonic wars, when, seeking to avoid involvement, we acted for some years under the so-called Embargo and Non-Intercourse Acts. That policy turned out to be a disastrous failure—First, because it brought our own nation close to ruin, and second, because it was the major cause of bringing us into active participation in European wars in our own War of 1812. It is merely reciting history to recall to you that one of the results of the policy of embargo and non-intercourse was the burning in 1814 of part of this Capitol in which we are assembled.

Our next deviation by statute from the sound principles of neutrality and peace through international law did not come for one hundred and thirty years. It was the so-called Neutrality Act of 1935—only four years ago—an act continued in force by the joint resolution of May 1, 1937, despite grave doubts expressed as to its wisdom by many Senators and Representatives and by officials charged with the conduct of our foreign relations, including myself. I regret that the Congress passed that act. I regret equally that I signed that act.

On July 14 of this year I asked the Congress in the course of peace and in the interest of real American neutrality and security to take action to change that act. I now ask again that such action be taken in respect to that part of the act which is wholly inconsistent with ancient precepts of the law of nations—the embargo provisions. I ask it because they are, in my opinion, most vitally dangerous to American neutrality, American security and American peace.

These embargo provisions, as they exist today, prevent the sale

to a belligerent by an American factory of any completed implements of war but they allow the sale of many types of uncom-
pleted implements of war, as well as all kinds of general material
and supplies. They, furthermore, allow such products of industry
and agriculture to be taken in American-flag ships to belligerent
nations. There in itself—under the present law—lies definite danger to our neutrality and our peace.

From a purely material point of view, what is the advantage to
us in sending all manner of articles across the ocean for final pro-
cessing there, when we could give employment to thousands by
doing it here? Incidentally, and again from the material point of
view, by such employment we automatically aid our own national defense. And if abnormal profits appear in our midst even
in time of peace, as a result of this increase of industry, I feel certain that the subject will be adequately dealt with at the coming
regular session of the Congress.

Let me set forth the present paradox of the existing legislation
in its simplest terms: If, prior to 1935, a general war had broken
out in Europe, the United States would have sold to and bought
from belligerent nations such goods and products of all kinds as
the belligerent nations, with their existing facilities and geographical situations, were able to buy from us or sell to us. This would
have been the normal practice under the age-old doctrines of international law. Our prior position accepted the facts of geography and of conditions of land power and sea power alike as they
existed in all parts of the world.

If a war in Europe had broken out prior to 1935, there would
have been no difference, for example, between our exports of
sheets of aluminum and airplane wings; today there is an artificial legal difference. Before 1935 there would have been no difference between the export of cotton and the export of gun cotton.
Today there is. Before 1935 there would have been no difference
between the shipment of brass tubing in piece form and brass
tubing in shell form. Today there is. Before 1935 there would have
been no difference between the export of a motor truck and an armored motor truck. Today there is.

Let us be factual and recognize that a belligerent nation often
needs wheat and lard and cotton for the survival of its population
just as much as it needs anti-aircraft guns and anti-submarine
depth charges. Let those who seek to retain the present embargo
position be wholly consistent and seek new legislation to cut off
cloth and copper and meat and wheat and a thousand other articles from all of the nations at war.

I seek a greater consistency through the repeal of the embargo
provisions, and a return to international law. I seek reenactment
of the historic and traditional American policy which, except for

159

the disastrous interlude of the Embargo and Non-Intercourse Acts, has served us well for nearly a century and a half.

Repeal Will Not Lead to War

It has been erroneously said that return to that policy might bring us nearer to war. I give to you my deep and unalterable conviction, based on years of experience as a worker in the field of international peace, that by the repeal of the embargo the United States will more probably remain at peace than if the law remains as it stands today. I say this because with the repeal of the embargo this government clearly and definitely will insist that American citizens and American ships keep away from the immediate perils of the actual zones of conflict.

Repeal of the embargo and a return to international law are the crux of this issue. The enactment of the embargo provisions did more than merely reverse our traditional policy. It had the effect of putting land powers on the same footing as naval powers, so far as sea-borne commerce was concerned. A land power which threatened war could thus feel assured in advance that any prospective sea-power antagonist would be weakened through denial of its ancient right to buy anything anywhere.

This, four years ago, gave a definite advantage to one belligerent as against another, not through his own strength or geographic position, but through an affirmative act of ours. Removal of the embargo is merely reverting to the sounder international practice, and pursuing in time of war as in time of peace our ordinary trade policies. This will be liked by some and disliked by others, depending on the view they take of the present war, but that is not the issue. The step I recommend is to put this country back on the solid footing of real and traditional neutrality.

When and if repeal of the embargo is accomplished, certain other phases of policy reinforcing American safety should be considered. While nearly all of us are in agreement on their objectives, the only question relates to method.

I believe that American merchant vessels should, so far as possible, be restricted from entering danger zones. War zones may change so swiftly and so frequently in the days to come that it is impossible to fix them permanently by act of Congress; specific legislation may prevent adjustment to constant and quick change. It seems, therefore, more practical to delimit them through action of the State Department and administrative agencies. The objective of restricting American ships from entering such zones may be attained by prohibiting such entry by the Congress; or the result can be substantially achieved by Executive proclamation that all such voyages are solely at the risk of the American owners themselves.

The second objective is to prevent American citizens from traveling on belligerent vessels, or in danger areas. This can also be accomplished either by legislation, through continuance in force of certain provisions of existing law, or by proclamation making it clear to all Americans that any such travel is at their own risk.

The third objective, requiring the foreign buyer to take transfer of title in this country to commodities purchased by belligerents, is also a result which can be attained by legislation or substantially achieved through due notice by proclamation .

The fourth objective is the preventing of war credits to belligerents. This can be accomplished by maintaining in force existing provisions of law, or by proclamation making it clear that if credits are granted by American citizens to belligerents our government will take no steps in the future to relieve them of risk or loss. The result of these last two will be to require all purchases to be made in cash and cargoes to be carried in the purchasers' own ships, at the purchasers' own risk. . . .

To those who say that this program would involve a step toward war on our part, I reply that it offers far greater safeguards than we now possess or have ever possessed to protect American lives and property from danger. It is a positive program for giving safety. This means less likelihood of incidents and controversies which tend to draw us into conflict, as they did in the last World War. There lies the road to peace. . . .

I should like to be able to offer the hope that the shadow over the world might swiftly pass. I cannot. The facts compel my stating, with candor, that darker periods may lie ahead. The disaster is not of our making; no act of ours engendered the forces which assault the foundations of civilization. Yet we find ourselves affected to the core; our currents of commerce are changing, our minds are filled with new problems, our position in world affairs has already been altered.

America's Interest

In such circumstances our policy must be to appreciate in the deepest sense the true American interest. Rightly considered, this interest is not selfish. Destiny first made us, with our sister nations on this hemisphere, joint heirs of European culture. Fate seems now to compel us to assume the task of helping to maintain in the Western World a citadel wherein that civilization may be kept alive. The peace, the integrity and the safety of the Americas—these must be kept firm and serene.

In a period when it is sometimes said that free discussion is no longer compatible with national safety, may you by your deeds show the world that we of the United States are one people, of one mind, one spirit, one clear resolution, walking before God in the light of the living.

VIEWPOINT 4

"In what respect is this country threatened by reason of the fact no sale of arms is being made?"

The Arms Embargo Should Not Be Repealed

William E. Borah (1865-1940)

William E. Borah served as a U.S. senator from Idaho from 1907 until his death in 1940. An opponent of Woodrow Wilson and the League of Nations in 1919, he remained in the Senate long enough to become an opponent of Franklin D. Roosevelt and his attempt to lead the country away from isolationism in 1939.

At issue in 1939 was the repealing of provisions in the 1937 Neutrality Act that barred Americans from selling arms and munitions to warring nations. Roosevelt wanted presidential discretion to authorize the selling of such goods to Great Britain and France. Throughout the summer of 1939 Roosevelt's calls for changes in the law were blocked by isolationists in Congress including Borah, who in July informed Roosevelt that he had received private information that war in Europe would not occur. When war did break out in September, Roosevelt called for a special session of Congress and reiterated his plea for lifting the arms embargo.

The following viewpoint is a radio address Borah made on September 14, after Roosevelt had called the special session, but before Congress convened. After citing the isolationist tradition of George Washington and America's disappointments following World War I, Borah accuses Roosevelt of laying the "foundation" for ultimate American intervention in the war in Europe. He argues that the arms embargo of the 1937 Neutrality Act is crucial for keeping America out of war in Europe. Repeal of the embargo, he warns, would inevitably lead to America's helping to arm one side of the war against the other—a step that would de-

William E. Borah, "Retain the Arms Embargo," a radio speech broadcast September 14, 1939. Reprinted in *Vital Speeches of the Day*, October 1, 1939.

stroy American neutrality and entangle America in the conflict. Borah's arguments failed to sway the majority of Congress, which repealed the arms embargo. He continued to advocate nonintervention until his death in January 1940.

Europe is again in the midst of war. The President of the United States has issued proclamations to the effect that in this war this nation shall stand neutral. But we all realize that laws and statutes and proclamations are not, and will not be, sufficient to maintain successfully a policy of neutrality. Only the united will of the people can accomplish this difficult task.

It is highly proper therefore that we openly and frankly discuss all phases of this question, which bears, and will bear, so heavily upon the great body of the people. I want to associate myself tonight with all those who believe we can and ought to remain neutral. I want to resolve with you that we will in good faith put forth our best thoughts and our best efforts to accomplish that great aim.

If we can succeed as a people, especially in the midst of conditions such as they now are, in establishing here upon this Western Continent a great neutral power, a power standing not for force, not for cruelty and injustice, but for peace, for fair dealing among nations, for reason and justice, we will not only have added honor to our own nation, happiness to our own people, but we will have rendered to all nations and all peoples a service far greater than it will ever be possible for us to render by joining any nation, or nations, in carrying on war.

Force is gradually undermining and destroying freedom everywhere. If we are not going to wholly surrender to a world governed by force, then we must establish somewhere a great power which speaks for and represents in act and deed the things which make for reason and justice.

Whatever may be the discouragements and however great may be the obstacles thrown in our way, let us make the effort, let us unite behind a policy which, if carried through in good faith upon the part of the government and with effectiveness upon the part of the people, will not only shelter our homes from mass murder, our people from poverty and premature graves, but will also go far toward guaranteeing anew the blessing of free institutions. It is an effort worthy of a great and free people.

We are met on the threshold of all debate, of all consideration, of this subject of neutrality with the statement often delivered and with an air of finality that we cannot be neutral, that Europe is now so near to the United States, owing to modern inventions and the mingling of business affairs, that neutrality is impracticable if not impossible.

This seems to me a spineless doctrine. It is not the doctrine inherited from our forebears. If true, we would be the most ill-fated nation on the earth instead of being, as we had long supposed, the most favorably circumstanced of any, or all, nations.

George Washington's Situation

How near was Europe, how smotheringly close, was the European system when Washington announced his policy of neutrality and published it to an astonished and enraged Europe? He thought neutrality both wise and practicable; in fact, he believed that such a policy was indispensable to a free America. Yes, how close was Europe to the United States at that time?

The United States was really looked upon by European powers as a part of the European system. Brazil at that time belonged to Portugal. Practically, if not all, the balance of South America was owned, or controlled, by the Spanish crown.

The West Indies belonged to England, France and Spain combined. European countries owned, or controlled, Central America, Mexico, also what was later known as Texas, Arizona, California, Florida, Louisiana, New Mexico and Alaska.

In fact, this continent might be said to have been at this time geographically a European-controlled continent. Our entire northern frontier was heavily garrisoned by European regulars. The Indians were being used by European powers to harass our people and all Europe mocked at the idea that this young Republic would long remain an independent government.

We were in actual contact, physical, political and spiritual—if I may use such a term in this connection—every day of our lives with Europe and affected likewise daily by the domination of the European system. But Washington said we will be neutral as to those European conflicts. And, had he not so declared and made good, does any one doubt the devastating effect upon freedom, upon liberty, upon this Republic?

But we have no alternative, it is in effect declared, after these 150 years of self-government, we must go in in some way or other into all these controversies, broils and wars of Europe. It is useless, we are told, to try to avoid this fate.

Though these wars are not our wars, though they are wars brought on through the manipulation and unconscionable schemes of remorseless rulers, though their national policies are not our policies, though their crimes are not our crimes, still, we have no alternative, so it is urged, but to sacrifice the wealth, the homes, the savings and the lives of our people whenever the conflicts arise.

Although our people have sought peace and now seek peace, still we must make war because European governments maintain an eternal saturnalia of human sacrifices. Though the law of our

Lindbergh and the Arms Embargo

Aviation hero Charles A. Lindbergh began speaking out against the foreign policy of the Roosevelt administration in the late 1930s. In this excerpt from an October 13, 1939, radio speech, Lindbergh voices his opposition to the lifting of the arms embargo. One of his arguments is that the bond between Europe and America is racial, not political; while America should not enter any wars in Europe over such political ideals as democracy, he says, intervention might be justified if the "white race" were threatened.

I do not believe that repealing the arms embargo would assist democracy in Europe, because I do not believe this is a war for democracy. This is a war over the balance of power in Europe—a war brought about by the desire for strength on the part of Germany and the fear of strength on the part of England and France.

The more munitions the armies obtain, the longer the war goes on, and the more devastated Europe becomes, the less hope there is for democracy.

That is a lesson we should have learned from our participation in the last war. If democratic principles had been applied in Europe after that war, if the "democracies" of Europe had been willing to make some sacrifices to help democracy in Europe while it was fighting for its life, if England and France had offered a hand to the struggling republic of Germany, there would be no war today.

If we repeal the arms embargo with the idea of assisting one of the warring sides to overcome the other, then why mislead ourselves by talk of neutrality?

Those who advance this argument should admit openly that repeal is a step toward war. The next step would be the extension of credit, and the next would be the sending of American troops. . . .

Our bond with Europe is a bond of race and not of political ideology. We had to fight a European army to establish democracy in this country. It is the European race we must preserve; political progress will follow.

Racial strength is vital—politics, a luxury. If the white race is ever seriously threatened, it may then be time for us to take our part in its protection, to fight side by side with the English, French and Germans, but not with one against the other for our mutual destruction.

Let us not dissipate our strength or help Europe to dissipate hers in these wars of politics and possession. For the benefit of Western civilization we should continue our embargo on offensive armaments.

land banishes racial and religious persecution from our common country, still, because Europe is "near," we must join in the racial and religious conflicts and sacrifice our people over conditions which our forebears long since rejected.

Though we seek no people's territory, nevertheless, because Europe is "near," we must sacrifice the savings of our people and the sons of our mothers in this endless imperialistic strife. Though we would take no part of the loot which was divided up at the close of the World War, we are now called upon to make sure the title to a vast amount of this loot. What a fateful doctrine to propose! Let us renounce it and make the effort at least to establish freedom from the European system.

A Foundation for Intervention

But, friends, the problem of maintaining neutrality under present conditions lies closer home. Let's go direct to its discussion. It is presented by this proposal to repeal the Arms Embargo Act. To those who are advocating repeal, I submit this question: Is it not your main purpose in securing repeal to enable us to furnish arms, munitions and implements of war to one group of nations and to deny them to another group of nations, which groups are now in mortal combat?

Is not this laying the foundation for intervention—in fact, is it not intervention—in the present European war? Is it not your purpose to take sides through the authority which will be available when the embargo law is repealed?

And if the purpose of repeal is to do these things, and we do them, is not neutrality broken down, destroyed, and are we not thenceforth by every rule of international law, by every dictate of common sense and common honesty, parties to a European conflict?

I further submit to those who hear me: Do you think the time has come when for reasons of humanity, or of national defense, we should take our place in another European war? I feel we are really considering in this debate the broad question of whether we are justified as a people in intervening in this conflict and meet the issues as they are being presented upon the battle fields of Europe, for we cannot escape that destination if we move along the lines now proposed.

Let me review a brief and recent piece of history. Four years ago there began an earnest discussion in this country of the subject of neutrality. It was taken up in Congress and fully debated. Every phase of it was presented. It was discussed in the open arenas of the nation.

Learned men in all walks of life brought their contribution to the consideration of the subject. Our people wanted, above all things, to cut out the sale of arms to warring nations. It was felt it would help to keep us out of foreign wars.

The 1937 Neutrality Act

Finally, in 1937, we passed a law which prohibited the sale of arms, munitions and the implements of war to any nation, or nations, engaged in war. This law met the approval of both houses of Congress, almost unanimously. It met the approval of the executive department. It met the approval overwhelmingly of the great majority of the American people.

At the time this law was passed and this policy of neutrality established, there was no war of any moment anywhere. Germany and Britain were upon comparatively friendly terms. Both as a matter of moral and as a matter of international law, as a sovereign right, we had the undoubted right to establish this policy of declining the sale of arms, munitions and implements of war to any nation engaged in war.

It is now proposed to repeal entirely this provision of the law. It is proposed to repeal it to enable this government to furnish arms to one side and to withhold them from the other. The proposal for repeal is based upon the program of taking sides in this furnishing of arms.

Undoubtedly, as I say, we had a right to pass the law and, undoubtedly, we have a right to repeal the law. But when we couple the repeal with the announced and declared program of furnishing arms and munitions to one side and withholding them from the other, such program will unquestionably constitute intervention in the present conflict in Europe.

It may be said to repeal the law is not unneutral. I think under the circumstance it is. However, let's not discuss technicalities. But when it is said to me as a Senator: I want you to carry through a program, the first step of which is repeal, the second step of which is the furnishing of arms and munitions to one side, openly, persistently and continually declared, then I know I am voting for intervention, I am helping to take this nation into a European war.

I cannot hide behind the fact that they are two different acts because both are a part of one plan, and that plan includes the furnishing of arms, which is beyond question intervention. All any one need to do to know that this is the real, the controlling, purpose of repeal is to read the literature on repeal down to the last forty-eight hours.

The talk here in Washington is no longer that of merely furnishing arms. It is said: We must prepare to fight. One of my colleagues, a most able and sincere Senator, declared a few nights ago publicly: "Let us give up this dream of impartiality, therefore, of neutrality. It is better," said he, "to take sides and fight."

He was speaking out boldly what is now heard from the same sources from which came the agitation of furnishing arms. And, if in a few months we can tear up the law which a nation almost universally approved, how long do you think it will take to put across the proposition of sending our young men into the trenches once we have intervened?

They may say to me: You cannot be sure that intervention will send our young men to Europe. Of course, I cannot be sure. But I cannot be sure that it will not. I say that would be the logic of the movement. But suppose I cannot be sure, I ask: Why risk it? Why trifle with foreign war? Why bring the American boys to the precipice where any incident of war may kick them over?

The plan now presented by the advocates of repeal is that the democracies of Europe are imperiled, that we must go to their rescue, that civilization is threatened, that we cannot ignore the problem presented. But, if the war continues and the imperiling of democracies and the threatening of civilization increase, what can we say, having once put our hand to the plow? Will we turn our backs to the whole situation?

I repeat, as I stated a moment ago, what we are really considering these days is the broad question: Has the time come when the United States must take a part in this European conflict? Why deceive ourselves as to what will happen once we enter the conflict. Why shut our eyes to the inevitable consequences which must flow?

Time will not permit a detailed discussion of what is known as the cash-and-carry plan. It is based upon the principle that those who want our arms and munitions or raw materials shall come and get them, pay cash and carry them away. But, while I cannot discuss it in detail, I want to take time to say that this plan does not change the situation, as I understand it, with reference to neutrality.

Repeal Means War

The cash-and-carry plan repeals the embargo law and enables our government to direct the arms and munitions to one side and withhold them from the other. Whatever merits, or demerits, this plan may have, it does not seem to me to bear, only most indirectly, upon the question which I have sought to have you consider this evening.

I am concerned at this time with one proposition, that of avoiding any act, or acts, which will embroil us in a European war. I do not believe the cash-and-carry plan has any considerable bearing upon that point, and I shall therefore content myself with this brief reference. . . .

The Question of Selling Arms

In conclusion, the President has called a special session of Congress for the purpose of removing the embargo on arms, munitions and implements of war. There are some of us who want to keep the old law—who insist that the sale of arms to all nations engaged in war shall continue to be prohibited. The only question in controversy, the only matter of difference that I know of, is the sole question of whether we shall sell arms or not sell arms.

We see that the supporters of repeal are anxious to put an embargo on ships going to war zones, on loans to all nations engaged in war, anxious to prohibit our citizens from traveling in war areas, all this and more is to be done in the name of neutrality in the effort to keep us out of war.

We most heartily support this entire program. We say in the name of peace: Do these things. Maintain neutrality as to all these matters. But we observe here that there is a sudden break in the embargo—the most threatening and disturbing of all factors, the most calculated to get us into trouble—arms, munitions and implements of war are to be let through. Embargo is not to apply. What is the significance?

We feel sincerely that this is an error. We stand where we stood two years ago, where Congress stood, where the Executive stood, and where the people stood. Why prohibit loans in the name of peace and for the protection of our people but not prohibit arms? Why place an embargo on all these other things mentioned but repeal it as to arms?

That is the sole matter of controversy. What we did two years ago we did in the name of humanity, in the name of peace, to protect our homes, our sons and daughters, and to help keep us out of war. Blame us not therefore if we are slow to surrender our convictions.

What we who oppose repeal are contending for is now the law of the land. It has been and is being enforced under the proclamation of the President. No arms, munitions and implements of war are being sold.

In what possible way can the United States be benefited by permitting the sale? Who is it that is to be benefited? In what respect is this country threatened by reason of the fact no sale of arms is being made? In what respect are the safety and security of the people imperiled?

This is the sole matter of controversy. We urge that the same rule, the same principle, be applied to the most deadly of disturbers, arms, along with the other things prohibited.

"It is now altogether clear that such assistance to those who resist attack is a vital part of our national self-defense."

The United States Should Extend Lend-Lease Aid to Great Britain

Cordell Hull (1871-1955)

Following the surrender of France in June 1940, Great Britain stood alone as the last major European power in a state of war with Nazi Germany (the Soviet Union had signed a nonaggression pact with Germany in 1939, which remained in effect until Germany invaded the Soviet Union in June of 1941). Germany launched an air war against Great Britain, which many people thought would be followed by an invasion. Following the repeal of arms embargo legislation in 1939, the United States sold arms and munitions to Great Britain on a "cash-and-carry" basis—Britain would pay for its purchases without loans, and would transport the goods on its own ships. Many hoped these restrictions would help avoid repeating the circumstances that led America into World War I.

Britain was able to withstand Germany's air assaults, but its cash reserves were being rapidly depleted. Shortly after Franklin D. Roosevelt was elected to an unprecedented third term as U.S. president in November 1940, he was informed by British prime minister Winston Churchill that the time was approaching "when we shall no longer be able to pay cash." Still barred by American neutrality laws from providing monetary loans to Great Britain, Roosevelt and his advisers came up with the idea of lend-lease

Cordell Hull, "The Defense of the United States," a speech to the House Foreign Affairs Committee, January 15, 1941. Reprinted in *Vital Speeches of the Day*, February 1, 1941.

aid. Under this proposal the United States would lend arms and other materials of war to nations deemed by the president vital to U.S. interests, with decisions concerning repayment deferred to the end of the war. The president introduced the policy in a press conference on December 17, and elaborated on the idea in a radio "fireside chat" on December 29, in which he called on the United States to "become the great arsenal of democracy."

For the next few months Roosevelt's lend-lease proposal was heatedly debated as Congress tried to decide whether to pass H.R. 1776, "An Act to Promote the Defense of the United States." Many isolationists viewed lend-lease as simply another step toward American involvement in a foreign war, while supporters of the bill argued that it would instead prevent direct American intervention. The following viewpoint is taken from a statement made on January 15, 1941, before the House Foreign Affairs Committee by Roosevelt's secretary of state, Cordell Hull. Citing the dangers to the United States posed by Germany, Japan, and other aggressive countries, he asserts that the lend-lease proposal is of critical importance to the nation. Should Great Britain fall, he argues, the Atlantic Ocean would come under the control of Germany and would offer America no protection against German invasion. Delay in implementing lend-lease, Hull warns, could be disastrous for the United States.

We are here to consider a bill designed to promote the defense of the United States. I shall not discuss the technical details of the proposed measure, since that will be done by other departments of the government more directly concerned with these matters. I shall place before you briefly the controlling facts relating to the manner in which the dangers that now confront this hemisphere and, therefore, this nation have arisen, and the circumstances which render imperative all possible speed in our preparation for meeting these dangers.

During the past eight years, our government has striven, by every peaceful means at its disposal, to secure the establishment in the world of conditions under which there would be a reasonable hope for enduring peace. We have proceeded in the firm belief that only if such conditions come to exist will there be a certainty that our country will be fully secure and safely at peace. The establishment of such conditions calls for acceptance and application by all nations of certain basic principles of peaceful and orderly international conduct and relations.

171

Accordingly, in the conduct of our foreign relations, this government has directed its efforts to the following objectives: (1) peace and security for the United States, with advocacy of peace and limitation and reduction of armament as universal international objectives; (2) support for law, order, justice and morality and the principle of non-intervention; (3) restoration and cultivation of sound economic methods and relations, based on equality of treatment; (4) development, in the promotion of these objectives, of the fullest practicable measure of international cooperation; (5) promotion of the security, solidarity and general welfare of the Western Hemisphere.

The Road to Tyranny

Observance and the advocacy of the basic principles underlying these policies and efforts toward their acceptance and application became increasingly important as three nations, one after another, made abundantly clear, by word and by deed, their determination to repudiate and destroy the very foundations of a civilized world order under law and to enter upon the road of armed conquest, of subjugation of other nations, and of tyrannical rule over their victims.

The first step in this fatal direction occurred in the Far East in 1931 with forceful occupation of Manchuria in contravention of the provisions of the [1922] nine-power treaty and of the [1928] Kellogg-Briand pact. The equilibrium in the Far East which had been established by the Washington Conference treaties of 1921-22 became seriously disturbed by the setting up by forceful means in a part of China of a regime under Japanese control under the name of "Manchukuo." This control over Manchuria has been marked by the carrying out of a policy of discrimination which has resulted in forcing out American and other foreign interests.

During the years that followed, Japan went steadily forward in her preparations for expansion by force of arms. In December, 1934, she gave notice of her intention to terminate the naval treaty of February 6, 1922. She then proceeded with intensified construction of military and naval armaments, at the same time undertaking, from time to time, limited actions directed toward an extension of her domination over China and involving disregard and destruction of the lawful rights and interests of other countries, including the United States.

In July, 1937, the armed forces of Japan embarked upon large-scale military operations against China. Invading forces of more than a million men occupied large areas along the seaboard and in the central provinces. . . .

It has been clear throughout that Japan has been actuated from the start by broad and ambitious plans for establishing herself in

172

a dominant position in the entire region of the western Pacific. Her leaders have openly declared their determination to achieve and maintain that position by force of arms and thus to make themselves masters of an area containing almost one-half of the entire population of the world. As a consequence, they would have arbitrary control of the sea and trade routes in that region.

Previous experience and current developments indicate that the proposed "new order" in the Pacific area means, politically, domination by one country. It means, economically, employment of the resources of the area concerned for the benefit of that country

In September 1940, Germany, Italy, and Japan signed a pact pledging themselves to form a military alliance against any power that might enter into war against them—a provision many Americans, including cartoonist Herbert L. Block, believed was directed at them.

and to the ultimate improvement of other parts of the area and exclusion of the interests of other countries. It means, socially, the destruction of personal liberties and the reduction of the conquered peoples to the role of inferiors.

It should be manifest to every person that such a program for the subjugation and ruthless exploitation by one country of nearly one-half of the population of the world is a matter of immense significance, importance and concern to every other nation wherever located.

Notwithstanding the course which Japan has followed during recent years, this government has made repeated efforts to persuade the Japanese government that her best interests lie in the development of friendly relations with the United States and with other countries which believe in orderly and peaceful processes among nations. We have at no time made any threats.

Aggression in Europe

In Europe, the first overt breach of world order was made by Italy when, in 1935, that country invaded and conquered Ethiopia, in direct contravention of solemnly accepted obligations under the covenant of the League of Nations and of the Kellogg-Briand pact. In 1939 Italy seized Albania in violation of unequivocal treaty obligations. In the summer of 1940 she entered the European war on the side of Germany with the openly avowed purpose of participating with that country in a remodeling of the world on the basis of a "new order" founded upon unlimited and unrestricted use of armed force. Finally, without provocation, she has attacked Greece.

Throughout this period the government of the United States made known to the government of Italy its anxious concern over the growing deterioration of peaceful international relationships. Both on the occasion of the Italo-Ethiopian controversy and during the period preceding Italy's entry into the European war, this government addressed numerous communications to the government of Italy in an effort to prevent new breaches of world order.

Germany, from the time that Hitler and his associates came to power in 1933, began feverishly to construct vast armaments, while following a program of repeatedly made and repeatedly broken promises as a part of a skillful diplomatic game designed to lull the suspicions of other countries. After employing for several months at the disarmament conference in Geneva tactics which have since become a distinct pattern of German policy—further demands as previous demands are met—Germany, in October, 1933, rendered impossible any effective international agreement for limitation of armaments by withdrawing from the disarmament conference. There then followed nearly six years during which Germany, having determined upon a policy of unlimited conquest, moved inevitably toward the catastrophe of war.

Germany's work of preparation followed two main lines. The first consisted in the creation of armed force. To this end her entire national economy was transformed into a highly regimented and highly disciplined war economy. Every phase of national activity became harnessed to the requirements of preparation for war. More than half of the national income was expended for military purposes. Foreign trade and foreign payments became rigidly controlled for the same purpose. The production of planes and tanks and guns and all the other countless accessories of a modern war machine became the immediate objective of the whole national effort.

America's Pledge

In his annual message to Congress on January 6, 1941, President Franklin D. Roosevelt calls for Congress to grant him executive authority to provide aid to Great Britain and other nations.

I ask this Congress for authority and for funds sufficient to manufacture additional munitions and war supplies of many kinds to be turned over to those nations which are now in actual war with aggressor nations.

Our most useful and immediate role is to act as an arsenal for them as well as for ourselves. They do not need man power, but they do need billions of dollars worth of the weapons of defense.

The time is near when they will not be able to pay for them all in ready cash. We cannot, and we will not, tell them that they must surrender, merely because of present inability to pay for the weapons which we know they must have. . . .

I recommend that we make it possible for those nations to continue to obtain war materials in the United States, fitting their orders into our own program. Nearly all their matériel would, if the time ever came, be useful for our own defense. . . .

Let us say to the democracies: "We Americans are vitally concerned in your defense of freedom. We are putting forth our energies, our resources and our organizing powers to give you the strength to regain and maintain a free world. We shall send you, in ever-increasing numbers, ships, planes, tanks, guns. This is our purpose and our pledge."

The second line consisted of a series of steps directed toward improving the strategic position of Germany. The first of these was the occupation and fortification of the Rhineland in 1936, in direct violation of the Locarno treaty, voluntarily entered into by Germany ten years earlier. Then followed, in rapid succession, the absorption of Austria, in direct violation of pledges given by Hitler to respect the sovereignty and independence of that country; the dismemberment and final seizure of Czecho-Slovakia, in spite of Hitler's assurances after the seizure of Austria that Germany desired no additional territory in Europe and in violation of a solemn pledge to respect the independence of that country, officially given in October, 1938; the annexation of Memel [a Lithuanian city], and, finally, on September 1, 1939, a brutal attack upon, and the devastation and partitioning of, Poland.

The period of the war has witnessed the invasion and occupation of Denmark, Norway, Holland, Belgium and Luxemburg, in violation of the scrupulously observed neutrality of these countries and in contravention, in the cases of some of these countries, of assurances expressly given by Germany of her intention to respect their independence and sovereignty; the invasion and partial occupation of France; the splitting up of Rumania and the German occupation of the remaining portion of that country.

These seizures have been accomplished through a combined use of armed force applied from without and of an almost unbelievable amount of subversive activity from within. Each of the invaded and occupied countries has been subjected to a reign of terror and despotism. By word and by deed, the invaders have made unmistakably clear their determination to impose permanently upon these unfortunate countries a rule of tyranny frequently reminiscent of the worst pages of ancient history.

So long as there seemed to remain even a faint hope of inducing the leaders of Germany to desist from the course which they were following, the government of the United States neglected no opportunity to make its voice heard in restraint. It went further, and repeatedly offered its assistance in economic readjustments which might promote solution of the existing difficulties by peaceful means. All hope disappeared when the Nazi legions struck at Poland and plunged Europe into a new war.

Since then, it has become increasingly apparent that mankind is today face to face, not with regional wars or isolated conflicts,but with an organized, ruthless and implacable movement of steadily expanding conquest. We are in the presence of forces which are not restrained by considerations of law or principles or morality; which have fixed no limits for their program of conquest; which have spread over large areas on land and are desperately struggling now to seize control of the oceans as an essential means of achieving and maintaining their conquest of the other continents.

Control of the high seas by law-abiding nations is the key to the security of the Western Hemisphere in the present-day world situation. Should that control be gained by the partners of the tripartite pact, the danger to our country, great as it is today, would be multiplied manyfold.

It is frequently said that there can be no danger of an invasion of the New World. It is said: As Germany has not been able to cross the British Channel, how can she cross the Atlantic?

German forces could cross the Channel in an hour's time were it not for the fact that Britain, now thoroughly prepared and well armed, is fighting every hour of the day to prevent that crossing, and is fortified with every known device to repel a landing. The twenty miles of water between continental Europe and Britain are under British, not German, control. Were Britain defeated, and were she to lose command of the seas, Germany could easily cross the Atlantic—especially the south Atlantic—unless we were ready and able to do what Britain is doing now. Were the Atlantic to fall into German control, the Atlantic would offer little or no assurance of security.

Under these conditions our national security would require the continuous devotion of a very great part of all our work and wealth for defense production, prolonged universal military service, extremely burdensome taxation, unending vigilance against enemies within our borders, and complete involvement in power diplomacy. These would be the necessities of a condition as exposed as ours would be.

Great Britain is today a veritable fortress. So will this country be when our preparations for armed defense are completed. Most likely, however, it will not be by direct and frontal attack that the would-be invaders will undertake the conquest of this country, if they ever have a chance to embark upon such an enterprise. It is rather to be anticipated that their efforts would first be directed against other portions of this hemisphere, more vulnerable than this country, and then against us.

Subversive forces are hard at work in many American countries, seeking to create internal dissension and disunion as a now-familiar prelude to armed invasion. Today these forces are held in check and are being steadily eradicated. But the entire situation would change if control of the high seas were to pass into the hands of the would-be attackers. Under such conditions, the difficulties of continental defense would demand from us vastly greater efforts than we are now called upon to envisage.

Aid to Great Britain

The most serious question today for this country is whether the control of the high seas shall pass into the hands of powers bent on a program of unlimited conquest. It is, in this light, above all, that we should order our present-day thinking and action with respect to the amount of material assistance which our country is prepared to furnish Great Britain.

On no other question of public policy are the people of this country so nearly unanimous and so emphatic today as they are on that of the imperative need, in our own most vital interest, to give Great Britain and other victims of attack the maximum of material aid in the shortest possible space of time. This is so because it is now altogether clear that such assistance to those who resist attack is a vital part of our national self-defense. In the face of the forces of conquest now on the march across the earth, self-defense is and must be the compelling consideration in the determination of wise and prudent national policy.

For us to withhold aid to victims of attack would not result in a restoration of peace. It would merely tend to perpetuate the enslavement of nations already invaded and subjugated and provide an opportunity for the would-be conquerors to gather strength for an attack against us.

The protagonists of the forces against which we are today forging the instrumentalities of self-defense have repudiated in every essential respect the long-accepted principles of peaceful and orderly international relations. They have disregarded every right of neutral nations, even of those to which they themselves had given solemn pledges of inviolability. Their constantly employed weapons for the government of their unfortunate victims are unrestricted terrorization, firing squads, deceit, forced labor, confiscation of property, concentration camps and deprivations of every sort.

The most scrupulous observance by peaceful countries of legal concepts provides today no security whatever. Many nations which trusted to the integrity of their intentions and the care with which they observed their legal obligations have been destroyed.

I am certain that the day will come again when no nation will have the effrontery and the cynicism to demand that, while it itself scoffs at and disregards every principle of law and order, its intended victims must adhere rigidly to all such principles—until the very moment when its armed forces have crossed their frontiers. But so long as such nations exist, we cannot and must not be diverted, either by their threats or by their hypocritical protests, from our firm determination to create means and conditions of self-defense wherever and in whatever form we find essential to our own security.

The Need for Speed

The present bill sets up machinery which will enable us to make the most effective use of our resources for our own needs and for the needs of those whom, in our own self-defense, we are determined thus to aid. The great problem of democracy is to organize and to use its strength with sufficient speed and completeness. The proposed legislation is an essential measure for that purpose. This bill will make it possible for us to allocate our resources in ways best calculated to provide for the security of this nation and of this continent in the complex and many-sided conditions of danger with which we are and are likely to be confronted. Above all, it will enable us to do all these things in the speediest possible manner. And, overwhelmingly, speed is our greatest need today.

"Under this bill, . . . it would be possible, without any doubt whatsoever, for circumstances to arise which would most certainly involve the United States in war."

The United States Should Not Extend Lend-Lease Aid to Great Britain

James F. O'Connor (1878-1945)

In January 1941, shortly after his election to a third term as president, Franklin D. Roosevelt presented to Congress H.R. 1776, "An Act to Promote the Defense of the United States," later known as the Lend-Lease Act. Prompted by British pleas for aid, it gave sweeping new powers to the president to provide assistance to any nation he designated as vital for America's defense, and appropriated $7 billion for that purpose. At a news conference held on December 29, 1940, Roosevelt drew an analogy between lending arms to the British and lending a garden hose to a neighbor whose house was on fire. Great Britain and other countries fighting Nazism should not be compelled to surrender "merely because of present inability to pay for the weapons which we know they must have," he argued.

The bill provoked a bitter debate in Congress, where it was strenuously opposed by isolationists. Robert A. Taft, an isolationist senator from Ohio, criticized Roosevelt's garden hose analogy, stating that lending war supplies was more akin to lending chewing gum—who would want it back? Another opponent of lend-lease was James F. O'Connor, whose January 21, 1941, remarks on the floor of Congress are reprinted in part here.

O'Connor, a Democrat and former rancher, banker, and judge,

James F. O'Connor, *Congressional Record*, 77th Cong., 1st sess. (January 21, 1941), pp. 211-13.

represented Montana in the House of Representatives from 1937 to 1945. In his speech he attacks the arguments of lend-lease supporters who maintained that providing military aid to Great Britain was the only alternative to sending U.S. soldiers abroad. O'Connor argues that the passage of the bill would instead be a direct step toward further intervention in Europe and would eventually cause the United States "to plunge headlong into war." He states that while he shares with others a desire for a British victory over Germany, such a goal is not worth risking American lives in a foreign conflict. Despite the efforts of O'Connor, Taft, and others, the Lend-Lease Act passed in March 1941 by wide margins in both houses of Congress. Eventually the United States sent $50 billion in lend-lease aid to Great Britain and other countries during World War II.

On its face, H.R. 1776 is a bill "to promote the defense of the United States."

If the 435 Members of this House believed that this really is a bill "to promote the defense of the United States" then this bill would be passed in a few minutes' time without a single vote being cast against it, because every one of us here believes in defending the United States.

I speak to you today, my colleagues, as one of many who feels that this legislation would not do what it proposes to accomplish, namely: "To promote the defense of the United States."

The decision this Congress makes in passing on this bill will affect the lives of millions of people throughout the world. I want that decision to be in favor of the American people.

I do not propose, myself, and I do not think that you intend, to support this, or any other measure that is not in the best interests of the American people.

There is not a question in my mind as to where the sympathies of our people lie in regard to the wars raging across the oceans. By thought, word, deed, and prayer Americans have indicated plainly they prefer that the victors of these wars shall be the democracies of Great Britain, China, and Greece.

The average American, in my opinion, is thinking something like this: "Let us give them anything we have in the way of materials that will help them win the war so long as it does not jeopardize the safety and security of the United States."

But the American people do not want this country to plunge headlong into war.

181

Help Britain? Help China? Help Greece? Emphatically "Yes."

But to the extent of sending troops their answer, a thousand times more emphatic, is "No."

This Nation has been committed to a policy, so far as the democracies are concerned, of "all aid short of war."

The people, at least up to now, have taken those words at their literal meaning.

Perhaps, now, they finally have come to realize that "short of war" is vague and may be misleading.

This bill, H.R. 1776, is an act to carry out the "short of war" policy.

Lend-Lease Will Lead to War

Under this bill, in its present form, it would be possible, without any doubt whatsoever, for circumstances to arise which most certainly would involve the United States in war.

Let me illustrate just one such circumstance.

Suppose we were to send our warships into danger zones or use them to convoy supply ships to Great Britain or Ireland. Is there any doubt whatever that Britain's foes would attempt to sink our vessels? Is there any doubt that such an attack on our ships would not plunge the United States into war?

And this is but one of similar situations that could arise.

And let me ask you this question, colleagues:

Would any of us whom the American people honored by election to public office last November be here today if, prior to election day, we had stood before the American voters and openly proclaimed:

"I am in favor of the United States entering war."

Or if we had proclaimed:

"I will support legislation that may involve the United States in war."

Of course we would not be here if we had made any such campaign statement. No Member here, I am confident, will dispute me on this point.

If, then, I gave my pledge to Montana voters to do my best to "promote the defense of the United States," and keep us out of war, how can I be expected to support a bill that my conscience tells me exposes the United States to the gravest danger of being forced into war?

As it now reads, this bill, in my opinion, would do just that. . . .

What condition exists now that did not exist last fall when I gave my pledge to Montana voters—except the emotional hysteria that has been manufactured by the press, the radio, and the motion-picture theaters? . . .

Congress passed the Neutrality Act for the precise purpose of keeping America out of war. Then, at the President's insistence, we amended that act to strengthen our position as a neutral.

Now, after election is over, we have before us a bill that many of us feel would serve to get us into—not keep us out of—war.

In the first place, passage of this bill would amount to a complete abdication of the legislative branch of the Government. Congress already has surrendered so much of its authority as to be virtually incapable of discharging its duty as the law-making representatives of the electorate.

By the unprecedented powers this bill gives to the Office of the Chief Executive, powers that easily could lead to involvement of the Nation in war, Congress would give up the authority vested in it, exclusively, under the Constitution, to decide when the United States shall go to war.

Let us, my friends, keep faith with our people. Let us take no affirmative action that seems to me, without a doubt, will cause our naval and military forces to go into this war in Europe. . . .

Already, out of the Constitution and the interpretations by our Supreme Court, the President has plenary power in our external affairs. He is the sole agency and representative of our policy with foreign nations. Pass this bill, as it stands, and it would give him the same total power over our domestic defense powers.

While I am 100 percent for the purpose of the bill—to promote the defense of the United States—I cannot support this bill in its present form.

Please understand that I do not contend that any course, in these days, is bulletproof against involvement of this Nation in war. The only thing Congress can do is keep its pledge to the people to try to keep them out of war. We cannot keep that pledge by supporting bills that permit aggressive and unneutral acts that are sure to get us into war.

Perhaps the course I suggest is wrong. I do not know. Only the future holds the answer. No human being has it.

Let us consider what are Britain's aims and what are our aims in this crisis.

Are not the words, "Hitlerism must be crushed" familiar to you? Do you not recall 25 years ago almost the same sort of excuse for war. Only then it was "Kaiserism."

What happened to the Kaiser after his army was defeated? He was placed in a little place of his own, which, according to good information, afforded him luxurious living. Of course, the cost to the German people was $70,000,000.

What is going to happen when "Hitlerism" is crushed? How much further will Britain want to go? Has Britain said she wants to restore the status quo in Europe as it existed as of August 31, 1939? Has she said that France, Poland, Austria, Belgium, Holland, Poland, Rumania, and the other countries are to be restored? Would Britain need troops to accomplish this? Would we be asked to supply them?

A Dark Future

If so, the future looks dark for the flower of American manhood.

If we are to attempt to right the wrongs of Europe, 3,000 miles away, God help America.

Let us think a little further.

Suppose Germany is licked. That will not mean she is conquered. Great nations never are conquered, unless they are exterminated, which is impossible.

France is prostrated today, but not conquered. The spirit of France will rise. On the ruins perhaps a greater nation than ever before will be born. France may profit by her mistakes.

If Germany should defeat Great Britain, would the English people be conquered? Oh, no; they are not made of faulty fiber. The fight would have just begun.

The seed for disorder in the world is planted by selfish, greedy, war-minded men who find themselves adrift from Christianity.

Europe is dark today because most of Europe has forsaken Christian principles.

As I see it, the duty of this Congress is not to take any step that might involve this Nation in war, but rather to assume a statesmanlike leadership toward the goal of peace.

Involving this Nation, the most powerful on earth, in war certainly is not a step toward peace. You cannot quench a fire by adding a huge amount of new fuel to it.

Peace is an active and positive thing. Peace is not merely a cessation of war through some peace treaty. History is filled with the fragments of broken pledges for peace. . . .

The First World War

Do you wonder, my friends, that I shudder at the prospects of America becoming embroiled in Europe's wars? At the prospect of having to pledge not only the lives of American young men but the homes of the people who have worked and saved a lifetime to own—in fact, their all—to prosecute a war in Europe?

The first World War, you will recall, was fought to "save democracy."

Today the same nations are taking part in another great conflict, eyed in the same purpose, only with added fury, cruelty, barbarity, hatred, and viciousness. What is it about? The same things that caused the first World War.

The picture is repainted, of course, by adding a touch here and there—but the face of the war monster is still vivid. The mask does not hide the horrid expression of greed, desire for power, trade, gold, land, hatred of fellow man, and the hideous gaunt jaws and empty eye sockets.

The President, in recent eloquent speeches, visualized a world of religious freedom, freedom of speech, freedom from want, freedom from fear.

What a great and happy world that would be. Christ visualized such a world. As I heard the President's words, I pondered the picture he painted.

Lend-Lease Would Be Ruinous

One of the harshest critics of lend-lease was Senator Burton K. Wheeler of Montana, as this excerpt from his January 12, 1941, radio speech demonstrates.

Approval of this legislation means war, open and complete warfare. I, therefore, ask the American people before they supinely accept it. Was the last World War worth while?

If it were, then we should lend and lease war materials. If it were, then we should lend and lease American boys. President Roosevelt has said we would be repaid by England. We will be. We will be repaid, just as England repaid her war debts of the first World War—repaid those dollars wrung from the sweat of labor and the toil of farmers with cries of "Uncle Shylock." Our boys will be returned—returned in caskets, maybe; returned with bodies maimed, returned with minds warped and twisted by sights of horrors and the scream and shriek of high-powered shells.

Considered on its merits and stripped of its emotional appeal to our sympathies, the lend-lease-give bill is both ruinous and ridiculous. Why should we Americans pay for war materials for Great Britain who still has $7,000,000,000 in credit or collateral in the United States? Thus far England has fully maintained rather than depleted her credits in the United States. The cost of the lend-lease give program is high in terms of American tax dollars, but it is even higher in terms of our national defense. Now it gives to the President the unlimited power to completely strip our air forces of its every bomber, of its every fighting plane.

But we are not living today in that God-like world. This is a world of chaos created by man's greed.

Can we wipe out want in Europe when we have not wiped out want here?

I can take you into any town, city, village, or county in this country and show you want.

Dare we set America up and commit her as the financial and military blood bank of the rest of the world when the proportion of want in this country is still so great that by doing this our country would become a victim of financial and military pernicious anemia? . . .

Should we not appreciate the fact that we cannot right every wrong in this man-made world? We cannot police this world. To do so would require many millions of soldiers and billions more dollars of armaments.

The forgotten man, to my way of thinking, was the American soldier of World War No. 1. When he came home he found his job gone. He had to abandon gradually the ideals he thought he had fought for. He saw his hope of material prosperity dwindle. He took any job he could get.

If he were so unfortunate as to be injured in body or in mind, he found himself, perhaps, in a hospital or confined in his own home. The help his Government extended was not too much.

If America gets into this world war we will have 10 times as many of these "forgotten men" when the conflict is concluded. Go back to the cause of the Russian revolution and see if that could not have been avoided had the powers that be not forgot to remember.

And we will have a bankrupt Nation—of that there can be no doubt.

To finance this war we already have seen what the cost would be. America would be economically annihilated.

Of course, I want to defend America. But I do not want to be a party to putting my country into such a position that if England sinks, or any other nation sinks the United States will go down with her.

I do not believe it is possible for any outside enemy to invade America successfully.

Is America Vulnerable?

Germany could not invade the United States, with any hope of victory, without enormous numbers of troops. How could she get them actually onto our shores— with our naval and military and aerial might to fend her off?

Could Germany—if she is victorious in the war in Europe— hold many more millions of people than there are Germans under her heel while she is attempting to conquer America? Would all the other nations abroad stand idle, totally helpless, if Germany were so foolish as to move her military machine off the European Continent to undertake a conquest of another continent?

No; my friends, I think military invasion of America by any outside enemy is fantastically impossible.

I fully realize that national defense in its broader sense means more than keeping hostile forces from this continent. It means, insofar as we can, protecting ourselves from other threats to our security. There is not a single doubt but what our interests—financial and economic—are tied in with Britain's victory, but I am not one of those who believes that we are tied in to such an extent that such a victory is essential to our economic existence and to the continuation of our way of life. Regardless of the outcome of this war, a new order is in the making with reference to our domestic economy and our trade with foreign nations. Our whole internal set-up is going to have to be revamped and revised to meet the change in world conditions. . . .

Unless peace can be can be brought about it is imperative, until we get in better shape to defend ourselves, that we do everything for the democracies that we possibly can within the framework of the Constitution and our laws to enable them to carry on, but I am not prepared to surrender the power of Congress under the Constitution and to jeopardize the future of my country to the point where we are going to populate the cemeteries of Europe again.

No, my friends, to me the role for us is clear. It is the role of peace seeker, not war seeker.

A warring world is a sick world. Peace is to the world body politic what health is to an individual.

Individuals rejoice when health is restored—not when they start a sickness.

Nations rejoice when peace is declared—not when they begin a war.

We must study the mistakes that have caused wars, if we are to prevent the spread of war and our involvement. No one nation ever has a monopoly on mistakes. Every nation lives in a glass house. At some time or other every nation has played the role of traitor to Christianity and the cause of peace. . . .

In conclusion I believe that we should proceed cautiously. . . .

I would feel that I would be untrue to myself, the laws of my country, and my country, were I to support this bill as written.

VIEWPOINT 7

"I have been forced to the conclusion that we cannot win this war for England, regardless of how much assistance we extend."

The United States Cannot Prevent a German Victory

Charles A. Lindbergh (1902-1974)

In September 1940 the America First Committee was founded to oppose President Franklin D. Roosevelt's foreign policies, which many people believed would lead to American intervention in World War II. Within a year the organization had grown to several hundred thousand members organized in 450 chapters around the country, with businessmen Henry Ford and Robert E. Wood and senators Gerald P. Nye and Burton K. Wheeler among its members. The organization's most famous spokesperson (and the only one who could rival Roosevelt in attracting the nation's attention) was aviator Charles A. Lindbergh, still lionized by much of the American public for his pioneering solo flight across the Atlantic Ocean in 1927. Lindbergh had opposed the Lend-Lease Act when Congress debated it in early 1941. After that bill passed he toured the nation making speeches against Roosevelt's foreign policy moves to aid Great Britain in its war with Germany. The following viewpoint is from a radio address Lindbergh made on April 23, 1941.

Lindbergh had lived in Europe for much of the 1930s, and had closely observed the rise of German military and aviation power (he had accepted a decoration from Marshall Hermann Goering, Germany's air force commander, and was accused by some of be-

Charles A. Lindbergh, *Congressional Record*, 77th Cong., 1st sess., appendix (April 23, 1941), pp. A2152-54.

ing a Nazi sympathizer). His observations convinced him of German military supremacy and the inevitability of Great Britain's defeat in the war. Saving Great Britain might be a worthy cause, he argues in this address, but it is a lost cause. The United States should stop interfering in the wars of Europe and instead concentrate on its own affairs, he concludes.

Lindbergh and others continued to stress this theme over the next months as America teetered on the edge of war. After being attacked by Roosevelt as an appeaser and defeatist, Lindbergh resigned from his position as colonel in the Army Air Corps. After America declared war on Germany and Japan, however, he supported the United States and flew fifty secret combat missions in the Pacific theater.

There are many viewpoints from which the issues of this war can be argued. Some are primarily idealistic. Some are primarily practical. One should, I believe, strive for a balance of both. But, since the subjects that can be covered in a single address are limited, tonight I shall discuss the war from a viewpoint which is primarily practical. It is not that I believe ideals are unimportant, even among the realities of war; but if a nation is to survive in a hostile world, its ideals must be backed by the hard logic of military practicability. If the outcome of war depended upon ideals alone, this would be a different world than it is today.

I know I will be severely criticized by the interventionists in America when I say we should not enter a war unless we have a reasonable chance of winning. That, they will claim, is far too materialistic a viewpoint. They will advance again the same arguments that were used to persuade France to declare war against Germany in 1939. But I do not believe that our American ideals and our way of life will gain through an unsuccessful war. And I know that the United States is not prepared to wage war in Europe successfully at this time. We are no better prepared today than France was when the interventionists in Europe persuaded her to attack the Siegfried Line.

I have said before and I will say again that I believe it will be a tragedy to the entire world if the British Empire collapses. That is one of the main reasons why I opposed this war before it was declared and why I have constantly advocated a negotiated peace. I did not feel that England and France had a reasonable chance of winning. France has now been defeated; and despite the propaganda and confusion of recent months, it is now obvious that England is losing the war. I believe this is realized even by the British government. But they have one last desperate plan remaining. They hope that they may be able to persuade us to send another American Expeditionary Force to Europe and to share with England militarily as well as financially the fiasco of this war.

Beware of English Propaganda

I do not blame England for this hope, or for asking for our assistance. But we now know that she declared a war under circumstances which led to the defeat of every nation that sided with her, from Poland to Greece. We know that in the desperation of war England promised to all those nations armed assistance that she could not send. We know that she misinformed them, as she has misinformed us, concerning her state of preparation, her military strength, and the progress of the war.

In time of war, truth is always replaced by propaganda. I do not believe we should be too quick to criticize the actions of a belligerent nation. There is always the question whether we, ourselves, would do better under similar circumstances. But we in this country have a right to think of the welfare of America first, just as the people in England thought first of their own country when they encouraged the smaller nations of Europe to fight against hopeless odds. When England asks us to enter this war, she is considering her own future and that of her Empire. In making our reply, I believe we should consider the future of the United States and that of the Western Hemisphere.

It is not only our right but it is our obligation as American citizens to look at this war objectively and to weigh our chances for success if we should enter it. I have attempted to do this, especially from the standpoint of aviation; and I have been forced to the conclusion that we cannot win this war for England, regardless of how much assistance we extend.

The Limits of American Power

I ask you to look at the map of Europe today and see if you can suggest any way in which we could win this war if we entered it. Suppose we had a large army in America, trained and equipped. Where would we send it to fight? The campaigns of the war show only too clearly how difficult it is to force a landing, or to maintain an army, on a hostile coast.

Suppose we took our Navy from the Pacific and used it to convoy British shipping. That would not win the war for England. It would, at best, permit her to exist under the constant bombing of the German air fleet. Suppose we had an air force that we could send to Europe. Where could it operate? Some of our squadrons

The Groups Who Want War

Charles A. Lindbergh's most controversial speech was given during an America First Committee rally at Des Moines, Iowa, on September 11, 1941. His audience of 8,000 had just heard President Franklin D. Roosevelt's "shoot on sight" speech broadcast on the radio, in which the president escalated American involvement in World War II by pledging to attack threatening German ships. Lindbergh responded to this new development by directly attacking the three groups that he believed were the main supporters of U.S. war intervention: the British, the Jews, and the Roosevelt administration. His attack on Jews was the most controversial. Criticized by many within and outside the America First Committee, it did much to discredit the isolationist movement.

The three most important groups who have been pressing this country toward war are the British, the Jewish and the Roosevelt administration. . . .

As I have said, these war agitators comprise only a small minority of our people; but they control a tremendous influence.

Against the determination of the American people to stay out of war, they have marshaled the power of their propaganda, their money, and their patronage. . . .

The second major group mentioned is the Jewish. It is not difficult to understand why Jewish people desire the overthrow of Nazi Germany. The persecution they suffered in Germany would be sufficient to make bitter enemies of any race. No person with a sense of the dignity of mankind can condone the persecution the Jewish race suffered in Germany. But no person of honesty and vision can look on their pro-war policy here today without seeing the dangers involved in such a policy, both for us and for them.

Instead of agitating for war the Jewish groups in this country should be opposing it in every possible way, for they will be among the first to feel its consequences. Tolerance is a virtue that depends upon peace and strength. History shows that it cannot survive war and devastation. A few farsighted Jewish people realize this and stand opposed to intervention. But the majority still do not. Their greatest danger in this country lies in their large ownership and influence in our motion pictures, our press, our radio, and our government. . . .

When hostilities commenced in Europe, in 1939, it was realized by these groups that the American people had no intention of entering the war. They knew it would be worse than useless to ask us for a declaration of war at that time. But they believed that this country could be enticed into the war in very much the same way we were enticed into the last one. They planned, first, to prepare the United States for foreign war under the guise of American defense; second, to involve us in the war, step by step, without our realization; third, to create a series of incidents which would force us into the actual conflict. These plans were, of course, to be covered and assisted by the full power of their propaganda.

might be based in the British Isles, but it is physically impossible to base enough aircraft in the British Isles alone to equal in strength the aircraft that can be based on the continent of Europe.

I have asked these questions on the supposition that we had in existence an army and an air force large enough and well enough equipped to send to Europe; and that we would dare to remove our Navy from the Pacific. Even on this basis, I do not see how we could invade the continent of Europe successfully as long as all of that continent and most of Asia is under Axis domination. But the fact is that none of these suppositions are correct. We have only a one-ocean Navy. Our Army is still untrained and inadequately equipped for foreign war. Our air force is deplorably lacking in modern fighting planes.

When these facts are cited, the interventionists shout that we are defeatists, that we are undermining the principles of democracy, and that we are giving comfort to Germany by talking about our military weakness. But everything I mention here has been published in our newspapers and in the reports of congressional hearings in Washington. Our military position is well known to the governments of Europe and Asia. Why, then, should it not be brought to the attention of our own people?

Interventionists Hurt Democracy

I say it is the interventionists in America, as it was in England and in France, who give comfort to the enemy. I say it is they who are undermining the principles of democracy when they demand that we take a course to which more than 80 percent of our citizens are opposed. I charge them with being the real defeatists, for their policy has led to the defeat of every country that followed their advice since this war began. There is no better way to give comfort to an enemy than to divide the people of a nation over the issue of foreign war. There is no shorter road to defeat than by entering a war with inadequate preparation. Every nation that has adopted the interventionist policy of depending on someone else for its own defense has met with nothing but defeat and failure.

When history is written, the responsibility for the downfall of the democracies of Europe will rest squarely upon the shoulders of the interventionists who led their nations into war, uninformed and unprepared. With their shouts of defeatism and their disdain of reality, they have already sent countless thousands of young men to death in Europe. From the campaign of Poland to that of Greece, their prophecies have been false and their policies have failed. Yet these are the people who are calling us defeatists in America today. And they have led this country, too, to the verge of war.

There are many such interventionists in America, but there are

192

We Should Not Convoy Materials to Europe

In a radio address on March 30, 1941, excerpted here, Republican congressman Hamilton Fish of New York speaks out against using American vessels to convoy shipments of supplies to Great Britain, a policy that was being implemented in steps by President Franklin D. Roosevelt.

My position is simply this: I am in favor of all aid to the democracies consistent with our own national defense, but opposed to our involvement in European or Asiatic wars unless attacked. I am willing to maintain that position until the cows come home.

I do not believe that the European war is our war, or that we had anything to do with starting it. If it is our war, then we are a lot of cowards and cravens for not having been in it a year and a half ago.

Let us get the convoy issue straight. Convoys mean shooting, and shooting means war. The convoying of ships into the war zones is an act of war. . . .

Somewhere between 83 and 90 per cent of the people, according to the various Gallup polls, are opposed to our entrance into war unless attacked. We are not in the war now, as some columnists and interventionists claim. That is defeatist and interventionist propaganda. No shots have been fired, no American ships have been sunk, no American has been killed, and no attack has been made on the American flag.

No member of Congress, whether he voted for or against the Lend-Lease Bill, wants to see any of the articles for the defense of England sunk. If the sinkings get worse we could transfer more of our merchant ships to the British, and possibly some more old destroyers for additional bases, but the responsibility for convoying and getting the war supplies across is up to the British navy. First, last and all the time.

Between losing a shipload of war materials which can be duplicated, and losing a ship load of American boys who cannot be duplicated on this earth, there can be only one answer. I do not propose by my vote to send American boys to watery graves trying to get to Europe, Africa or Asia.

However, the signal bell ringing in the engine room of an American naval vessel to start the first convoy would be equivalent to a declaration of an undeclared war by the President.

more people among us of a different type. That is why you and I are assembled here tonight. There is a policy open to this nation that will lead to success—a policy that leaves us free to follow our own way of life and to develop our own civilization. It is not a new and untried idea. It was advocated by Washington. It was incorporated in the Monroe Doctrine. Under its guidance the United States became the greatest nation in the world.

It is based upon the belief that the security of a nation lies in the strength and character of its own people. It recommends the maintenance of armed forces sufficient to defend this hemisphere from attack by any combination of foreign powers. It demands faith in an independent American destiny. This is the policy of the America First Committee today. It is a policy not of isolation but of independence; not of defeat but of courage. It is a policy that led this nation to success during the most trying years of our history, and it is a policy that will lead us to success again.

We have weakened ourselves for many months, and, still worse, we have divided our own people by this dabbling in Europe's wars. While we should have been concentrating on American defense we have been forced to argue over foreign quarrels. We must turn our eyes and our faith back to our own country before it is too late. And when we do this a different vista opens before us. Practically every difficulty we would face in invading Europe becomes an asset to us in defending America. Our enemy, and not we, would then have the problem of transporting millions of troops across the ocean and landing them on a hostile shore. They, and not we, would have to furnish the convoys to transport guns and trucks and munitions and fuel across 3,000 miles of water. Our battleships and submarines would then be fighting close to their home bases. We would then do the bombing from the air and the torpedoing at sea. And if any part of an enemy convoy should ever pass our Navy and our air force, they would still be faced with the guns of our coast artillery and behind them the divisions of our Army.

The United States is better situated from a military standpoint than any other nation in the world. Even in our present condition of unpreparedness no foreign power is in a position to invade us today. If we concentrate on our own defenses and build the strength that this nation should maintain, no foreign army will ever attempt to land on American shores.

War is not inevitable for this country. Such a claim is defeatism in the true sense. No one can make us fight abroad unless we ourselves are willing to do so. No one will attempt to fight us here if we arm ourselves as a great nation should be armed. Over 100 million people in this nation are opposed to entering the war. If the principles of democracy mean anything at all, that is reason enough for us to stay out. If we are forced into a war against the wishes of an overwhelming majority of our people, we will have proved democracy such a failure at home that there will be little use fighting for it abroad.

The time has come when those of us who believe in an independent American destiny must band together and organize for strength. We have been led toward war by a minority of our people. This minority has power. It has influence. It has a loud voice. But it does not represent the American people.

During the last several years I have traveled over this country from one end to the other. I have talked to many hundreds of men and women, and I have letters from tens of thousands more who feel the same way as you and I. Most of these people have no influence or power. Most of them have no means of expressing their convictions except by their vote, which has always been against this war. They are the citizens who have had to work too hard at their daily jobs to organize political meetings. Hitherto, they have relied upon their vote to express their feelings; but now they find that it is hardly remembered except in the oratory of a political campaign.

These people, the majority of hard-working American citizens, are with us. They are the true strength of our country. And they are beginning to realize, as you and I, that there are times when we must sacrifice our normal interests in life in order to insure the safety and the welfare of our nation.

Such a time has come. Such a crisis is here. That is why the America First Committee has been formed—to give voice to the people who have no newspaper or newsreel or radio station at their command; to the people who must do the paying and the fighting and the dying if this country enters the war.

Whether or not we do enter the war rests upon the shoulders of you in this audience; upon us here on this platform; upon meetings of this kind that are being held by Americans in every section of the United States today. It depends upon the action we take and the courage we show at this time. If you believe in an independent destiny for America, if you believe that this country should not enter the war in Europe, we ask you to join the America First Committee in its stand. We ask you to share our faith in the ability of this nation to defend itself, to develop its own civilization, and to contribute to the progress of mankind in a more constructive and intelligent way than has yet been found by the warring nations of Europe. We need your support, and we need it now. The time to act is here.

"One peaceful nation after another has met disaster because each refused to look the Nazi danger squarely in the eye, until it actually had them by the throat. The United States will not make that fatal mistake."

The United States Should Try to Prevent a German Victory

Franklin D. Roosevelt (1882-1945)

As 1941 progressed, President Franklin D. Roosevelt took several steps that brought the United States closer to war against Japan and Germany. Tensions rose especially in the North Atlantic, where German submarines threatened the shipments of American food, munitions, and other supplies promised to Great Britain under the terms of the new lend-lease program. Since under the terms of the Neutrality Act lend-lease aid could not be sent on American ships, Secretary of War Henry Stimson proposed to have the U.S. Navy escort foreign ships carrying goods to Great Britain. Roosevelt, mindful that isolationists in Congress and elsewhere would strongly oppose such a move, did not immediately embrace such a policy, but the steps he took gradually escalated America's commitment to Great Britain and placed the United States on a collision course with Germany. These steps included extending America's "hemispheric defense" zone to Greenland, and then to Iceland. Within these zones American warships would escort British ships, as well as radio to the British the locations of German submarines they spotted. In May, Roosevelt declared an economic emergency, froze German assets in the United States, and seized German ships in American ports.

Abridged from "The Time for Active Defense Is Now," Franklin D. Roosevelt's radio address broadcast September 11, 1941. Reprinted in *Vital Speeches of the Day*, October 1, 1941.

Historian Irwin Unger writes in *These United States:*

> Each action brought the nation a trifle closer to outright bel-
> ligerency, but still the president was reluctant to throw the
> country's full weight behind Britain. He believed war must
> come; but fearing the wrath of the isolationists, he felt unable to
> start it himself. Instead he waited impatiently for the Germans
> to move offensively against the United States.

In early September, a German submarine fired on the American
destroyer *Greer*, which had been following the submarine and ra-
dioing its location to the British. President Roosevelt describes
the incident in the following viewpoint, taken from his September 11, 1941, radio address to the nation. Neglecting to mention
what the *Greer* was doing at the time of attack, Roosevelt calls the
German attack an act of "piracy" and announces a new policy:
American ships will "shoot on sight" all German and Italian
ships and submarines.

Roosevelt then goes beyond the specific incident to make the
general argument that Germany must be defeated. Responding at
least in part to the views of Charles Lindbergh and other isolationists, Roosevelt argues that allowing Germany to emerge victorious from the war would be extremely detrimental to the
United States. He maintains that he still does not seek a "shooting
war with Hitler," but hearkens back to historical American claims
of the rights of navigation and trade to buttress his assertions that
an "active defense" is necessary.

My Fellow Americans: The Navy Department of the United
States has reported to me that on the morning of September 4 the
United States destroyer *Greer*, proceeding in full daylight toward
Iceland, had reached a point southeast of Greenland. She was car-
rying American mail to Iceland. She was flying the American
flag. Her identity as an American ship was unmistakable.

She was then and there attacked by a submarine. Germany admits that it was a German submarine. The submarine deliberately
fired a torpedo at the *Greer*, followed later by another torpedo attack. In spite of what Hitler's propaganda bureau has invented,
and in spite of what any American obstructionist organization
may prefer to believe, I tell you the blunt fact that the German
submarine fired first upon this American destroyer without
warning, and with deliberate design to sink her.

Our destroyer, at the time, was in waters which the Government
of the United States had declared to be waters of self-defense, sur-

rounding outposts of American protection in the Atlantic.

In the north of the Atlantic, outposts have been established by us in Iceland, in Greenland, in Labrador and in Newfoundland. Through these waters there pass many ships of many flags. They bear food and other supplies to civilians; and they bear material of war, for which the people of the United States are spending billions of dollars, and which, by Congressional action, they have declared to be essential for the defense of our own land.

An Act of Piracy

The United States destroyer, when attacked, was proceeding on a legitimate mission.

If the destroyer was visible to the submarine when the torpedo was fired, then the attack was a deliberate attempt by the Nazis to sink a clearly identified American warship.

On the other hand, if the submarine was beneath the surface of the sea and, with the aid of its listening devices, fired in the direction of the sound of the American destroyer without even taking the trouble to learn its identity, as the official German communique would indicate, then the attack was even more outrageous. For it indicates a policy of indiscriminate violence against any vessel sailing the seas, belligerent or non-belligerent.

This was piracy, piracy legally and morally. It was not the first nor the last act of piracy which the Nazi government has committed against the American flag in this war, for attack has followed attack.

A few months ago [May 21, 1941] an American flag merchant ship, the *Robin Moor*, was sunk by a Nazi submarine in the middle of the South Atlantic, under circumstances violating long-established international law and violating every principle of humanity. The passengers and the crew were forced into open boats hundreds of miles from land, in direct violation of international agreements signed by nearly all nations, including the government of Germany. No apology, no allegation of mistake, no offer of reparations has come from the Nazi government.

In July, 1941, nearly two months ago, an American battleship in North American waters was followed by a submarine which for a long time sought to manoeuvre itself into a position of attack upon the battleship. The periscope of the submarine was clearly seen. No British or American submarines were within hundreds of miles of this spot at the time so the nationality of the submarine is clear. . . .

In the face of all this we Americans are keeping our feet on the ground. Our type of democratic civilization has outgrown the thought of feeling compelled to fight some other nation by reason of any single piratical attack on one of our ships. We are not becoming hysterical or losing our sense of proportion. Therefore, what I am thinking and saying tonight does not relate to any isolated episode.

The Job in Hand

Major General John F. O'Ryan, a veteran of World War I, argues in a March 1941 radio address that the United States should take whatever steps are necessary, including convoying, to deliver lend-lease materials to Great Britain.

When the American people gave their support to the "Lease-Lend Bill" they confirmed their conviction that Britain's fight is our fight, and as well the fight of other peoples not yet blitzkrieged into submission to the Hitler will. Obviously their purpose was to give to Britain war materials and food supplies needed to keep their people going while we create and train forces adequate to meet the Hitler challenge for world domination. Further I believe it is the purpose of the American people to insure the delivery of these war materials to the British, and not to permit them to be destroyed while en route to Britain. The British cannot spare the shipping or naval craft to enable them to "come and get it." To *give*, is to "deliver." Any other policy would be fatuous. It would mean an invitation to Hitler to make of the cargoes, fireworks, or food for the fishes. Therefore we are certain to convoy such shipments.

The job in hand is to arm the British, feed them, sustain them, and so soon as we can, support them with all our power, for Britain is now playing the role of the lone policeman battling on behalf of all civilized peoples against the forces of evil. We have no other choice, for Britain at the moment is standing between us and potential disaster.

There exists at present no world organization for the maintenance of world law and order, and the wolves are on the loose. . . .

This is not a European war. Hitler has not confined his ambitions to Europe. His troops and bombers are now in North Africa. An army of Fifth Column experts are hard at work in South America, in Mexico and here in our own homeland. His ships of war are at large in the North Atlantic. In the Far East he counts on the cooperation of Japan to do for him there what he cannot do himself.

In the present state of the world only resolute and forthright peoples who will fight and sacrifice for their freedom and rights, can survive. We propose to survive. Re-read our war history.

Instead, we Americans are taking a long-range point of view in regard to certain fundamentals, a point of view in regard to a series of events on land and on sea which must be considered as a whole, as a part of a world pattern.

It would be unworthy of a great nation to exaggerate an isolated incident, or to become inflamed by some one act of violence.

But it would be inexcusable folly to minimize such incidents in the face of evidence which makes it clear that the incident is not isolated, but part of a general plan.

The important truth is that these acts of international lawlessness are a manifestation of a design, a design that has been made clear to the American people for a long time. It is the Nazi design to abolish the freedom of the seas and to acquire absolute control and domination of these seas for themselves.

For with control of the seas in their own hands, the way can become obviously clear for their next step, domination of the United States, domination of the Western Hemisphere by force of arms. Under Nazi control of the seas no merchant ship of the United States or of any other American republic would be free to carry on any peaceful commerce, except by the condescending grace of this foreign and tyrannical power.

The Atlantic Ocean, which has been and which should always be a free and friendly highway for us, would then become a deadly menace to the commerce of the United States, to the coasts of the United States and even to the inland cities of the United States.

The Hitler government, in defiance of the laws of the sea, in defiance of the recognized rights of all other nations, has presumed to declare, on paper, that great areas of the seas, even including a vast expanse lying in the Western Hemisphere, are to be closed and that no ships may enter them for any purpose, except at peril of being sunk. Actually they are sinking ships at will and without warning in widely separated areas both within and far outside of these far-flung pretended zones.

This Nazi attempt to seize control of the oceans is but a counterpart of the Nazi plots now being carried on throughout the Western Hemisphere, all designed toward the same end. For Hitler's advance guards, not only his avowed agents but also his dupes among us, have sought to make ready for him footholds and bridgeheads in the New World, to be used as soon as he has gained control of the oceans.

His intrigues, his plots, his machinations, his sabotage in this New World are all known to the Government of the United States. Conspiracy has followed conspiracy.

For example, last year a plot to seize the government of Uruguay was smashed by the prompt action of that country, which was supported in full by her American neighbors. A like plot was then hatching in Argentina, and that government has carefully and wisely blocked it at every point. More recently an endeavor was made to subvert the government of Bolivia and within the past few weeks the discovery was made of secret air landing fields in Colombia within easy range of the Panama Canal. I could multiply instance upon instance.

To be ultimately successful in world mastery, Hitler knows that he must get control of the seas. He must first destroy the bridge of ships which we are building across the Atlantic and over which we shall continue to roll the implements of war to help destroy him, to destroy all his works in the end. He must wipe out our patrol on sea and in the air if he is to do it. He must silence the British Navy.

I think it must be explained over and over again to people who like to think of the United States Navy as an invincible protection that this can be true only if the British Navy survives. And that, my friends, is simple arithmetic.

For if the world outside of the Americas falls under Axis domination, the shipbuilding facilities which the Axis powers would then possess in all of Europe, in the British Isles and in the Far East would be much greater than all the shipbuilding facilities and potentialities of all of the Americas, not only greater, but two or three times greater—enough to win.

Even if the United States threw all its resources into such a situation, seeking to double and even redouble the size of our Navy, the Axis powers, in control of the rest of the world, would have the man power and the physical resources to outbuild us several times over.

No Peace in a Nazi-Dominated World

It is time for all Americans of all the Americas to stop being deluded by the romantic notion that the Americas can go on living happily and peacefully in a Nazi-dominated world.

Generation after generation, America has battled for the general policy of the freedom of the seas. And that policy is a very simple one—but a basic, a fundamental one. It means that no nation has the right to make the broad oceans of the world at great distances from the actual theatre of land war unsafe for the commerce of others.

That has been our policy, proved time and time again, in all our history.

Our policy has applied from the earliest days of the republic and still applies, not merely to the Atlantic but to the Pacific and to all other oceans as well.

Unrestricted submarine warfare in 1941 constitutes a defiance—an act of aggression—against that historic American policy.

It is now clear that Hitler has begun his campaign to control the seas by ruthless force and by wiping out every vestige of international law, every vestige of humanity.

His intention has been made clear. The American people can have no further illusions about it.

To tender whisperings of appeasers that Hitler is not interested in the Western Hemisphere, no soporific lullabies that a wide ocean protects us from him can long have any effect on the hard-headed, far-sighted and realistic American people.

Because of these episodes, because of the movements and operations of German warships, and because of the clear, repeated proof that the present government of Germany has no respect for treaties or for international law, that it has no decent attitude toward neutral nations or human life—we Americans are now face to face not with abstract theories but with cruel, relentless facts.

This attack on the *Greer* was no localized military operation in the North Atlantic. This was no mere episode in a struggle between two nations. This was one determined step toward creating a permanent world system based on force, on terror and on murder.

And I am sure that even now the Nazis are waiting, waiting to see whether the United States will by silence give them the green light to go ahead on this path to destruction.

The Nazi danger to our Western World has long ceased to be a mere possibility. The danger is here now—not only from a military enemy but from an enemy of all law, all liberty, all morality, all religion.

There has now come a time when you and I must see the cold inexorable necessity of saying to these inhuman, unrestrained seekers of world conquest and permanent world domination by the sword—"You seek to throw our children and our children's children into your form of terrorism and slavery. You have now attacked our own safety. You shall go no further."

The Limits of Diplomacy

Normal practices of diplomacy—note writing—are of no possible use in dealing with international outlaws who sink our ships and kill our citizens.

One peaceful nation after another has met disaster because each refused to look the Nazi danger squarely in the eye, until it actually had them by the throat.

The United States will not make that fatal mistake.

No act of violence, no act of intimidation will keep us from maintaining intact two bulwarks of defense: First, our line of supply of material to the enemies of Hitler, and second, the freedom of our shipping on the high seas.

No matter what it takes, no matter what it costs, we will keep open the line of legitimate commerce in these defensive waters of ours.

We have sought no shooting war with Hitler. We do not seek it now. But neither do we want peace so much that we are willing to pay for it by permitting him to attack our naval and merchant ships while they are on legitimate business.

I assume that the German leaders are not deeply concerned tonight, or any other time, by what the real Americans or the American Government says or publishes about them. We cannot bring about the downfall of nazism by the use of long-range invective.

But when you see a rattlesnake poised to strike, you do not wait until he has struck before you crush him.

These Nazi submarines and raiders are the rattlesnakes of the Atlantic. They are a menace to the free pathways of the high seas. They are a challenge to our own sovereignty. They hammer at our most precious rights when they attack ships of the American flag—symbols of our independence, our freedom, our very life.

It is clear to all Americans that the time has come when the Americas themselves must now be defended. A continuation of attacks in our own waters, or in waters which could be used for further and greater attacks on us, will inevitably weaken American ability to repel Hitlerism.

Do not let us be hair-splitters. Let us not ask ourselves whether the Americas should begin to defend themselves after the first attack, or the fifth attack, or the tenth attack, or the twentieth attack.

The time for active defense is now.

Do not let us split hairs. Let us not say, "We will only defend ourselves if the torpedo succeeds in getting home, or if the crew and the passengers are drowned."

This is the time for prevention of attack.

If submarines or raiders attack in distant waters, they can attack equally well within sight of our own shores. Their very presence in any waters which America deems vital to its defense constitutes an attack.

In the waters which we deem necessary for our defense American naval vessels and American planes will no longer wait until Axis submarines lurking under the water, or Axis raiders on the surface of the sea, strike their deadly blow—first.

Upon our naval and air patrol—now operating in large number over a vast expanse of the Atlantic Ocean—falls the duty of maintaining the American policy of freedom of the seas—now. That means, very simply, very clearly, that our patrolling vessels and planes will protect all merchant ships—not only American ships but ships of any flag—engaged in commerce in our defensive waters. They will protect them from submarines; they will protect them from surface raiders.

This situation is not new. The second President of the United States, John Adams, ordered the United States Navy to clean out European privateers and European ships of war which were infesting the Caribbean and South American waters, destroying

American commerce.

The third President of the United States, Thomas Jefferson, ordered the United States Navy to end the attacks being made upon American and other ships by the corsairs of the nations of North Africa.

A Warning

My obligation as President is historic; it is clear; yes, it is inescapable.

It is no act of war on our part when we decide to protect the seas that are vital to American defense. The aggression is not ours. Ours is solely defense.

But let this warning be clear. From now on, if German or Italian vessels of war enter the waters the protection of which is necessary for American defense, they do so at their own peril.

The orders which I have given as Commander in Chief of the United States Army and Navy are to carry out that policy—at once.

The sole responsibility rests upon Germany. There will be no shooting unless Germany continues to seek it.

That is my obvious duty in this crisis. That is the clear right of this sovereign nation. This is the only step possible, if we would keep tight the wall of defense which we are pledged to maintain around this Western Hemisphere.

I have no illusions about the gravity of this step. I have not taken it hurriedly or lightly. It is the result of months and months of constant thought and anxiety and prayer. In the protection of your nation and mine it cannot be avoided.

The American people have faced other grave crises in their history—with American courage, with American resolution. They will do no less today. They know the actualities of the attacks upon us. They know the necessities of a bold defense against these attacks. They know that the times call for clear heads and fearless hearts.

And with that inner strength that comes to a free people conscious of their duty, conscious of the righteousness of what they do, they will—with divine help and guidance—stand their ground against this latest assault upon their democracy, their sovereignty and their freedom.

CHAPTER 5

The End of Isolationism

Chapter Preface

The attack on Pearl Harbor by the Japanese on December 7, 1941, sounded a death knell for isolationism. The foundation of much isolationist argument up to that time was the assertion that the United States, surrounded by oceans on two sides, was not vulnerable to direct attack. This impregnability, many argued, made foreign alliances and interventions unnecessary to protect the safety and basic interests of Americans. Pearl Harbor undercut this reasoning. Michigan senator Arthur H. Vandenberg, a leading isolationist throughout the 1930s, wrote in his diary sometime after the attack:

> My convictions regarding international cooperation and collective security for peace took firm form on the afternoon of the Pearl Harbor attack. That day ended isolationism for any realist.

The America First Committee, the nation's preeminent isolationist group that had opposed American entry into World War II, dissolved shortly after the Pearl Harbor attack, and most of its members and other isolationists joined in supporting the American war effort. This did not prevent them from being investigated by the Federal Bureau of Investigation for "subversive" activities during the war, nor did it protect them from charges of being Nazi sympathizers during and after the conflict. The term "isolationist" became a smear word often denied by those so accused, and isolationism in general became discredited during and after World War II.

World War II ended with America's dropping two atomic bombs on Japan. The beginning of the Atomic Age was only one aspect of a vastly changed world. Most of the powerful nations that had competed for world influence prior to the war—Japan, Great Britain, France, Germany, Italy—were so devastated by war as to be no longer significant players on the world scene, unable even to maintain their colonial empires in Africa and Asia. The United States found itself in the position of being one of two superpowers in the entire world. The other was the Soviet Union, which after World War II moved to create a permanent division of Germany (which had been divided into war zones occupied by the World War II allies) and to dominate eastern Europe by establishing "satellite" regimes in the countries occupied by Soviet soldiers during the conflict.

Disputes over American foreign policy now focused on U.S.-

Soviet relations. Some Americans, such as former vice president Henry Wallace, argued that the United States should work to build on its cooperative wartime relationship with the Soviet Union and create a system of collective security based on the League of Nations model. Others, such as diplomat George Kennan, argued that the United States should confront and "contain" the expansionist and ideologically dangerous Soviet Union, and should, in order to achieve that goal, enter into alliances with other countries. Neither side advocated U.S. withdrawal or neutrality in world affairs. Manfred Jonas writes that, given America's position as one of two superpowers, a policy of neutrality as advocated by isolationists in the 1930s was no longer feasible.

> Neutrality was impossible in any future war, if for no other reason than that the Soviet Union regarded the United States as its primary foe. The United States could clearly not be indifferent to the outcome of any new war in Europe or Asia, since such a war would inevitably affect the world balance of power and, therefore, the safety of the United States. The argument regarding America's impregnability was no longer convincing after the experience at Pearl Harbor and the development of nuclear weapons.

As a result the United States took a series of actions that would have been unthinkable fifty—or even ten—years earlier. Rather than repeat its refusal to join the League of Nations, it instead joined the United Nations, a new international organization created to replace Woodrow Wilson's failed dream. Rather than insist on collecting debts and reparations from European countries (as it had following World War I), it instead provided additional economic assistance to former wartime allies and foes in the form of the Marshall Plan and other programs. Rather than eschew "foreign entanglements," it helped form the nation's first peacetime military alliance: the North Atlantic Treaty Organization. A few remaining isolationists opposed all these steps, but they found their arguments belittled by Congress and the American people. Instead of going back to the policies of the 1930s, the United States began its four-decade crusade against the Soviet Union and international communism.

VIEWPOINT 1

"A withdrawal from the problems and responsibilities of the world after this war would be sheer disaster."

The United States Should Help Create a New Global Organization

Wendell L. Willkie (1892-1944)

Even before the United States entered World War II, it was grappling with the questions of its place in the world following the war's end and whether to participate in forming a replacement for the failed League of Nations. The August 14, 1941, Atlantic Charter, a statement of general war aims and goals signed by President Franklin D. Roosevelt and British prime minister Winston S. Churchill, included a provision calling for the establishment of a "permanent system of general security." In January 1942, the United States, having just entered the war, joined twenty-five other countries in signing a *Declaration by United Nations*, a pledge of mutual support in the fight against the Axis Powers of Germany, Italy, and Japan. The 1942 document marked the first time the term *United Nations* (a phrase suggested by Roosevelt) was used officially. On October 30, 1943, representatives of China, Great Britain, the United States, and the Soviet Union signed the Moscow *Declaration on General Security*, which included a pledge to work toward the establishment of a comprehensive global organization.

Many questioned whether the American public would be more accepting of a new United Nations than it had been of the League of Nations following World War I. Addressing this question was an influential book written by Roosevelt's opponent in the 1940 presidential election, Wendell L. Willkie. Willkie, a utility executive, was a harsh critic of Roosevelt's New Deal domestic programs. But he was also a past supporter of Woodrow Wilson and the League of Nations, and after the 1940 election he spoke in support of Roosevelt's war preparedness policies. In 1942, he went on a round-the-world tour as a personal envoy for Roosevelt, providing a symbolic gesture of American support in such places as the Middle East, the Soviet Union, and China. His bestselling 1943 book, *One World,* based on his travel experiences, was primarily meant to encourage the Allied war effort, but it also included a stirring call for postwar international cooperation. In the excerpts from the book reprinted here, Willkie argues that the nations participating in the 1942 anti-Axis pact should, after the war, establish a "common council" to plan the postwar world and work to prevent future wars. He asserts that American nonparticipation in the League of Nations after World War I was a grievous mistake that helped lead to World War II, and that America, far from attempting to isolate itself from world affairs, should instead take a leadership role.

People in the United States are apt to conclude that there is no such thing as public opinion or the operation of its power in countries under absolute forms of government. As a matter of fact, in every absolutely governed country I visited, the government had elaborate methods of determining what the people were thinking. Even [Soviet dictator Joseph] Stalin has his form of "Gallup poll," and it is recorded that Napoleon at the height of his power, as he sat astride his white horse amid the smoldering ruins of Moscow, anxiously waited for his daily courier's report of what the mobs in Paris were thinking.

In every country I saw around the world, I found some kind of public opinion operating powerfully both on the course of the war and on the slowly emerging ideas of peace. In Bagdad [Iraq], I found it in the conversation in every coffeehouse, and there are a multitude of them. In Russia, it was expressed in great factory meetings and in the talk of Russians everywhere, who, however contrary it may seem to our notion of Soviet Russia, exchange ideas in private conversation almost as freely as we do. In China, newspapers, though not as unrestricted as ours, nevertheless with a surprising freedom reflect and lead public opinion. No man I talked to in China, whether he was the leader of the Communist party, a factory worker, a college professor, or a soldier, seemed to have any hesitancy about expressing his views, and many of the views were in conflict with some of the policies of the government.

In every country I found worry and doubt in the hearts and minds of people behind the fighting fronts. They were searching for a common purpose. This was plain in the questions they asked about America after the war, about Great Britain, and, when I was in China, about Russia. The whole world seemed to me in an eager, demanding, hungry, ambitious mood ready for incredible sacrifices if only they could see some hope that those sacrifices would prove worth while. . . .

Why a World Organization Is Necessary

In an essay written for the August/September 1943 issue of Congressional Digest, *Clark M. Eichelberger, national director of the League of Nations Association, argues that the reasons for the creation of the League of Nations after World War I still apply.*

A glance at the purposes for which the League of Nations was established will quickly reveal that the same impelling reasons exist today, only more urgent as a result of the experience of the second world war. Institutions are created to give effect to newly formed rules of human conduct; new rules of human conduct grow out of necessity. What were some of the necessities that found expression in the institutions of the League?

The first principle on which the League was founded is that means for the peaceful settlement of disputes must be substituted for the war system. The second principle was that there must be some sacrifice of national sovereignty accompanied by group responsibility for the enforcement of peace. The third principle was that permanent world peace is partly dependent upon a continuous and ever-expanding process of establishing international social and economic justice. The scope of these principles may not have been thoroughly understood at the time, but as the blackout of another dark age descended upon Europe and Asia, with its deepening shadow over the Western Hemisphere, a glance backward at the 1920's makes that decade seem very bright indeed.

The above three principles are as valid today and must be the very basis of the world organization of the future.

The people must define their purposes during the war. I have quite deliberately tried to provoke discussion of those purposes among the peoples of the various countries of the world. For I live in a constant dread that this war may end before the people of the world have come to a common understanding of what they fight for and what they hope for after the war is over. I was a soldier in the last war and after that war was over, I saw our bright dreams disappear, our stirring slogans become the jests of the cynical, and all because the fighting peoples did not arrive at any common postwar purposes while they fought. It must be our resolve to see that that does not happen again. . . .

Neither the proclamations of leaders nor the opinion of the people of the world, however articulate, can accomplish anything unless we plan while we fight and unless we give our plans reality.

The United Nations Pact

When the [1942] United Nations pact was announced, hundreds of millions of men and women in South America, in Africa, in Russia, in China, in the British Commonwealth, in the United States, in the conquered countries of Europe, perhaps even deep in Germany and Italy, thought they saw a vision of the nations signatory to that pact joining as partners in a common struggle to work together to free mankind. They thought that those nations would, during the war, sit in common council of strategy, of economic warfare, of planning for the future. For they knew that thus the war would be brought to a speedier end. They also knew that to learn to work together now would be the best insurance that the nations would learn to live together in the future.

More than a year has passed since the signing of the pact. Today the United Nations is a great symbol and a treaty of alliance. But we must face the fact that if hopeful billions of human beings are not to be disappointed, if the world of which we dream is to be achieved, even in part, then today, not tomorrow, the United Nations must become a common council, not only for the winning of the war but for the future welfare of mankind. . . .

It is idle to talk about creating after the war is over a machinery for preventing economic warfare and promoting peace between nations, unless the parts of that machinery have been assembled under the unifying effort and common purpose of seeking to defeat the enemy. . . .

What we need is a council today of the United Nations—a common council in which all plan together, not a council of a few, who direct or merely aid others, as they think wise. We must have a council of grand military strategy on which all nations that are bearing the brunt of the fighting are represented. Perhaps we might even learn something from the Chinese, who with so little have fought so well, so long. Or from the Russians who have recently seemed to know something about the art of war.

A Common Council

We must have a common council to amalgamate the economic strength of the United Nations toward total war production and to study jointly the possibilities of future economic co-operation.

And most important of all, as United Nations, we must formulate now the principles which will govern our actions as we move step by step to the freeing of the conquered countries. And we must set up a joint machinery to deal with the multiple problems that will accompany every forward step of our victorious armies. Otherwise we will find ourselves moving from one expediency to another, sowing the seeds of future discontents—racial, religious, political—not alone among the peoples we seek to free, but even among the United Nations themselves. It is such discontents that have wrecked the hopes of men of good will throughout the ages. . . .

An International Ideal

It was only a short time ago—less than a quarter of a century—that the allied nations gained an outstanding victory over the forces of conquest and aggression then led by imperial Germany.

But the peace that should have followed that war failed primarily because no joint objectives upon which it could be based had been arrived at in the minds of the people, and therefore no world peace was possible. The League of Nations was created full-blown; and men and women, having developed no joint purpose, except to defeat a common enemy, fell into capricious arguments about its structural form. Likewise, it failed because it was primarily an Anglo-French-American solution, retaining the old colonial imperialisms under new and fancy terms. It took inadequate account of the pressing needs of the Far East, nor did it sufficiently seek solution of the economic problems of the world. Its attempts to solve the world's problems were primarily political. But political internationalism without economic internationalism is a house built upon sand. For no nation can reach its fullest development alone. . . .

For years many in both parties have recognized that if peace, economic prosperity, and liberty itself were to continue in this world, the nations of the world must find a method of economic stabilization and co-operative effort.

These aspirations at the end of the First World War, under the presidency of Woodrow Wilson, produced a program of international co-operation intended to safeguard all nations against military aggression, to protect racial minorities, and to give the oncoming generation some confidence that it could go about its affairs without a return of the disrupting and blighting scourge of war. Whatever we may think about the details of that program, it was definite, affirmative action for world peace. We cannot state positively just how effective it might have proved had the United States extended to it support, influence, and active participation.

But we do know that we tried the opposite course and found it altogether futile. We entered into an era of strictest detachment from world affairs. Many of our public leaders, Democratic and Republican, went about the country proclaiming that we had been tricked into the last war, that our ideals had been betrayed, that never again should we allow ourselves to become entangled in world politics which would inevitably bring about another armed outbreak. We were blessed with natural barriers, they maintained, and need not concern ourselves with the complicated and unsavory affairs of an old world beyond our borders.

We shut ourselves away from world trade by excessive tariff barriers. We washed our hands of the continent of Europe and displayed no interest in its fate while Germany rearmed. . . . And in so doing, we sacrificed a magnificent opportunity for leadership in strengthening and rehabilitating the democratic nations, in fortifying them against assault by the forces of aggression which at that very moment were beginning to gather. . . .

If our withdrawal from world affairs after the last war was a contributing factor to the present war and to the economic instability of the past twenty years—and it seems plain that it was—a withdrawal from the problems and responsibilities of the world after this war would be sheer disaster. Even our relative geographical isolation no longer exists.

At the end of the last war, not a single plane had flown across the Atlantic. Today that ocean is a mere ribbon, with airplanes making regular scheduled flights. The Pacific is only a slightly wider ribbon in the ocean of the air, and Europe and Asia are at our very doorstep.

American Choices

America must choose one of three courses after this war: narrow nationalism, which inevitably means the ultimate loss of our own liberty; international imperialism, which means the sacrifice of some other nation's liberty; or the creation of a world in which there shall be an equality of opportunity for every race and every nation. I am convinced the American people will choose, by overwhelming majority, the last of these courses. To make this choice effective, we must win not only the war, but also the peace, and we must start winning it now.

To win this peace three things seem to me necessary— first, we must plan now for peace on a world basis; second, the world must be free, politically and economically, for nations and for men, that peace may exist in it; third, America must play an active, constructive part in freeing it and keeping its peace.

When I say that peace must be planned on a world basis, I mean quite literally that it must embrace the earth. Continents and oceans are plainly only parts of a whole, seen, as I have seen them, from the air. England and America are parts. Russia and

213

China, Egypt, Syria and Turkey, Iraq and Iran are also parts. And it is inescapable that there can be no peace for any part of the world unless the foundations of peace are made secure throughout all parts of the world.

This cannot be accomplished by mere declarations of our leaders, as in an Atlantic Charter. Its accomplishment depends primarily upon acceptance by the peoples of the world. For if the failure to reach international understanding after the last war taught us anything it taught us this: even if war leaders apparently agree upon generalized principles and slogans while the war is being fought, when they come to the peace table they make their own interpretations of their previous declarations. So unless today, while the war is being fought, the people of the United States and of Great Britain, of Russia and of China, and of all the other United Nations, fundamentally agree on their purposes, fine and idealistic expressions of hope such as those of the Atlantic Charter will live merely to mock us as have Mr. Wilson's Fourteen Points. The Four Freedoms will not be accomplished by the declarations of those momentarily in power. They will become real only if the people of the world forge them into actuality. . . .

Our Western world and our presumed supremacy are now on trial. Our boasting and our big talk leave Asia cold. Men and women in Russia and China and in the Middle East are conscious now of their own potential strength. They are coming to know that many of the decisions about the future of the world lie in their hands. And they intend that these decisions shall leave the peoples of each nation free from foreign domination, free for economic, social, and spiritual growth.

Economic freedom is as important as political freedom. Not only must people have access to what other peoples produce, but their own products must in turn have some chance of reaching men all over the world. There will be no peace, there will be no real development, there will be no economic stability, unless we find the method by which we can begin to break down the unnecessary trade barriers hampering the flow of goods. Obviously, the sudden and uncompromising abolition of tariffs after the war could only result in disaster. But obviously, also, one of the freedoms we are fighting for is freedom to trade. I know there are many men, particularly in America, where our standard of living exceeds the standard of living in the rest of the world, who are genuinely alarmed at such a prospect, who believe that any such process will only lessen our own standard of living. The reverse of this is true.

Many reasons may be assigned for the amazing economic development of the United States. The abundance of our national resources, the freedom of our political institutions, and the char-

214

acter of our population have all undoubtedly contributed. But in my judgment the greatest factor has been the fact that by the happenstance of good fortune there was created here in America the largest area in the world in which there were no barriers to the exchange of goods and ideas.

One World

And I should like to point out to those who are fearful one inescapable fact. In view of the astronomical figures our national debt will assume by the end of this war, and in a world reduced in size by industrial and transportation developments, even our present standard of living in America cannot be maintained unless the exchange of goods flows more freely over the whole world. It is also inescapably true that to raise the standard of living of any man anywhere in the world is to raise the standard of living by some slight degree of every man everywhere in the world.

Finally, when I say that this world demands the full participation of a self-confident America, I am only passing on an invitation which the peoples of the East have given us. They would like the United States and the other United Nations to be partners with them in this grand adventure. They want us to join them in creating a new society of independent nations, free alike of the economic injustices of the West and the political malpractices of the East. But as partners in that great new combination they want us neither hesitant, incompetent, nor afraid. They want partners who will not hesitate to speak out for the correction of injustice anywhere in the world.

Our allies in the East know that we intend to pour out our resources in this war. But they expect us now—not after the war—to use the enormous power of our giving to promote liberty and justice. Other peoples, not yet fighting, are waiting no less eagerly for us to accept the most challenging opportunity of all history—the chance to help create a new society in which men and women the world around can live and grow invigorated by independence and freedom.

VIEWPOINT 2

"I know it is argued times have changed; . . . distances have been annihilated; we cannot rely on old doctrines and principles. . . . This argument is fallacious. The oceans are just as wide as ever."

The United States Should Not Help Create a New Global Organization

William P. Elmer (1871-1956)

In January 1942, twenty-six countries including the United States signed the *Declaration by United Nations*, in which they pledged mutual support both in fighting the Axis nations of Germany, Italy, and Japan, and in working toward a future world without war. In June 1943 Congress was debating a resolution written by Congressman J. William Fulbright of Arkansas advocating U.S. participation in an international organization to maintain peace. In contrast to the struggles over the League of Nations following World War I, Congress overwhelmingly passed the Fulbright Resolution by a vote of 360-29. The Senate followed suit in November by a vote of 85-5.

One of the few congressmen to cast a negative vote was William P. Elmer, a Missouri Republican who served a single term in the House of Representatives, from 1943 to 1945. In the following viewpoint, taken from his speech in Congress on June 30, 1943, Elmer reiterates classic American isolationist themes, arguing that the United States has maintained a successful "Americanist" policy of isolationism since the days of George Washington, that the United States should not fight to preserve the British empire, and that the country is still protected by the Atlantic and Pacific

William P. Elmer, *Congressional Record*, 78th Cong., 1st sess., appendix (June 30, 1943), pp. A3441-43.

Oceans. Elmer attacks any future international organization as a threat to America's sovereignty and freedom.

Despite the concerns of Elmer and others, work toward forming the United Nations continued. In 1944, at meetings in Dumbarton Oaks, near Washington, D.C., the United States, China, Great Britain, and the Soviet Union agreed to a basic framework for the structure of the new organization. The United States hosted and participated in a 1945 conference in San Francisco, which resulted in the writing of the United Nations Charter. After six days of debate in July 1945 (compared to eight months' debate on the League of Nations), the U.S. Senate voted to ratify the charter and American membership in the United Nations. Among the senators casting votes in support were pre–World War II isolationists Arthur H. Vandenberg of Michigan, who argued in the senatorial debates that the United Nations in its final form did *not* threaten American sovereignty, and Burton K. Wheeler of Montana, who dismissed the charter as "a declaration of pious nonsense" but voted for it anyway.

I speak on the Fulbright resolution, as follows:

> *Resolved by the House of Representatives (the Senate concurring).* That the Congress hereby expresses itself as favoring the creation of appropriate international machinery with power adequate to establish and to maintain a just and lasting peace among the nations of the world, and as favoring participation by the United States therein.

I am a nationalist. I am not an internationalist or interventionist. I believe in the principles of the American Government. You may call me an isolationist if you please if that term means adhering to and practicing the principles enunciated by our founding fathers and under which we have operated a successful Government for 150 years.

As derisively defined by those who seek advantage, I declare there are no isolationists in this country, and no political party of consequence has ever declared for isolationism. Nor has any such party declared for internationalism. The declarations of party platforms have been nearer to the isolation idea than to the international one, and will be in 1944. No party dares to declare for internationalism. The membership of this House dare not so declare. Some will play around in the shallows with milk-water resolutions like this one to test out the sentiment of voters, with the illuminating thought if it falls it doesn't mean anything anyway.

217

If this resolution is right in the minds of its proponents; if it means military force to police the world; if it means international-ism; the change in our form of government in any way; the sur-render of some of our sovereignty; the abolition of our national life or any part of it, why not come out in boldness and say so? Why not set out the plan in detail and advocate its immediate adoption? If it is so good and beneficial, why delay till the war is over? Maybe its beneficent effects will convert our enemies, for they say, like us, they are waging the war for eternal peace.

Surely we do not want to creep up on the American people with an olive branch in one hand and a stiletto in the other to slit their throats. Let us declare for political nationalism or political internationalism so the people will know whither we are trying to lead them. Let the issues be clear cut and not be clouded. I have talked to and read letters from hundreds of soldiers, some here, some from abroad, and they have never seen anything yet worth fighting for in any foreign country. One wrote: "I am in the land where Christ was born; I wish to Christ I was in the land where I was born." When these boys return home—if they do—they will be full to overflowing with national patriotic spirit and they will start a crusade of America for Americans that will sweep aside all the other isms and schisms from our way of life. It will be the death knell of that internationalism whose main objective is world trade at the sacrifice of national sovereignty. The same thing will be true of all nations. Even China will have a national spirit after this war ends.

Yet this has never meant and does not now mean we or any of these nations are living in a state of isolation, or that we are hous-ing ourselves within a shell. That illustration is often used by those who have run out of reasons. It is just an excuse to silence the fearful and ridicule the patriot. The rule has ever been to as-sume our place in the galaxy of nations in every way except to tie our destiny with theirs. Between isolationism and international-ism we have plowed our course of national Americanism; it has kept us free from wars and preserved our peace. It was the devia-tion from our true course that involved us in two world wars.

This resolution violates our national rule. Walter Lippmann in his new book on this subject, *United States Foreign Policy*, says iso-lationism is misnamed. That it really means insolvency. That we never have had and do not now have a national or international policy. That our Monroe Doctrine is incapable of performance and defense, by us. That it would bankrupt us to fulfill its obliga-tions. All of this because of the international urge. May I ask if we had no policy, nation or international, by what chance have we grown to stature? How did we become the richest and best Na-tion of the earth? If the form of Government we adopted is wrong why so long in discovering it?

Why did it come with two world wars, the origin of which is so far hidden in the remote background of history, we can only speculate as to their cause? Would it bankrupt us to enforce the implications of the Monroe Doctrine? We have done so since 1824, by virtue of national prestige until it is now an accepted international fact. It has cost us little and saved us much. If we could not enforce the Monroe Doctrine without insolvency, how can we then enforce all the implications of this resolution to cover all the world and still remain solvent? Can we by uniting with the insolvent nations of the world—and all of them broke—better our political and financial condition over the more limited sphere of our present commitments?

The questions, without argument, give the answer. We are the only nation now solvent but we are fast approaching that dismal abyss. We constantly solace ourselves by talking about our great natural resources, our national income, and cite them as to our ability to finance, police, and govern the whole world. Yet we cannot enforce the Monroe Doctrine and could not defend ourselves without an alliance with Britain. This war is depleting our natural resources; discouraging our people in the production of wealth. We are taxing and borrowing, mounting our national debt, spend it and call it income. The extravagances it produces we call prosperity. We are at our lowest ebb, but will go lower, in real national wealth.

Have we spent this money to defend the Monroe Doctrine or to save the British Empire from destruction? How much will we spend to uphold and maintain that Empire if we adopt the international policy of forever weaving our destiny with that of Britain and all other nations? That is just the international policy Lippmann writes about and this resolution contemplates. It means insolvency and destruction for us. How different is this idea from that of [Winston] Churchill. He said the greatest day's work of his life was getting America on their side of this war. And it was. That was said when his country was gasping for breath. Later, when India was gasping for her independence, he said he was not appointed Prime Minister to liquidate the British Empire. I admire him for both statements. Both are patriotic, national; they exalt the welfare of his country, above all others. That is why I am an American nationalist.

Where did this resolution come from? It is not native-born. It doesn't have the birthmarks of Americanism. It is not inspired by our system of national life. It is born across the sea, but not in a manger. It is a foreigner, steeped in a mixture of marxism, fascism, naziism, and world-wide commerce. Its application would render us a subservient and subaltern nation. The action of the

219

committee in bringing the resolution to this floor has been described as "vastly important and historic." I say it is vastly destructive of American ideals. . . .

The basic idea of the League of Nations and of this resolution and all other similar schemes is power and force that was the heart of the covenant of the League. It meant then, and means now, the establishment of an international army powerful enough to enforce peace by coercing or subduing any other combination of nations. No other nation shall maintain an army for defensive or offensive purposes. The direction of this force will have to be vested in the whole League, else it is a mere balance of power. This means the surrender of sovereignty by the individual nations. No reservation can save it. The government of Washington and Jefferson will be merged in a super government of the world. It is the United States of America or One World.

Lessons of World War I

We often hear: "We won World War No. 1, but lost the peace." That is just a saying without foundation. We won nothing in World War No. 1 except debt, destruction, and death. After the war we intermeddled unofficially in the affairs of Europe; directed their commerce; loaned money to and financed the politicians on both sides; tried social experiments; loaned to foreign governments; supplied foreign corporations with money and machinery to rehabilitate themselves; and rebuilt her cities. This was not isolationism; it was interventionist meddling where we had no business. We were helping them keep out that dreaded monster, Russian communism. Then they traded with everybody else but us. American-loaned money was used to pay German indemnities and the Allied Nations used this money to pay us on the war loans. They really paid nothing. They have paid nothing yet.

In South America we loaned money, bought worthless government bonds, so they could trade with Europe. We did everything but join the League of Nations and back it with our military power. The failure to do this is the basis of that cry, "We lost the peace." That is a false cry, too. The League of Nations was composed of the victorious Allies who were the preferred powers. They had complete control and the military power to coerce Germany. They had the peace. Our signing the covenant would only have added our unneeded wealth and power to the League. When it was completed there existed the same old balance of power that had troubled Europe for centuries. Our joining the League would not have changed it. Just made the balance of it a little more unbalanced without changing the peace terms.

The same old jealousies, hates, rivalries, selfishness, and double-crossings took place as of old. England double-crossed France and finally permitted Germany to rearm. All of them watched Italy ravish their sister member, Ethiopia. England, France, and Russia secretly took sides in the civil war in Spain, and England never protested the use of military aid by Germany and Italy to Franco. . . . What peace did we lose in this set-up? We merely lost a chance of getting into this maelstrom of hell 2 years earlier than we did. If the powers had so decreed, these tares of war could have been uprooted, and they did not need our help to do it. Each one distrusted and sought advantage of the other.

The United States hosted the San Francisco Conference in 1945 in which the charter of the United Nations was written and adopted. President Harry S. Truman is pictured here delivering the closing address on June 28.

Today we are allied with England in World War No. 2. England is hated with venomous hate by more people on this earth than any other power. She lost her East India possessions to Japan, and has to hold India down by the sword because of this hatred. Even the Chinese rejoiced when the English were jailed by the Japs. I believe the present strife in north Africa between the French generals is partly due to England's covetous eyes on north Africa as a colonial possession. She knows France cannot resist, and the others will not. She has double-crossed all nations—even us. Do we want to cast our lot into this inferno? With all of this as known history what can we hope to gain by joining in a world-wide league, assuming more obligations and expense, with a surrender of sovereignty?

What is our formula for peace? We have the best one ever devised. And that is to stay at home and mind our own business. It worked for 130 years, and would work today if we observed it. Our Constitution says in order to form a more perfect Union, establish justice, insure domestic tranquility, provide for the common defense, promote the general welfare and secure the blessings and liberty to ourselves and our posterity, we established our Government. It has done these things. We never have needed an international alliance to carry out these beneficent ideas. We have done it by a national policy. I know some now regard our founding fathers as fossils; their principles worn out; that the world is in a new era and needs new governments. But a compass is still used on the modern ship and its needle points to the North Star; an anchor is still used to hold the ship steady; a loyal crew is necessary to insure a safe voyage; the well-known and tried routes are the safest. We know who laid the keel of our ship and we know the material of which it is built. I am not in favor of sabotaging it to embark in a new boat built by unknown workmen without plan or design, with no compass, or anchor, with a mixed crew of jabbering internationalists on a strange sea and on untried routes with a lot of co-owner nations who have heretofore, if not now, been international pirates, schemers, oppressors, and exploiters of weak people. The Bible says, "Remove not the ancient landmarks which thy fathers have set." That is good advice to us as a nation.

I know it is argued times have changed; modern inventions have made the world small; distances have been annihilated; we cannot rely on old doctrines and principles. Our own power is not enough to save us. We need alliances—even world-wide—not with all nations—just with those whom we want to share this power with us to boss the world. This argument is fallacious. The oceans are just as wide as ever. . . .

We have the guns, ships, planes, submarines, and millions of men. We can detect enemy ships, submarines, and planes on the distant high seas. Not a one of them could come within 500 miles of our coast without detection and destruction. All the ships in the world cannot land an army and equipment on our shores and invade us if we are not asleep. There would have been no Pearl Harbor if we had been awake. If we can fight an aggressive war where the first battle line of defense is 3,000 miles from our shores, I know we can defend our homes. If we cannot, we are unworthy of the name we bear and our country will fall. I verily believe the airplane is the greatest security of the ages against cross-sea invasion. With planes, submarines, and coast defenses, no enemy can land ships. We can still thank God the "land was divided" and the oceans bound us on either side.

I now there is an insistent demand for world-wide coalition. We want peace. It is so desired we are apt to close our eyes and grab for it. But the words of Patrick Henry should ring in our ears. We established and saved our country by war at home. The only real menace we ever had was in 1861-65, when we divided ourselves.

This was the only real war ever fought. Hand to hand, man to man, with a bravery and ferociousness in battle never equalled in world history. Many of us in this House are descended from those men who fought that war of division. Now we stand united under one flag and for one purpose—to defend our common country. No one could object to world agreements for peace. Our country has had them from the beginning. The objection is in tying ourselves through political alliances with other nations and putting our reliance for national safety in an armed force, controlled by them. That is a loss of sovereignty and would soon lose our independence and safety. World commerce and even world peace are not worth it. We have already heard the utter abjectness preached here, that we must join with England to "save ourselves." That was a cowardly and false doctrine. It was preached as an excuse to enter the war to save England, not ourselves. That abjectness was not shared by all, but if our national safety depends on superpower world force then abjectness becomes a national policy and spirit. Nationalism would be dead. It is a disturbing thought that world peace is always linked by internationalists and interventionists with world commerce, the cause of most wars.

American Declarations

Our national policy in dealing with foreign nations was firmly established by our first five Presidents. We have followed their advice in its true sense. Washington spent 4 years in writing his farewell address and submitted it to all the leading statesmen of his time. It is a chart for our foreign policy. He said:

> Observe good faith and justice toward all nations; cultivate peace and harmony with all; . . . the greatest rule of conduct for us in regard to foreign nations is, in extending our commercial relations to have with them as little political connections as possible; . . . it is our true policy to steer clear of permanent alliances with any portion of the foreign world.

That is a definite foreign policy.

Thomas Jefferson said:

> Peace, commerce, and honest friendship with all, entangling alliances with none.

That is a definite foreign policy.

Monroe promulgated another foreign policy which in effect said: We will not meddle in European affairs and they shall not meddle in ours, or America for Americans. We have woven this foreign policy inextricably with and as a part of our national policy. It is not isolation, intervention, or international. It is American, a distinct policy, separate from all world politics, and intended so to be.

The Republican national platform of 1940 said:

> The Republican Party is firmly opposed to involving this Nation in foreign war. . . . The Republican Party stands for Americanism, preparedness, and peace . . . and also to efficiently uphold in war the Monroe Doctrine.

The Democratic national platform of 1940 said:

> We will not participate in foreign wars, and we will not send our Army, Navy, or Air Forces to fight in foreign lands outside of the Americas, except in case of attack. We favor and shall rigorously enforce and defend the Monroe Doctrine.

These are declarations of foreign policy. There is no internationalism in them. Objectors to this policy mean they want national alliances in peace and war instead of American policies. Regardless of all ingenious theories, plans, and schemes, and arguments made to undermine or overcome, it is the fixed policy and sentiment of the American people. Unscrambling entangling alliances, as once proposed, or alliances made with one or more countries for physical security, as now proposed, are not American. They are byproducts of war diseases.

I am an American. I am proud of it. It means something. When the old Apostle Paul was tied to the post and the soldier was ready to lash him he said: "Is it lawful for thee to scourge a Roman citizen uncondemned?" The whip fell from that soldier's hand and he ran to the captain and said: "Take heed what thou doest, this man is a Roman citizen." The captain of the hosts ran, he did not walk, and said to Paul: "Art thou a Roman?" The little, old, baldheaded, weak-eyed, epileptic, hunchback straightened himself up to the full stature of his chains and proudly said: "I am." The centurion said: "With a great price bought I that freedom." Paul said: "I was free born." In that day it was greater to be a Roman than to be a king. Today it is greater to be a freeborn American than to be a king. Shall we lose that birthright of kingship? Shall we trade it for a miserable mess of international peace pottage steeped in the viciousness of world politics? Or shall we preserve it for ourselves and transmit it to our posterity to live by and, if need be, to die for? We are Americans. We are nationalists. We are not internationalists. We do not want the flag to come trailing back some time after we have tried this fallacy. We don't want the flag to leave here.

"The paramount purposes of the pact are peace and security."

The United States Should Join the North Atlantic Treaty Organization

Dean G. Acheson (1893-1971)

By 1948 fear of the Soviet Union's dominating Europe was a major concern of American foreign policy. The division of Europe between eastern (Soviet-controlled) and western halves extended into Germany itself, where Great Britain, France, and the United States announced plans in June 1948 to end their occupation of their respective military zones in Germany and create the Federal Republic of Germany, or West Germany. The three occupying powers sought to create an independent and relatively strong Germany, in contrast to the Soviet Union's desire for Germany to remain weak and divided.

The Soviet Union under its leader Joseph Stalin reacted to the creation of West Germany by forming the German Democratic Republic, or East Germany, and by blockading all land and water traffic to West Berlin (the Anglo-American–controlled section of the former German capital, which lay wholly within the Soviet-controlled zone). The United States under President Harry S. Truman responded with the Berlin Airlift, which in the winter of 1948/49 flew in tons of food and supplies to the 2.5 million residents of West Berlin. The Soviet Union backed down from its blockade in the spring of 1949, but Germany remained a focal point of tensions between the two world powers.

Concern generated by the Berlin blockade and other events in Europe helped stimulate the desire for a mutual defense pact

From "The Atlantic Pact," Dean G. Acheson's radio address broadcast March 18, 1949. Reprinted in *Vital Speeches of the Day*, April 1, 1949.

against Soviet aggression. On April 4, 1949, the United States and eleven other countries (Great Britain, France, Belgium, the Netherlands, Luxembourg, Denmark, Portugal, Italy, Norway, Iceland, and Canada) signed a treaty forming the North Atlantic Treaty Organization, or NATO, which declared that an armed attack against one of the countries was an attack against all. A key implication of the treaty was the United States' promise to respond immediately to an attack (presumably by the Soviet Union) on one or more of NATO's member nations. Unlike its neutrality at the beginnings of World War I and of World War II, the United States had pledged itself to immediately intervene in the event of a third war in Europe.

The North Atlantic Treaty had to be ratified by the U.S. Senate, where it was expected to be strenuously opposed by isolationists. The following viewpoint on NATO is by Dean G. Acheson, a lawyer who had served as assistant and under secretary of state before being appointed secretary of state by Truman in January 1949. In a March 18, 1949, radio address, Acheson defends the treaty as necessary to preserve peace in Europe and the principles of democracy and liberty shared by the countries signing the agreement. He argues that the United Nations, established after World War II, has not lived up to all its goals of collective security, and that additional agreements and organizations such as NATO are necessary. He contends that the pact does not abrogate the section in the United States Constitution giving Congress the power to declare war, but provides the U.S. government with needed flexibility in providing for the national defense. The Senate ratified the treaty on July 21, 1949. For the first time in its history, the United States had committed itself to an "entangling alliance" with other nations in a time of peace.

The text of the proposed North Atlantic pact was made public today. I welcome this opportunity to talk with my fellow citizens about it. . . .

I think the American people will want to know the answers to three principal questions about the pact: How did it come about and why is it necessary? What are its terms? Will it accomplish its purpose?

The paramount purposes of the pact are peace and security. If peace and security can be achieved in the North Atlantic area, we shall have gone a long way to assure peace and security in other areas as well.

The achievement of peace and security means more than that in the final outcome we shall have prevented war and brought about the settlement of international disputes by peaceful means. There must be conviction of people everywhere that war will be prevented and that disputes will be settled peacefully. In the most practical terms, true international peace and security require a firm belief by the peoples of the world that they will not be subjected to unprovoked attack, to coercion and intimidation, to interference in their own affairs. Peace and security require confidence in the future, based on the assurance that the peoples of the world will be permitted to improve their conditions of life, free from fear that the fruits of their labor may be taken from them by alien hands.

These are goals of our own foreign policy which President Truman has emphasized many times, most recently in his inaugural address when he spoke of the hope that we could help create "the conditions that will lead eventually to personal freedom and happiness for all mankind." These are also the purposes of the United Nations, whose members are pledged "to maintain international peace and security" and to promote "the economic and social advancement of all peoples."

These purposes are intimately related to the origins of the United Nations. As the second world war neared its end, the peoples who bore the brunt of the fighting were sick of the horror, the brutality, the tragedy of war. Out of that revulsion came the determination to create a system that would go as far as humanly possible in insuring international peace and security.

The United Nations

The United Nations seeks to maintain peace and security by enjoining its members from using force to settle international disputes. Moreover, it insists that they acknowledge tolerance and co-operation as the guiding principles for the conduct of nations.

The members are expected to settle differences by the exercise of reason and adjustment, according to the principles of justice and law. This requires a spirit of tolerance and restraint on the part of all the members.

But, as in any other institution which presupposes restraint, violence or obstruction can be used to defeat the basic understanding. This happens in personal relations, in families, communities, churches, politics, and everywhere in human life. If the system is used in ways it was not intended to be used, there is grave danger that the system will be disrupted.

That applies to the United Nations. The system is not working as effectively as we hoped because one of its members has attempted to prevent it from working. By obstructive tactics and the misuse of the veto, the Soviet Union has seriously interfered with the work of the Security Council in maintaining international peace and security.

But the United Nations is a flexible instrument. Although the actions of the Soviet Union have disturbed the work of the United Nations, it is strong enough to be an effective instrument for peace. It is the instrument by which we hope world peace will be achieved. The Charter recognizes the importance of regional arrangements consistent with the purposes and principles of the charter. Such arrangements can greatly strengthen it.

The Atlantic pact is a collective self-defense arrangement among the countries of the North Atlantic area. It is aimed at coordinating the exercise of the right of self-defense especially recognized in Article 51 of the United Nations Charter. It is designed to fit precisely into the framework of the United Nations and to assure practical measures for maintaining peace and security in harmony with the Charter.

It is the firm intention of the parties to carry out the pact in accordance with the provisions of the United Nations Charter and in a manner which will advance its purposes and principles. . . .

It is important to keep in mind that the really successful national and international institutions are those that recognize and express underlying realities. The North Atlantic community of nations is such a reality. It is based on the affinity and natural identity of interests of the North Atlantic powers.

The North Atlantic treaty which will formally unite them is the product of at least three hundred and fifty years of history, perhaps more. There developed on our Atlantic coast a community, which has spread across the continent, connected with Western Europe by common institutions and moral and ethical beliefs. Similarities of this kind are not superficial, but fundamental. They are the strongest kind of ties, because they are based on moral conviction, on acceptance of the same values in life.

The very basis of western civilization, which we share with the other nations bordering the North Atlantic, and which all of us share with many other nations, is the ingrained spirit of restraint and tolerance. This is the opposite of the Communist belief that coercion by force is a proper method of hastening the inevitable. Western civilization has lived by mutual restraint and tolerance. This civilization permits and stimulates free inquiry and bold experimentation. It creates the environment of freedom, from which flows the greatest amount of ingenuity, enterprise and accomplishment.

These principles of democracy, individual liberty and the rule of law have flourished in this Atlantic community. They have universal validity. They are shared by other free nations and find expression on a universal basis in the Charter of the United Nations; they are the standards by which its members have solemnly agreed to be judged. They are the elements out of which are forced the peace and welfare of mankind.

Added to this profoundly important basis of understanding is another unifying influence—the effect of living on the sea. The sea does not separate people as much as it joins them, through trade, travel, mutual understanding and common interests.

Common Interests

For this second reason, as well as the first, North America and Western Europe have formed the two halves of what is in reality one community, and have maintained an abiding interest in each other.

It is clear that the North Atlantic pact is not an improvisation. It is the statement of the facts and lessons of history. We have learned our history lesson from two world wars in less than half a century. That experience has taught us that the control of Europe by a single aggressive, unfriendly power would constitute an intolerable threat to the national security of the United States. We participated in those two great wars to preserve the integrity and independence of the European half of the Atlantic community in order to preserve the integrity and independence of the American half. It is a simple fact, proved by experience that an outside attack on one member of this community is an attack upon all members.

We have also learned that if the free nations do not stand together they will fall one by one. The stratagem of the aggressor is to keep his intended victims divided, or, better still, set them to quarreling among themselves. Then they can be picked off one by one without arousing unified resistance. We and the free nations of Europe are determined that history shall not repeat itself in that melancholy particular.

As President Truman has said: "If we can make it sufficiently clear, in advance, that any armed attack affecting our national security would be met with overwhelming force, the armed attack might never occur."

The same thought was expressed by the Foreign Relations Committee of the Senate last year in its report recommending approval of Senate Resolution 239. "The committee is convinced," the report said, "that the horrors of another world war can be avoided with certainty only by preventing war from starting. The experience of World War I and World War II suggests that the best deterrent is the certainty that immediate and effective counter-measures will be taken against those who violate the peace." That resolution, adopted by an overwhelming vote of the

Senate, expressly encourages the development of collective self-defense and regional arrangements within the United Nations framework and the participation of the United States in these arrangements.

What are the principal provisions of the North Atlantic pact? I should like to summarize them.

Principal Provisions

First, the pact is carefully and conscientiously designed to conform in every particular with the Charter of the United Nations. This is made clear in the first article of the pact, which reiterates and reaffirms the basic principle of the Charter. . . .

The second article is equally fundamental. The associated countries assert that they will preserve and strengthen their free institutions and will see to it that the fundamental principles upon which free institutions are founded are better understood everywhere. They also agree to eliminate conflicts in their economic life and to promote economic co-operation among themselves. Here is the ethical essence of the treaty—the common resolve to preserve, strengthen and make understood the very basis of tolerance, restraint and freedom—the really vital things with which we are concerned.

This purpose is extended further in Article 3, in which the participating countries pledge themselves to self-help and mutual aid. In addition to strengthening their free institutions, they will take practical steps to maintain and develop their own capacity and that of their partners to resist aggression. They also agree to consult together when the integrity or security of any of them is threatened. The treaty sets up a council, consisting of all the members, and other machinery for consultation and for carrying out the provisions of the pact.

Successful resistance to aggression in the modern world requires modern arms and trained military forces. As a result of the recent war, the European countries joining in the pact are generally deficient in both requirements. The treaty does not bind the United States to any arms program. But we all know that the United States is now the only democratic nation with the resources and the productive capacity to help free nations of Europe to recover their military strength.

Therefore, we expect to ask the Congress to supply our European partners some of the weapons and equipment they need to be able to resist aggression. We also expect to recommend military supplies for other nations which will cooperate with us in safeguarding peace and security.

In the compact world of today, the security of the United States cannot be defined in terms of boundaries and frontiers. A serious threat to international peace and security anywhere in the world is of direct concern to this country. Therefore it is our policy to help free people to maintain their integrity and independence, not only in Western Europe or in the Americas, but wherever the aid we are able to provide can be effective. Our actions in supporting the integrity and independence of Greece, Turkey and Iran are expressions of that determination. Our interest in the security of these countries has been made clear, and we shall continue to pursue that policy.

In providing military assistance to other countries, both inside and outside the North Atlantic pact, we will give clear priority to the requirements for economic recovery. We will carefully balance the military assistance with the capacity and requirements of the total economy, both at home and abroad.

But to return to the treaty, Article 5 deals with the possibility, which unhappily cannot be excluded, that the nations joining together in the pact may have to face the eventuality of an armed attack. In this article, they agree that an armed attack on any of them, in Europe or North America, will be considered an attack on all of them. In the event of such an attack, each of them will take, individually and in concert with the other parties, whatever action it deems necessary to restore and maintain the security of the North Atlantic area, including the use of armed force.

Not Committed to Fight

This does not mean that the United States would be automatically at war if one of the nations covered by the pact is subjected to armed attack. Under our Constitution, the Congress alone has the power to declare war. We would be bound to take promptly the action which we deemed necessary to restore and maintain the security of the North Atlantic area. That decision would be taken in accordance with our Constitutional procedures. The factors which would have to be considered would be, on the one side, the gravity of the armed attack; on the other, the action which we believed necessary to restore and maintain the security of the North Atlantic area. That is the end to be achieved. We are bound to do what in our honest judgment is necessary to reach that result. If we should be confronted again with a calculated armed attack such as we have twice seen in the twentieth century, I should not suppose that we would decide any action other than the use of armed force effective either as an exercise of the right of collective self-defense or as necessary to restore the peace and security of the North Atlantic area. That decision will rest where the Constitution has placed it.

This is not a legalistic question. It is a question we have frequently faced, the question of faith and principle in carrying out treaties. Those who decide it will have the responsibility for taking all appropriate action under the treaty. Such a responsibility requires the exercise of will—a will disciplined by the undertaking solemnly contracted to do what they decide is necessary to restore and maintain the peace and security of the North Atlantic area. That is our obligation under this Article 5. It is equally our duty and obligation to the security of our own country.

All of these provisions of the pact are subject to the overriding provisions of the United Nations Charter. Any measure for self-defense taken under the treaty will be reported to the Security Council of the United Nations. These measures will continue only until the Security Council, with its primary responsibility, takes the necessary action to restore peace and maintain security.

Article 5

One of the key provisions of the North Atlantic Treaty between the United States, Canada, and ten European nations was Article 5, reprinted below. The clause commits all countries to the defense of one another in case of attack.

The Parties agree that an armed attack against one or more of them in Europe or North America shall be considered an attack against them all; and consequently they agree that, if such an armed attack occurs, each of them, in exercise of the right of individual or collective self-defense recognized by Article 51 of the Charter of the United Nations, will assist the Party or Parties so attacked by taking forthwith, individually and in concert with the other Parties, such action as it deems necessary, including the use of armed force, to restore and maintain the security of the North Atlantic area.

Any such armed attack and all measures taken as a result thereof shall immediately be reported to the Security Council. Such measures shall be terminated when the Security Council has taken the measures necessary to restore and maintain international peace and security.

The treaty has no time limit, but after it has been in effect twenty years any member can withdraw on one year's notice. It also provides that after it has been in existence ten years, it will be reviewed in the circumstances prevailing at that time.

Additional countries may be admitted to the pact by agreement of all the parties already signatories.

These are the principal provisions of the treaty.

Will the pact accomplish its purpose?

No one can say with certainty. We can only act on our convictions. The United States government and the governments with

232

which we are associated in this treaty are convinced that it is an essential measure for strengthening the United Nations, deterring aggression, and establishing the sense of security necessary for the restoration of the economic and political health of the world.

The nations joining in the pact know that war does not pay. Others may not be as deeply convinced of this as we are. The North Atlantic treaty should help convince them also that war does not pay.

It seems absurd that it should be necessary, in this era of popular education and highly developed communications, to deal with allegations which have no relation to the truth and could not stand even the crudest test of measurement against realities. Nevertheless, the power and persistence with which the lie is today employed as a weapon of international policy is such that this cannot always be avoided.

No Aggressive Designs

I refer here to the allegations that this treaty conceals aggressive designs on the part of its authors with respect to other countries. Any one with the most elementary knowledge of the processes of democratic government knows that democracies do not and can not plan aggressive wars. But for those from whom such knowledge may have been withheld I must make the following categoric and unequivocal statement for which I stand with the full measure of my responsibility in the office I hold:

This country is not planning to make war against any one. It is not seeking war. It abhors war. It does not hold war to be inevitable. Its policies are devised with the specific aim of bridging by peaceful means the tremendous differences which beset international society at the present time. . . .

This treaty is designed to help toward the goal envisioned by President Truman when he said:

> As our stability becomes manifest, as more and more nations come to know the benefits of democracy and to participate in growing abundance, I believe that those countries which now oppose us will abandon their delusions and join with the free nations of the world in a just settlement of international differences.

To bring that time to pass, we are determined, on the one hand, to make it unmistakably clear that immediate and effective counter measures will be taken against those who violate the peace, and, on the other, to wage peace vigorously and relentlessly.

Peace is Positive

Too often peace has been thought of as a negative condition— the mere absence of war. We know now that we cannot achieve peace by taking a negative attitude. Peace is positive, and it has to be waged with all our thought, energy and courage, and with the conviction that war is not inevitable.

Under the leadership of President Truman, the United States is waging peace with a vigor and on a scale without precedent. While the war was being fought, this country took the initiative in the organization of the United Nations and related agencies for the collective and co-operative conduct of international affairs. We withdrew our military forces, except those required for occupation duties, and quickly reduced our military establishment to about one-tenth its war-time size. We contributed generously to post-war relief and rehabilitation.

When events called for firmness as well as generosity the United States waged peace by pledging its aid to free nations threatened by aggression, and took prompt and vigorous action to fulfill that pledge. We have actively sought and are actively seeking to make the United Nations an effective instrument of international co-operation. We proposed, and with the eager co-operation of sixteen other nations, put into effect a great concerted program for the economic recovery and spiritual reinvigoration of Europe [the Marshall Plan]. We joined the other American republics, and we now join with Western Europe, in treaties to strengthen the United Nations and insure international peace and security.

The United States is waging peace by promoting measures for the revival and expansion of world trade on a sound and beneficial basis. . . . We are preparing to carry out an energetic program to apply modern skills and techniques to what President Truman has called the "primitive and stagnant" economies of vast areas, so that they will yield a better and richer life for their people.

The United States is waging peace by throwing its full strength and energy into the struggle, and we shall continue to do so.

We sincerely hope we can avoid strife, but we cannot avoid striving for what is right. We devoutly hope we can have genuine peace, but we cannot be complacent about the present uneasy and troubled peace.

A secure and stable peace is not a goal we can reach all at once and for all time. It is a dynamic state, produced by effort and faith, with justice and courage. The struggle is continuous and hard. The prize is never irrevocably ours.

To have this genuine peace we must constantly work for it. But we must do even more. We must make it clear that armed attack will be met by collective defense, prompt and effective.

This is the meaning of the North Atlantic pact.

VIEWPOINT 4

"I cannot vote for a treaty which, in my opinion, will do far more to bring about a third world war than it will ever maintain the peace of the world."

The United States Should Not Join the North Atlantic Treaty Organization

Robert A. Taft (1889-1953)

Robert A. Taft, son of former U.S. president (and League of Nations supporter) William H. Taft, served in the U.S. Senate from 1939 to 1953. He was widely identified as one of the Senate's leading isolationists, although his actual record was not purely an isolationist one. He supported the war effort against Germany and Japan after the United States declared war against those countries, although he had previously argued against U.S. intervention in World War II. Following World War II he was caught between his desire to trim the U.S. military and President Harry S. Truman's call for a cold war against the Soviet Union. Taft somewhat reluctantly gave his support to Truman in 1947 when the president asked for aid for Greece and Turkey and issued his Truman Doctrine committing the nation to the "containment" of Soviet power and influence in the world. But when the president asked the Senate to ratify the April 4, 1949, treaty forming the North Atlantic Treaty Organization (NATO), in which the United States pledged to come to the defense of Canada and ten European nations if attacked (presumably by the Soviet Union), Taft balked. He explains his concerns in the following viewpoint, ex-

Robert A. Taft, *Congressional Record*, 81st Cong., 1st sess. (July 11, 1949), pp. 9205-209.

cerpted from a speech made on the Senate floor on July 11, 1949. While he says he would support a U.S. policy of pledging to come to Europe's defense in case of an attack by the Soviet Union, he argues that the treaty creating NATO is much too broad. He is especially critical of what he sees as a U.S. commitment to provide arms to countries in Europe, which he believes would increase the risks of starting a third world war.

It is with great regret that I have come to my conclusion [to vote against the North Atlantic Treaty], but I have come to it because I think the pact carries with it an obligation to assist in arming, at our expense, the nations of western Europe, because with that obligation I believe it will promote war in the world rather than peace, and because I think that with the arms plan it is wholly contrary to the spirit of the obligations we assumed in the United Nations Charter. I would vote for the pact if a reservation were adopted denying any legal or moral obligation to provide arms.

The purpose of American foreign policy, as I see it, is to maintain the freedom of the people of this country and, insofar as consistent with that purpose, to keep this country at peace. We are, of course, interested in the welfare of the rest of the world because we are a humane nation. Our huge economic aid, however, is based on the belief that a world which is prosperous and well off is less likely to engage in war than one in which there are great inequities in the economic condition of different people.

In the past, we have considered that the best method of preserving the peace and security of this country is the maintenance of American armed forces sufficient to defend us against attack, and a wise diplomatic policy which does not antagonize other nations. Those still are the main essentials to the maintenance of peace in the world of today.

But as the world shrinks in size, as new weapons are developed, as we inevitably become more involved in the affairs of other countries, it has become apparent that these weapons alone will not assure peace. And so we have committed ourselves to the principle of an association of sovereign nations banded together to preserve peace by preventing and punishing aggression. In the United Nations Charter we accepted the principle that we would go to war in association with other nations against a nation found by the Security Council to be an aggressor. That was a tremendous departure from our previous policy, but one which I have

236

always urged and approved from the days of the League of Nations. I believe that all nations must ultimately agree, if we are to have peace, to an international law defining the duties and obligations of such nations, particularly with reference to restraint from aggression and war. I believe that there should be international courts to determine whether nations are abiding by that law, and I believe that there should be a joint armed force to enforce that law and the decisions of that court. I believe that in the end, the public opinion of the world will come to support the principle that nations like individuals are bound by law, and will insist that any nation which violates the law be promptly subjected to the joint action of nations guided by a determination to enforce the laws of peace.

It is quite true that the United Nations Charter as drafted does not as yet reach the ideals of international peace and justice which I have described, but it goes a long way in that direction. It is defective principally because any one of the large nations can veto the action of the Security Council, and because there is not sufficient emphasis on law and justice as a guide to the action of the Security Council. But we have advised the President that prompt action should be taken to improve the Charter. Senate Resolution No. 239, adopted by the Senate on June 11, 1948, contained three clauses proposing improvement in the United Nations Charter: First, a voluntary agreement to remove the veto from many questions; second, maximum efforts to obtain agreement for a United Nations armed force and the reduction of national armaments; and third, a review of the Charter by a general conference called under article 109 of the Charter. As far as I know, the State Department has disregarded these injunctions of Senate Resolution 239 and concentrated only on that clause of the resolution which proposed a compact under article 51, based on the defects of the United Nations Charter. . . .

The Atlantic Treaty as drawn is certainly no improvement over the United Nations, nor can it by any stretch of the imagination be regarded as a perfection of or supplement to that Charter. From the point of view of an international organization, it is a step backward. . . .

What is the nature of that treaty?

It is obviously, and I do not think it can be questioned, a defensive military alliance between certain nations, the essence of which is an obligation under article 5 to go to war if necessary with any nation which attacks any one of the signers of the treaty. Such an attack may come from outsiders or it may come from one of the signers of the treaty itself. The obligation is completely binding for a period of 20 years. It imposes an obligation upon the United States to each member nation whether or not there is consultation or joint action by the Council, or a finding by any court that an unjustified armed attack has occurred. Our obligation is self-executing upon the occurrence of an armed attack.

Some doubt will always remain as to whether the Congress must declare war before our armed forces actually take part. I am inclined to think such action is not necessary if the President chooses to use our armed forces when an ally is attacked. But whether it is or not, the obligation to go to war seems to me binding upon the United States as a nation, so that Congress would be obligated to declare war if that were necessary to comply with the provisions of the treaty. It is pointed out that the President could fail to act and Congress could refuse to declare war, but certainly we are not making a treaty on the theory that we expect to violate it in accordance with our own sweet will.

It is correctly pointed out that the exact measures which we are obligated to take will be determined by us, and that it may not be necessary to go to the extent of a declaration of war. We do reserve a certain discretion, but as I see it, we do not reserve any discretion on the question, for instance, whether the armed attack is justified, as a reason for supporting it. If one of the members of the pact provokes an attack, even by conduct which we disapprove, we would still apparently be bound to go to its defense. By executing a treaty of this kind, we put ourselves at the mercy of the foreign policies of 11 other nations, and do so for a period of 20 years. The Charter is obviously aimed at possible Russian aggression against western Europe, but the obligation assumed is far broader than that. I emphasize again that the obligation is much more unconditional, much less dependent on legal processes and much less dependent on joint action than the obligation of the United Nations Charter.

A Question of Arms

And yet in spite of these dangers, I have wanted to vote in favor of the Atlantic Pact for one reason and would still do so if the question of arms were not involved. I fully agree with the effective argument in favor of the pact made by the distinguished Senator from Michigan [Arthur H. Vandenberg] because of its warning to the U.S.S.R. I think we should make it clear to the U.S.S.R. that if it attacks western Europe, it will be at war with us.

I agree that if the [German] Kaiser had known that England and the United States would be in the war, the First World War might never have begun. I agree that if Hitler had known the United States would be in the war, the Second World War might not have begun. I favor the extension of the Monroe Doctrine under present circumstances to western Europe.

It is said that the Atlantic Treaty is simply another Monroe Doctrine. I wish it were. That would be much more acceptable to me than the Atlantic pact, arms or no arms. Let me point out the vital differences. The Monroe Doctrine was a unilateral declaration. We were free to modify it or withdraw from it at any moment. This treaty, adopted to deal with a particular emergency today, is binding upon us for 20 years to cover all kinds of circumstances which cannot possibly be foreseen. The Monroe Doctrine left us free to determine the merits of each dispute which might arise and to judge the justice and the wisdom of war in the light of the circumstances at the time. The present treaty obligates us to go to war if certain facts occur. The Monroe Doctrine imposed no obligation whatever to assist any American Nation by giving it arms or even economic aid. We were free to fight the war in such a manner as we might determine, or not at all. This treaty imposes on us a continuous obligation for 20 years to give aid to all the other members of the pact, and, I believe, to give military aid to all the other members of the pact. . . .

The present treaty is a military alliance. The present treaty does contemplate a peacetime renewal of the old, open-ended lend-lease formula. The present treaty assumes unilateral responsibility for the fate of western Europe. We are obligated to go to the defense of any nation whether the other members of the pact do so or not, or whatever their consultation may advise. . . .

In spite of my belief that the treaty goes much too far and should have been confined to a mere declaration on our part that we would go to war if Russia attacked western Europe, I would still vote for the treaty except for my belief that the pact commits us to the arming of all the other signers of the pact. There is no question that the arms program and the treaty were negotiated together. There is no question in my mind that foreign nations which signed the treaty regarded the providing of arms as an essential part of it. . . .

Objections

First. With the arms in the pact it is even more clear that the pact is a military alliance, a treaty by which one nation undertakes to arm half the world against the other half, and in which all the pact members agree to go to war if one is attacked. It cannot be described otherwise than a military alliance. Of course, it is not like some of the alliances in the past, although many of them, such as the Franco-British alliance prior to World War I, were entirely defensive in character, or purported to be. Others were offensive and defensive alliances. I quite agree that the purpose of this alliance is not offensive, and that we have no offensive purpose in mind. But it is exactly like many defensive military alliances of the past. . . .

While this is not an offensive alliance, the line between defense and offense today is indeed a shadowy one. The Maginot Line was the essence of pure defense. Today it is the target of ridicule. Every good defense includes elements of offense. We cannot have an adequate armament for defense which cannot be converted overnight into a weapon of offense. We talked of defense for years before entering World War II while our preparation was really for offense. The result is, that no matter how defensive an alliance may be, if it carries the obligation to arm it means the building up of competitive offensive armament. This treaty, therefore, means inevitably an armament race, and armament races in the past have led to war. . . .

Second. The pact standing by itself would clearly be a deterrent to war. If Russia knows that if it starts a war it will immediately find itself at war with the United States, it is much less likely to start a war. I see and believe in the full force of that argument. That is why I would favor the extension of the Monroe Doctrine to Europe. But if Russia sees itself ringed about gradually by so-called defensive arms, from Norway and Denmark to Turkey and Greece, it may form a different opinion. It may decide that the arming of western Europe, regardless of its present purpose, looks to an attack upon Russia. Its view may be unreasonable, and I think it is. But from the Russian standpoint it may not seem

240

unreasonable. They may well decide that if war is the certain result, that war might better occur now rather than after the arming of Europe is completed. In 1941, Secretary [of State Cordell] Hull sent a message to Japan in the nature of an ultimatum which said, in effect, that if Japan did not withdraw from China, sooner or later they would face a war with the United States. The Japanese appear to have concluded that if ultimately there was to be such a war, it was to their interest to have it occur at once.

The arming of western Europe cannot be achieved overnight—in fact, it will be years before the European nations could resist an all-out Russian attack. During that period, I feel that the arms policy is more likely to incite war than to deter it. . . .

I think this arms program will very likely force the Russians into an acceleration of their arms program, so that we face an armament race, which in the past has seldom failed ultimately to produce war.

Third. The pact with the arms obligation, I believe, violates our obligations under the United Nations. . . .

An undertaking by the most powerful nation in the world to arm half the world against the other half goes far beyond any "right of collective self-defense if an armed attack occurs." It violates the whole spirit of the United Nations Charter. That Charter looks to the reduction of armaments by agreement between individual nations. I do not claim that there is any direct violation of the Charter, but the Atlantic Pact moves in exactly the opposite direction from the purposes of the Charter and makes a farce of further efforts to secure international peace through law and justice. It necessarily divides the world into two armed camps. It may be said that the world is already so divided, but it cannot be said that by enforcing that division we are carrying out the spirit of the United Nations.

Fourth. The obligation to furnish arms is either a mere token obligation, or it is one of vast extent. I do not know enough about modern military equipment to make any estimate. I have heard that to provide 60 divisions, which is said to be the very minimum necessary and perhaps completely inadequate against Russian attack, would cost a total of $24,000,000,000. We are entering on a new lend-lease. The history of the obligations has been that once begun, they cannot be easily brought to an end. Furthermore if the Russian threat justifies arms for all of western Europe, surely it justifies similar arms for Nationalist China, for Indochina, for India, and ultimately for Japan; and in the Near East for Iran, for Syria, and for Iraq. There is no limit to the burden of such a program, or its dangerous implications. . . .

I am quite willing to consider providing arms for a particular nation to meet a particular emergency. I voted for the Greek and

Turkish loans to provide arms. There may be other cases. I think today the providing of arms in support of Nationalist China, where war is actually going on, is something that I would approve, but that is a very different thing from building up a tremendous armament for 11 different nations, implying so far as I can see the obligation to do the same thing in the rest of the world.

Keep America Strong

In any war the result will not come from the battle put up by the western European countries. The outcome will finally depend on the armed forces of America. Let us keep our forces strong. Let us use the money we have for armament in building up the American Army, the American Air Forces, and the American Navy. Let us keep our forces strong, and spend the money that is available for arms for those forces, because in the last analysis, we will win a war only if the United States wins the war, no matter how we assist other nations. They may be of assistance here and there. We cannot be certain that they will fight. We cannot be sure what their position may be at the time. We cannot be sure that Communists will not take control in those nations. I believe very strongly, as Winston Churchill said, that the world depends on the strength of the American Army, and the weapons which the American Army has. . . .

Fifth. The justification for the arms aid rests on the necessity of defense against Russia, but remember that once these arms are provided, they are completely within the control of the nation receiving them. They are subject to the orders of those who, at the time, control the government of the country. Those governors may be Communists or Fascists, they may be peace-loving, or they may be aggressors. In future years, these arms may be used against us instead of on our side. If Russia should choose to go to war within the next year or two, they might easily be captured by the Russians and turned against us. We would be playing a dangerous game if we encouraged every country in Europe to arm itself to the teeth. Modern arms are not toys. . . .

Sixth. By approving this pact with the arms program, I believe we are committing ourselves to a particular course of action in war which may be unwise at the time when a war may actually develop. It is one thing to agree to go to war with Russia if it attacks western Europe. It is another to send American ground troops to defend Norway or Denmark or Holland or Italy or even France and England. I cannot assert positively that we are committing ourselves to a particular type of war, but I am inclined to think that we are. . . .

It may be that we should conduct a war on the Continent of Europe, even though it involves again the sending of millions of

American boys to fight Russians who, on land, will outnumber them four to one. But I do not think we should commit ourselves at the present time to any such program to make any such promise to our allies. We may find, if war ever comes, that our part in the war should be conducted from the air alone. We may find that the occupation of an enemy country is vain and useless if the war can be won otherwise, by the destruction of all of their military potentials. We should not commit ourselves by the ratification of this pact to the military assistance program and the plan of campaign which has apparently been promised the members of the pact. . . .

A Reluctant Conclusion

Mr. President, since I feel that this pact is inextricably linked with the arms program, and since I believe that, so linked, the program is a threat to the welfare of the people of the United States, I shall vote against this treaty.

I am quite willing to consider the providing of assistance to particular countries, at particular times, if such aid seems at that time a real deterrent to war, and on that principle I voted for aid to Greece and Turkey. But that is a very different thing from an obligation to build up the armed forces of 11 countries, and a commitment on the American taxpayer for 20 years to give continued aid under circumstances of which we have not the slightest conception today. It is a very different thing from arming half the world against the other half.

My conclusion has been reached with the greatest discomfort. When so many disagree with that conclusion, I must admit that I may be completely wrong. I do not claim to be an expert in question of foreign policy. I would like to be able to vote for a policy that will commit us to war if Russia attacks western Europe. I would be glad to join in an agreement to occupy Germany indefinitely to guard against a third attack from that quarter. I would waive my other objections to the Atlantic Pact if I did not feel that it was inextricably involved with the arms program. But I cannot escape the logic of the situation as I see it, and therefore I cannot vote for a treaty which, in my opinion, will do far more to bring about a third world war than it will ever maintain the peace of the world.

CHAPTER 6

Historians Debate the Decision to Enter World War II

Chapter Preface

After the United States ended its military alliance with France in 1800, it refrained from entering any other such alliance until 1947. Between 1947 and 1955 the United States created defensive alliances with 44 nations. This dramatic break with the traditional avoidance of "entangling alliances" had bipartisan support as America sought allies in its "cold war" with the Soviet Union. The United States, vaulted from relative isolationism into international preeminence by World War II, now chose to remain intimately involved in world affairs as the leader of the fight against global communism. While aspects of U.S. foreign policy during the Cold War were often criticized over the next four decades, most notably during the Vietnam War, the broad consensus among foreign policy leaders (and historians) concerning isolationism was that it was an inadequate response to America's global responsibilities as a world power.

That consensus has been increasingly questioned following the collapse of the Soviet Union in 1991. The end of the Cold War has resulted in a renewed debate over America's proper place in the world. Some, such as President Bill Clinton, have argued that the United States still has a responsibility to actively intervene in the world. In a March 1993 speech, Clinton favorably compares American actions after World War II with the isolationist upswing following World War I.

> I submit to you that we stand at the third great moment of deci
> sion in the 20th century. Will we repeat the mistaken of the
> 1920s or the 1930s by turning inward, or will we repeat the suc-
> cesses of the 1940s and the 1950s by reaching outward and im-
> proving ourselves as well?

But other observers have questioned the implications of America's actions as a world superpower, including the stationing of thousands of American soldiers in Europe under the North Atlantic Treaty Organization (NATO), U.S. participation in and funding of the United Nations, and American interventions abroad. In doing so, these critics have echoed many past isolationist themes—the advantage of the favored geographical position of the United States, the problems of intervening in another country's affairs, the dangers of surrendering U.S. sovereignty to international bodies, the false promise of using military force to spread democracy. Many have, like Clinton, cited lessons from

U.S. history to bolster their arguments.

The historical study of isolationism itself has become more nuanced than it was at the height of the Cold War. Historian Ronald Radosh, writing in 1974 as a leftist historian opposed to the Vietnam War, summarized the conventional Cold War wisdom:

> The "isolationists" were the bad guys—severe nationalists, whose desire to see America first led them to try to prevent the U.S. from fulfilling its international responsibilities. The "internationalists" were the good guys—men of maturity and responsibility, who knew that America could not continue to be an island unto itself. Globalism was an idea whose time had come. Its opponents had to be stopped.

Radosh labels these descriptions a "fairy tale"; he and other historians, including Justus D. Doenecke and Wayne S. Cole, have argued that the historical judgment of isolationists as close-minded and mistaken is simplistic and unjustified.

Many people have studied the history of isolationism, and American foreign policy in general, in order to learn what lessons it has to teach in making present-day choices. However, the lessons of history are not always clear. Disagreements over isolationism do not just affect America's foreign policy decisions; they affect the historical record of those decisions. The following pair of viewpoints offer a striking example of how differences in opinion over isolationism can lead two historians to offer strikingly contrasting pictures of America's last significant pre–Cold War foreign policy decision—the determination to enter World War II. The historians disagree not only on President Franklin D. Roosevelt's actions, but also on both the popularity and validity of the positions taken by isolationists during this critical time.

"[Roosevelt] had already committed beyond recall the United States to take part in the war then raging in Europe but he could not afford in the summer of 1940 to let this fact become known."

Franklin D. Roosevelt Instigated U.S. Involvement in World War II

Charles Callan Tansill (1890-1964)

Charles Callan Tansill was a professor of diplomatic history at Georgetown University in Washington, D.C. Part of an isolationist-leaning group of historians that included Charles A. Beard and William Henry Chamberlin, he wrote the 1938 book *America Goes to War* in which he criticized the American decision to enter World War I. In his 1952 *Back Door to War*, he argues that President Franklin D. Roosevelt machinated U.S. involvement in World War II.

The excerpts from *Back Door to War* reprinted here focus on U.S.-German relations after the start of World War II in 1939, but before America formally entered the conflict. Tansill argues that German leader Adolf Hitler was bending over backward to avoid antagonizing the United States, but that Roosevelt was actively aiding Great Britain and searching for an excuse to engage Germany in a naval war, even as he was promising the American people that he would not send American soldiers abroad. The American people were still strongly isolationist in the early 1940s,

Tansill argues, and it took devious and questionable methods by Roosevelt and his administration to engage the United States in war in Europe again.

Immediately after the outbreak of World War II, President Roosevelt made a radio address in which he reminded the American people that they should master "at the outset a simple but unalterable fact in modern foreign relations. When peace has been broken anywhere, peace of all countries everywhere is in danger." This theme of a "one world" he emphasized again and again: "Passionately though we may desire detachment, we are forced to realize that every word that comes through the air, every ship that sails the sea, every battle that is fought does affect the American future." In order to relieve the apprehensions that millions of Americans must have felt as a result of this stress upon the one-world concept, he then glibly gave the following assurance: "Let no man or woman thoughtlessly or falsely talk of America sending its armies to European fields. At this moment there is being prepared a proclamation of American neutrality." This assurance was followed by a reference to the "historic precedent that goes back to the days of the administration of President George Washington." America would remain "a neutral nation." But he closed his address with a curtain line that had an ominous implication: "*As long as it remains within my power to prevent*, there will be no blackout of peace in the United States.". . .

Before the Nazi armed forces had scored an important success in the Norway campaign, President Roosevelt began a series of endeavors to keep Italy out of the war. On April 29 [1940] he sent a telegram to [Italian leader Benito] Mussolini in which he expressed his deepest satisfaction with reference to "the policy of the Italian Government in exerting every effort to prevent war from spreading to southern and southeastern Europe." A further extension of the area of hostilities would bring into the war "still other nations which have been seeking to maintain their neutrality." He could see "no reason to anticipate that any one nation or any one combination of nations" could successfully "dominate either the continent of Europe . . . or a greater part of the world." He earnestly hoped that the powerful influence of Italy would continue to be exercised "in behalf of the negotiation of a just and stable peace."

[But] while the President was pleading with Mussolini to remain neutral in the great conflict that was wrecking Europe, he himself was pushing America down the road to war. On April 16 it was reported that the Anglo-French Purchasing Commission could obtain planes of almost any type then being produced for the armed forces of the United States. This news encouraged the French Premier, Paul Reynaud, to send to Washington (May 14) the startling request that the American Government arrange for the "sale or lease of old destroyers." On the following day Winston Churchill, who displaced Chamberlain as Prime Minister on May 10, sent a more ambitious request that was quite breath-taking:

> All I ask now is that you [President Roosevelt] should proclaim non-belligerency, which would mean that you would help us with everything short of actually engaging armed forces. Immediate needs are: First of all, the loan of forty or fifty of your older destroyers; . . . Secondly, we want several hundred of the latest types of aircraft; . . . Thirdly, anti-aircraft equipment and ammunition. . . . Fourthly, the fact that our ore supply is being compromised from Sweden, from North Africa and perhaps from Northern Spain, makes it necessary to purchase steel in the United States. . . . I should like to feel reasonably sure that when we can pay no more, you will give us the stuff all the same. Fifthly, . . . the visit of a United States Squadron to Irish ports . . . would be invaluable.

The President replied that he could not make a deal concerning the destroyers "without authorization from Congress." Moreover, America "needed the destroyers" for its "own defences." Churchill greatly regretted this negative answer but he still hoped to get "at the earliest possible date" the "largest possible number of Curtiss P-40 fighters." In conclusion he sounded a loud note of alarm that he knew would profoundly affect the President. If Britain were "left by the United States to its fate," there was a definite danger that the British fleet might be turned over to the Germans as a bargaining point. . . .

Churchill stated that he sent "nine hundred and fifty" of these cablegrams to the President and received "about eight hundred in reply." His relations with the American Chief Executive "gradually became so close that the chief business between our two countries was virtually conducted by these personal interchanges between him and me. . . . As head of the State as well as Head of the Government, Roosevelt spoke and acted with authority in every sphere."

It is obvious that Churchill regarded Roosevelt as an American dictator who had little concern for the opinions of Congress and the American people. With reference to the matter of war the Churchill cablegrams reveal that he believed that Roosevelt could plunge America into the conflict in Europe at any time he desired. The French Cabinet apparently had the same viewpoint.

The urgency of Churchill was translated into hysteria by Premier Reynaud. On May 18, [U.S. ambassador to France William] Bullitt was informed by Alexis Léger, Secretary-General of the French Foreign Office, that Reynaud was about to request President Roosevelt to ask Congress for a declaration of war against Germany. Bullitt frankly informed Léger that such a request would be worse than useless: Congress would almost unanimously vote against such a declaration. The President then talked to Bullitt over the telephone and instructed him to say that "anything of this nature was out of the question." But Reynaud continued to press for the impossible. On May 22 he told Bullitt that the German tide was growing more menacing every minute. There was grave danger that the French public would insist upon a separate peace with Germany. In that event a German victory over Britain "would follow in a few weeks." After this dire event the Panama Canal would be destroyed by air bombardment and the "American Army would be able to offer little resistance." Prompt action by the American Government was "the only real guarantee that Hitler would not some day be in the White House.". . .

Churchill Complains

Churchill was critical of the President's continued refusal to send old destroyers to the Allies. On June 5 he remarked to [Canadian prime minister] Mackenzie King that although the American Chief Executive was an excellent friend he had sent "no practical help" to Britain. He had not expected any military aid from the Americans "but they have not even sent any worthy contribution in destroyers or planes." It would be expedient "not to let Americans view too complacently prospect of a British collapse, out of which they would get the British Fleet and the guardianship of the British Empire."

On the day that Churchill sent this letter to Mackenzie King, the Germans began the final phase of the Battle of France. In five days they blazed a path to Paris. With a crushing defeat staring him in the face, Reynaud sent another plea to President Roosevelt. Its tone was quite epic but there was a strong feeling that the French Premier was like some frightened boy whistling loudly as he walked down a very dark alley: "For six days and six nights our divisions have been fighting without one hour of rest against an army which has a crushing superiority in numbers and material. Today the enemy is almost at the gates of Paris. We shall fight in front of Paris; we shall fight behind Paris; we shall close ourselves in one of our provinces to fight and if we should be driven out of it we shall establish ourselves in North Africa to continue the fight and if necessary in our American possessions." To make matters even worse, at this tragic hour Italy had "stabbed France in the back." The Allies were in desperate straits and required at once all the material support of the United States "short of an expeditionary force."

Reynaud's allusion to Italy's entrance into the war was turned by Roosevelt into a sharp thrust at Mussolini. That evening, in an address at Charlottesville, Virginia, the President alluded to the sweep of the tides of war across the Continent of Europe and the consequent menace to America of such a martial flood. Then, adopting a graphic phrase from Reynaud's plea earlier in the day, he suddenly remarked with dramatic intensity: "On this tenth day of June, 1940, the hand that held the dagger has struck it into the back of its neighbor." This unexpected interpolation directed at the Duce indicated the President's bitterness towards a dictator to whom he had made four futile pleas for nonintervention.

But Reynaud needed more than bitter allusions. Churchill rushed to France and tried to recall to Marshal Pétain the glorious stand of the Allied armies in the spring of 1918. The Marshal replied very quietly "that in those days he had a mass of manoeuvre of upwards of sixty divisions; now there was none." In 1918 there had been "sixty British divisions in the line." In 1940 the story was tragically different and Pétain was "haunted" by the grief he felt "that Britain, with her forty-eight million population had not been able to make a greater contribution to the land war against Germany."

The remarks of Marshal Pétain irritated Churchill considerably. On June 12 he sent to President Roosevelt the latest news from the French front and in this communication he permitted his resentment to color his message: "The aged Marshal Pétain, who was none too good in April and July, 1918, is, I fear, ready to lend his name and prestige to a treaty of peace for France." This was the moment for the President to "tip the balance in favour of the best and longest possible French resistance." In the White House it was believed that Reynaud's arm might be strengthened by brave words and bright promises. The Premier was assured that the American Government was "doing everything in its power" to make available to the Allied powers the war matériel they so urgently needed. The "magnificent resistance of the French and British armies" had profoundly impressed the American people.

When Ambassador [Joseph P.] Kennedy brought to Churchill a copy of this Presidential salute to Allied courage, the Prime Minister pressed for its immediate publication. It could play a "decisive part in turning the course of world history." At the very least it would "decide the French to deny Hitler a patched-up peace with France." In a hurried note to Reynaud, Churchill indicated the compromising character of the Roosevelt message. If France, on the basis of this assurance from the American Chief Executive, would continue in the war, it should be obvious that the United

States was "committed beyond recall to take the only remaining step, namely, becoming a belligerent in form as she has already constituted herself in fact."

The President realized the truth of this Churchill statement. He had already committed beyond recall the United States to take part in the war then raging in Europe but he could not afford in the summer of 1940 to let this fact become known. His campaign for re-election as President would soon take shape and he knew he could not hope for success if the voters knew that he was secretly putting America into World War II. He quickly sent word to Churchill explaining that he could not agree to the publication of his message to Reynaud. The Department of State saw in such publication the "gravest dangers." Churchill would not take this "disappointing telegram" as a final answer from the White House. On June 15 he frankly told the President that events in Europe were moving "downward at a pace where they will pass beyond the control of American public opinion." Eventually America would enter the struggle; why not now? It would be expedient to remember that if the Churchill Government fell a new cabinet might give the British fleet to Hitler. What would the United States do in that event? There was desperate need for the delivery of thirty-five destroyers at once. This matter should not be delayed.

Reynaud realized that he could not wait for several months until American assistance reached France. It was now or never. On June 14 he sent a message to Roosevelt that plumbed the depths of despair. German troops had just burst into Paris. Would it pay France to "continue to sacrifice her youth in a hopeless struggle?" Unless America could rush to France's aid with armed force she would "go under like a drowning man and disappear after having cast a last look towards the land of liberty from which she awaited salvation." When Roosevelt replied with a warm encomium upon the "resplendent courage" of the French armies but with no promise of immediate military aid, Reynaud requested Churchill to release his Government from its obligations not to negotiate a separate peace. The Prime Minister hastened to France in a vain effort to save the situation, but Reynaud had resigned by the time he reached Bordeaux. Marshal Pétain now assumed the burden of leadership and forwarded to Berlin a request for an armistice. . . .

The Destroyer Deal

The fall of France imparted a sense of urgency to the Administration's program for aiding Britain by the sale or lease of war matériel. The President's qualms about constitutional limitations slowly disappeared under the drumfire of repeated requests from

Churchill. Moreover, he brought into his Cabinet certain new members who were not averse to a prowar inclination. This was particularly true of the new Secretary of War, Henry L. Stimson, who was a notorious war hawk. It is apparent that after June 1940 the Administration embarked upon a phony bipartisan policy that pointed directly to American intervention in the European conflict. . . .

There was no doubt in Churchill's mind that any transfer of American destroyers to Britain would be a "decidedly unneutral act by the United States." It would justify a declaration of war by Hitler. Such action would be eminently agreeable to Churchill who would ardently welcome American help in the struggle against the dictatorships. But the situation had to be handled carefully. When Lord Lothian (August 6) cabled that the President was exceedingly anxious for a pledge that the British fleet would not be turned over to the Germans in the event that Britain fell, Churchill refused to give one. The British nation would "not tolerate any discussion of what we should do if our island were overrun." It would be best to couple the transfer of destroyers with the lease of naval and air bases in Newfoundland and on some British islands in the Caribbean.

On August 13 the essential paragraphs in this agreement were worked out during a conference between the President, Secretaries [Frank] Knox, [Henry] Morgenthau, and Stimson, and Sumner Welles. In the meantime [newspaper editor] William Allen White had received assurances from [Republican presidential candidate] Wendell Willkie that he would "not make a campaign issue of the transfer." The services of General [John J.] Pershing were next enlisted. The old warrior warned the American public in a broadcast that Britain needed immediate aid. This could best be given by placing at the disposal of the British and Canadian governments "at least fifty over-age destroyers which are left from the days of the World War.". . .

On September 2 notes were exchanged between Secretary [Cordell] Hull and Lord Lothian which first recited that the British Government, freely and without consideration, granted to the United States a lease for the "immediate establishment and use of naval and air bases and facilities" on the Avalon Peninsula and on the southern coast of Newfoundland, and on the east coast and on the Great Bay of Bermuda. The second item dealt with the establishment by the United States of air and naval bases on certain British territory in the Caribbean (Bahamas, Jamaica, Saint Lucia, Trinidad, Antigua, and British Guiana) in exchange "for naval and military equipment and material which the United States Government will transfer to His Majesty's Government." The leases would run for a period of 99 years. At the same time Churchill also gave an assurance that the British fleet would not be scuttled or surrendered. This assurance was not to be published. . . .

From the viewpoint of international law the destroyer deal was definitely illegal. . . . The whole matter was correctly described by the *St. Louis Post-Dispatch* in a pertinent headline: "Dictator Roosevelt Commits an Act of War."

Propaganda Efforts

During the years 1914 to 1917, British propaganda played a significant part in preparing the American mind for intervention in the World War. In the period prior to American intervention in World War II the British Government did not have to bear a heavy burden of propaganda: there were thousands of Americans who eagerly assumed this responsibility. The colorful story of these merchants of death has been told in such detail that it will be given merely a brief mention in these pages.

Rev. Harry Emerson Fosdick gave Roosevelt an excellent cue when he remarked that "of all the ways for Christians to make a war seem holy, the simplest way is to get Jesus into it." The President followed this tip on January 4, 1939, when he addressed Congress on the state of the nation. Storms from abroad were challenging three institutions "indispensable to Americans, now as always. The first is religion. It is the source of the other two—democracy and international good faith. . . . We have learned that God-fearing democracies of the world which observe the sanctity of treaties and good faith in their dealings with other nations cannot safely be indifferent to international lawlessness anywhere. They cannot forever let pass, without effective protest, acts of aggression against sister nations.". . .

Catholic leaders did not respond to this summons to enlist the churches in a movement towards intervention. Catholic cardinals like [William] O'Connell and [Denis] Dougherty were strongly opposed to America's entry into World War II, and the Catholic press was outspoken in its criticism of the implications in the President's policy. The *Catholic World* thought Americans "were in no position to save anyone. We shall be lucky to save ourselves. . . . What kind of madness has got hold of those who advocate our settling the quarrels of the world, changing the habits of nations that have been fighting for the last thousand years? Who do we think we are?" The *Ave Maria* was equally opposed to intervention: "The people of this country do not want war at this moment; they can see no transgression against our safety or honor to justify a war. . . . They have no commission, human or divine, to challenge aggression not directed against them."

The *Ave Maria* was particularly sharp in its criticism of William Allen White, famous Kansas editor, who was "doing everything humanly possible to get us into the European conflict." It was certainly true that White had been very busy in the fight against fascism. He was a member of the Union for Concerted Peace Efforts, the American Committee for Non-participation in Japanese Aggression, the National Refugee Service, the Council Against Intolerance, and the Non-partisan Committee for Peace through the Revision of the Neutrality Law. This last organization was an active pressure group in favor of sabotaging existing neutrality legislation.

After this work had been carried to a successful conclusion, White helped to launch the Committee to Defend America by Aiding the Allies. The implications of this movement should have been evident to him. In December 1939, [noted playwright] Robert Sherwood wrote to White to express the view that "it was necessary for the United States to intervene in a military way to check aggression by dictators." In his reply White remarked that he had always stood with Sherwood "in spirit" but had been constrained "by an old man's fear and doubt when it comes to lifting my voice for war."

In the spring of 1940 after this new organization had begun its activities, White became feverish in his anxiety to speed the gift of munitions of war to the hard-pressed Allies. In July he and the members of the Committee to Defend America by Aiding the Allies bent every effort to secure "the release of fifty or sixty overage but recently reconditioned American destroyers to England." When the President failed to show any great enthusiasm to push through a destroyer deal, White felt that "he had, as it were, lost his cud." Contact was made with large numbers of influential persons throughout the United States and they were urged to exert pressure upon the Chief Executive. The committee with its six hundred local chapters and thousands of volunteer workers was able to inundate the Capitol in Washington with a flood of letters and telegrams favoring the destroyer deal. The President owed a big debt to White who was so naive as to believe that America could walk halfway down the road to war and then stop. . . .

White . . . failed to understand the real intentions of the Committee to Defend America by Aiding the Allies. Its real drive was towards war, not peace. . . . He had been used as a convenient façade by an organization that had talked of peace while rushing down the road to war. He was the symbol of millions of Americans.

Lend-Lease

It was entirely fitting that lend-lease legislation should have a prelude of promises by the President that American boys would not be sent abroad to die along far-flung frontiers. It had been evident to the President in the summer of 1940 that American involvement in World War II might be just around the corner of the

255

next year. Senator [Burton K.] Wheeler had read between the lines of the President's pronouncements and when he saw the word *war* written in bold letters he tried to block such a contingency by a strongly-worded plank in the Democratic platform. But the pledge to keep out of "foreign wars" was nullified by the pregnant phrase—"except in case of attack." It would not be difficult for an Administration seeking war to push one of the Axis powers to the point where an attack was inevitable.

But the American people, like William Allen White, had to be fooled by pacific phrases. When the election currents in the fall of 1940 appeared to be making a turn towards Wendell Willkie, the President made some new pledges at Philadelphia on October 23: "To every man, woman and child in the nation I say this: Your President and your Secretary of State are following the road to peace. . . . We are arming ourselves not for any purpose of conquest or intervention in foreign disputes." A week later, in Boston, his pledge became more specific: "While I am talking to you mothers and fathers, I give you one more assurance. I have said this before, but I shall say it again and again and again: Your boys are not going to be sent into any foreign wars."

Robert Sherwood who helped to prepare this Boston speech had some qualms of conscience in later years: "For my own part, I think it was a mistake for him [the President] to go so far in yielding to the hysterical demands for sweeping reassurance, but, unfortunately for my own conscience, I happened at the time to be one of those who urged him to go the limit on this. . . . I burn inwardly whenever I think of those words 'again—and again—and again.'"

In the spring of 1941 these fires of conscience were burning very low in the President's entourage. Under the impact of appeals from Churchill in England the entire structure of American neutrality was finally demolished by the legislative bomb of lend-lease. This bomb was many months in the making. On November 6, 1940, Churchill wrote to Roosevelt to express his profound relief at the election results: "I feel you will not mind my saying that I prayed for your success and that I am truly thankful for it. . . . I must avow my sure faith that the lights by which we steer will bring us all safely to anchor." Those lights would lead America into the war.

On December 8, 1940, Churchill sent another long letter in which he outlined in great detail the pressing needs of Britain. In Churchill's eyes these needs were also America's needs because Britain was fighting our war as well as hers. The safety of the United States was "bound up with the survival and independence of the British Commonwealth of Nations." Therefore, America should rush to Britain war matériel of specified kinds to-

Roosevelt's Incitements to War

Charles Callan Tansill's contention that Franklin D. Roosevelt plotted the United States into World War II is echoed in historian Robert Smith Thompson's 1991 study, A Time for War: Franklin Delano Roosevelt and the Path to Pearl Harbor.

Did the United States enter the war just because of Pearl Harbor? No. America was in a naval war with Germany from the middle of 1941 on and in an economic war with Japan from even earlier; and America's plans to firebomb Japan no later than early 1942 were an open secret. . . .

Did the United States provoke Germany into its declaration of war and Japan into its Pearl Harbor attack? Yes.

- Despite the neutrality acts, the United States had *not* been neutral. It was giving support to the Chinese, the British, the Soviets, and others from well before Pearl Harbor.
- Speaking in public, President Roosevelt had invoked the word "victory.". . .
- By mid-1941, U.S. war production was soon to be outpacing those of Germany and Japan. . . .

At the later Tokyo War Crime Trial, General Tojo Hideki stated: "To adopt a policy of patience and perseverance under such impediment [the American pressure] was tantamount to self-annihilation of our nation. Rather than await extinction, it was better to face death by breaking through the encircling ring and find a way for existence." Here was no mere deterrence; here was deterrence that amounted to provocation.

Was the provocation deliberate? Three times, twice to [British ambassador] Lord Halifax and once to Prime Minister Churchill, Roosevelt intimated that he was trying to force "an incident" that would lead America more deeply into the fray. He may have hated war, but he presided over policies that came to be indistinguishable from incitements to war.

gether with the gift or loan "of a large number of American vessels of war." It was useless to expect Britain to pay for these loans. The moment was approaching when the British Government would "no longer be able to pay cash for shipping and other supplies." The few dollars Britain had left were badly needed for domestic requirements. It would be wrong "in principle" for Britain to be "divested of all saleable assets, so that after the victory was won with our blood, civilisation saved, and the time gained for the United States to be fully armed against all eventualities, we should stand stripped to the bone." America should bear a large part of the financial burden for a new crusade in Europe.

Roosevelt received this communication while he was cruising in the Caribbean. When he returned on December 16 he signified his ardent approval of aid to Britain at America's expense. On the following day, at a press conference, he recited an interesting parable:

> Suppose my neighbor's house catches fire and I have a length of garden hose four or five hundred feet away. If he can take my garden hose and connect it up with his hydrant, I may help him to put out the fire. Now what do I do? I don't say to him before that operation, "Neighbor, my garden hose cost me fifteen dollars; you have to pay me fifteen dollars for it." No! What is the transaction that goes on? I don't want fifteen dollars—I want my garden hose back after the fire is over. . . . What I am trying to do is to eliminate the dollar sign.

What he really meant to say was that he was trying to eliminate the dollar sign so far as Britain was concerned. The American taxpayers would have it before their anxious eyes for the next generation. But before they had time to make any estimates, a lend-lease bill was introduced in the House of Representatives. It bore the significant number H.R. 1776. In that year we declared our independence from Britain; in 1941 we put it into grave peril by giving Britain a blank check which Churchill filled in with great gusto and then sent back to Washington for Roosevelt's indorsement. Harry Hopkins was the contact man in this regard and while still in Britain he heard Churchill's famous broadcast in which the following dangerous nonsense was beamed to rapt American listeners:

> It seems now to be certain that the Government and the people of the United States intend to supply us with all that is necessary for victory. In the last war the United States sent two million men across the Atlantic. But this is not a war of vast armies, firing immense masses of shells at one another. We do not need the gallant armies which are forming throughout the American Union. We do not need them this year, nor next year, nor any year that I can foresee.

These assurances of Churchill were of the same stripe as the Roosevelt assurances during the last days of his campaign for re-election. He probably remembered Lord Northcliffe's sharp indictment of the American masses during the World War: "What sheep!" They could be sheared once more for British benefit by constant repetition of the old propaganda line about Britain fighting America's fight. Roosevelt repeated this line on December 29 in a "fireside chat" to the American people. Aid to Britain was now a question of "national security." If Britain were conquered, "all of us in the Americas would be living at the point of a gun.". . .

On January 2, 1941, Edward Foley, Morgenthau's general counsel, and his assistant, Oscar Cox, began the arduous task of drafting the bill. When opposition to the bill developed in certain circles in the State Department, Secretary Knox remarked to Morgenthau in his best seriocomic manner: "Let's organize a hanging bee over there someday and hang the ones that you and I pick out." Some of the clique around the President probably would have regarded the matter of a hanging bee very seriously when Senator Wheeler began a series of blasts against lend-lease legislation. On January 4, 1941, he asked some very pertinent questions: "If it is our war, how can we justify lending them stuff and asking them to pay us back? If it is our war, we ought to have the courage to go over and fight it, but it is not our war." A week later, in a radio broadcast, he feathered a shaft that evoked an immediate cry of pain from the sensitive President. He regarded the lend-lease program as "the New Deal's 'triple A' foreign policy—to plow under every fourth American boy." The President deeply resented these prophetic words and denounced the Wheeler comment upon lend-lease as the "rottenest thing that has been said in public life in my generation."

Although Admiral [H.R.] Stark expressed on January 13 the opinion that "we are heading straight for this war," the lend-lease program was sold to the American people as a form of peace insurance. On March 11, 1941, the lend-lease bill was signed by the President, and it was not long before a forecast of Senator [Robert A.] Taft was proved correct: "I do not see how we can long conduct such a war [undeclared war] without actually being in the shooting end of the war."

Hitler and the United States

This "shooting end of the war" was greatly feared by Hitler who strove in every way to avoid any incident that might lead to war with the United States. In order to conciliate public opinion in neutral countries, submarine commanders, from the very beginning of the war, had been directed "to conform to the Hague Convention." Passenger lines were not to be torpedoed even when under escort.

In September and October 1939, Hitler had high hopes that America might be induced to accept the role of mediator and thus bring to an early close a war that he had entered with many misgivings. . . .

Hitler was exceedingly anxious not to have war with America. [That] is clear in the testimony given during the Nürnberg trials. [Foreign minister Joachim von] Ribbentrop insisted upon the pacific disposition of the Führer concerning the United States, and [Baron Ernst von] Weizsäcker confirmed this fact: "No German desired to be at war with the United States or looked for trouble in that direction. . . . We were not to let ourselves be provoked to be the ones who bring the conflict to the open daylight. Wherever there would be unfriendly acts, . . . we would not be the ones who start."

The German press, under strict instructions, stopped its sharp criticism of the United States and of prominent American officials. Nazi officials became increasingly careful about any statements that might offend American sensibilities, and the German chargé d'affaires in Washington (Dr. Hans Thomsen), in a press release, went so far as to call President Roosevelt "high-minded" and to praise his admonitions of neutrality. In April 1940, General Walther von Brauchitsch assured representatives of the press that he had always admired the youthful strength of the United States and its people to which he attributed the "gigantic success of the new continent."

The new American neutrality law (November 4, 1939) gave certain satisfaction to Hitler who assured leading Nazis that it would render the United States harmless. Under this law the waters around the British Isles and the entire European coast from Bergen to the Spanish border were closed to American ships. These restrictions pleased the Führer who decreed on December 30, 1939, that American crews were to be treated "with the greatest consideration." In this same spirit Admiral [Erich] Raeder issued instructions that American ships were not to be pursued or sunk in order that "all difficulties which might result from trade war between the United States and Germany might be avoided at the very beginning." But this German policy of conciliation was sorely tried by incidents arising out of the establishment of a neutrality zone announced by the Panama Conference, October 3, 1939. This safety belt around the Americas south of Canada varied in width from 300 to 1000 miles. Belligerents were warned to refrain from naval action within that area, but no armed forces were stationed along the safety belt to enforce this regulation.

In order to conciliate America the German Admiralty issued orders designed to prevent naval engagements within this safety belt. When the Admiralty wished to recede from this position, Hitler refused to permit any change of orders. Moreover, the Führer adhered to this conciliatory policy even when American vessels adopted a course that must have enraged him. In December 1939 the German liner *Columbus* left Veracruz and was closely trailed by the U.S.S. *Tuscaloosa* which constantly broadcasted her position. This action compelled the Nazi captain to scuttle his ship some 450 miles east of Cape May. The same tactics were pursued by the U.S.S. *Broome* in trailing the *Rhein*, which also was scuttled by her captain. The freighter *Idarwild* was followed by the *Broome* until it was destroyed by H.M.S. *Diomede* (November 1940), with the *Broome* standing by to watch the result of her pursuit. The German Government refrained from filing any protest at these actions.

At a naval conference on March 18, Admiral Raeder was finally able to secure an important concession from the Führer. This took the form of a new blockade order (March 25, 1941) which not only included Iceland but went as far as the waters of Greenland. The first naval incident in the North Atlantic would soon take place.

The background for such an incident had been carefully filled in by President Roosevelt. In August 1940 he had sent Admiral Robert L. Ghormley, Major General D. C. Emmons, and Major General George V. Strong to London for exploratory conversations concerning eventual "armed co-operation with the British Commonwealth." After some months of conversations with important officers in the British armed services, Admiral Ghormley, in October 1940, sent to Admiral [Harold R.] Stark a full report on his mission. Stark, in turn, presented to Secretary Knox on November 12 a memorandum on national objectives. One of the most important items in this memorandum was "the prevention of the disruption of the British Empire." In order to achieve this objective, in January 1941 a series of secret staff conversations began in Washington. Two months later (March 27, 1941), the ABC-1 Staff Agreement was consummated which envisaged a "full-fledged war co-operation when and if Axis aggression forced the United States into the war."

One of the sections of this agreement was aimed at creating an incident that would "force the United States into the war." It contained the following explosive phraseology: "Owing to the threat to the sea communications of the United Kingdom, the principal task of the United States naval forces in the Atlantic will be the protection of shipping of the Associated Powers." In order to carry out this task the Royal Navy hastened to give the United States Navy the "benefit of its experience, and of the new devices and methods for fighting submarines that had already been evolved." The responsibility "now assumed by the United States Navy meant the organization of a force for escort-of-convoy." On February 1, 1941, this patrol force was given "the new and appropriate designation of Atlantic Fleet," and its commander, Rear Admiral Ernest J. King, was promoted to the rank of Admiral and designated Commander in Chief Atlantic Fleet. The first naval incident was almost at hand.

On April 10, 1941, the destroyer *Niblack* (Lieutenant Commander E. R. Durgin), in the waters off Iceland, picked up three boatloads of survivors from a torpedoed Netherlands freighter. As the last men were being pulled aboard, the sound operator made contact on a submarine. The division commander, D.L. Ryan, immediately assumed that the submarine was approaching for an attack so he ordered Mr. Durgin to drop some depth charges which caused the submarine to retire. This was the first action between United States and German armed forces. . . .

On April 25, during a press conference, the President expressly denied that naval escorts were being provided for fleets carrying lend-lease goods, and he developed at great length the difference between patrolling and convoying. A month later (May 27), in a national broadcast, he insisted that the delivery of war matériel to Britain was "imperative" and then stated that he had extended "our patrol in north and south Atlantic waters.". . .

While these exercises in double talk were being carried on, the President was taking active measures to see that Greenland [a colony of Denmark] did not fall into German hands. On January 9, 1941, the Department of State issued a release indicating that an American consulate had been established at Godthaab, and that provision had been made for the purchase in the United States of small arms for the Greenland police. These steps were followed by the signature (April 9, 1941) of an agreement authorizing the United States to occupy Greenland for defensive purposes. Inasmuch as the Danish Minister in Washington (Henrik Kauffmann) had no authority to conclude such an agreement, he was recalled by the Nazi-controlled Danish Foreign Office. He preferred to remain in Washington and was recognized by Secretary Hull as the regularly accredited minister. Needless to say, from the viewpoint of international law, this whole transaction was legally indefensible. . . .

The next naval incident involving German-American relations was the sinking of the American merchant ship (May 21, 1941) *Robin Moor*, New York to Cape Town, by a German submarine. There was no visit or search but the crew and passengers were allowed to take to open lifeboats. As the sinking occurred outside the blockade zone it is evident that the submarine commander disregarded orders concerning American ships. Admiral Raeder immediately issued orders to prevent further incidents of this nature, and Hitler, after confirming these instructions, remarked that he wished to "avoid any incident with the U.S.A." On June 20 the President sent a message to Congress in which he bitterly criticized Germany as an international outlaw. He followed this message with another move in the direction of war. On July 7 he ordered American occupation of Iceland. Two days later Secretary Knox gave a statement to the press which implied that the American patrol force in the North Atlantic had the right to use its guns when the occasion arose.

The *Greer* Incident

This occasion arose on September 4, 1941, when the destroyer *Greer*, bound for Iceland, was informed by a British plane that a submerged U-boat lay athwart her course some ten miles ahead. The *Greer* at once laid a course for the reported submarine, and after having made sound contact with it, kept it on her bow for more than three hours. During this period a British plane dropped four depth charges in the vicinity of the submarine without effect. Finally, the submarine commander grew tired of this game of hide-and-seek and launched a torpedo which the *Greer* was able to dodge. When the *Greer* counterattacked with depth charges, the submarine launched another torpedo which was avoided. When sound contact with the submarine could not be reestablished, the *Greer* resumed course for Iceland.

On September 11 the President gave a broadcast which presented a distorted version of the *Greer* incident. He conveniently forgot to tell that the initiative had been taken by the *Greer:* "She [the *Greer*] was flying the American flag. Her identity as an American ship was unmistakable. She was then and there attacked by a submarine. Germany admits that it was a German submarine. . . . We have sought no shooting war with Hitler. . . . The aggression is not ours. Ours is solely defense." American vessels would now shoot at sight.

In the face of this serious incident that clearly showed the aggressive character of American naval patrolling, Hitler maintained his policy of avoiding difficulties with the United States. On September 17 orders concerning American merchant vessels exempted them from attack, even when in convoy, in all zones except that immediately surrounding the British Isles. In the Pan-American safety belt "no warlike acts" were to be carried out on German initiative.

The American answer to these pacific gestures was to authorize escort duty for American destroyers. It was arranged that an American escort group, based on Argentia [Newfoundland], should take over from a Royal Canadian Navy escort at a designated place off Newfoundland and hand over the convoy to a Royal Navy escort at an agreed mid-ocean meeting place. Convoying was now an established practice, and it should be kept in mind that Secretary Knox, during the lend-lease hearings, had frankly admitted that he regarded convoying as an "act of war."

This *de facto* war in the Atlantic soon produced another incident. On October 16 five American destroyers rushed from Reykjavik, Iceland, to the help of a convoy that was being attacked by submarines. On the following day, while in the midst of the fighting, the destroyer *Kearny* was struck by a torpedo and slowly made its way back to Iceland. It had deliberately moved into the center of a pitched battle between German submarines and British and Canadian warships and had taken the consequences. It was not long before President Roosevelt gave to the American people a twisted account of the incident. On October 27 he recounted the happenings on October 16 and 17 and asserted that

263

he had "wished to avoid shooting." America had "been attacked. The U.S.S. *Kearny* is not just a Navy ship. She belongs to every man, woman, and child in this Nation. . . . Hitler's torpedo was directed at every American." In order to give additional over-tones of villainy to his description of Nazi wickedness he then stated that he had a secret map made in Germany which dis-closed Hitler's plan to put all the continent of South America un-der his domination. But that was not all. He had in his possession another document made in Germany that revealed Hitler's inten-tion, if he was victorious, to "abolish all existing religions." It should be evident that the "forward march of Hitlerism" should be stopped. . . . We are pledged to pull our own oar in the de-struction of Hitlerism." The American Navy had been given or-ders to "shoot on sight." The Nazi "rattlesnakes of the sea" would have to be destroyed.

This declaration of war was confirmed by the *Reuben James* inci-dent. On October 31, while the *Reuben James* was escorting a con-voy to Iceland, some German submarines were encountered about 600 miles west of that island. The American destroyer was struck by a torpedo and rapidly sank. Only 45, out of a crew of about 160, were saved. When the news of the sinking of the *Reuben James* reached Germany, Hitler remarked: "President Roo-sevelt has ordered his ships to shoot the moment they sight Ger-man ships. I have ordered German ships not to shoot when they sight American vessels but to defend themselves when attacked." On November 13, 1941, the directives for conduct of German warships when encountering American naval vessels remained pacific: "Engagements with American naval or air forces are not to be sought deliberately; they are to be avoided as far as possi-ble. . . . If it is observed before a convoy is attacked that it is being escorted by American forces, the attack is not to be carried out."

Germany was trying desperately to stay out of war with the United States. America's attitude was clearly stated by Sumner Welles at Arlington on November 11: "Beyond the Atlantic a sin-ister and pitiless conqueror has reduced more than half of Europe to abject serfdom. It is his boast that his system shall prevail even unto the ends of the earth. . . . The American people after full de-bate . . . have determined upon their policy. They are pledged . . . to spare no effort and no sacrifice in bringing to pass the final de-feat of Hitlerism and all that which that evil term implies. . . . We cannot know, we cannot yet foresee, how long and how hard the road may be which leads to that new day when another armistice will be signed."

To the mind of Welles and to others in the White House group it was obvious that America was really in the war. But the Ameri-can people did not realize that momentous fact, nor did they know that they were pledged "to spare no effort and no sacrifice in bringing to pass the final defeat of Hitlerism." It was easy for Mr. Welles to speak glibly of sacrifice. He had long enjoyed wealth and high social position. The word "sacrifice" had always been excluded from his dictionary. As the spokesman for the President he was suddenly breaking to the American people the dread news that they had become involved in a war they had ardently wished to avoid. The war hawks of 1941 were never tired of sneering at the majority of Americans as benighted isolationists who had tried to build a Chinese wall around the United States and thus cut it off from all foreign contacts. They knew their sneers were patent lies. America had never been isolated from the social, economic, religious, and cultural forces that shaped the modern world. Thanks to its geographical position it had escaped the recurring tides of conflict that had crumbled the walls of ancient civilizations and washed away the heritage men had earned through dauntless courage and high endeavor. Americans had been isolationists only against war and its evident evils, and their country had grown prosperous beyond the dreams of the founding fathers. But in 1915, President Wilson began to nurse the thought of sharing America's ideals and wealth with the rest of the world, and two years later he led us into a foreign war that he hoped would make the world safe for democracy. But this theme song turned sour in American ears when it led to the great parade of 1917 which ended for many men in the vast cemeteries in France. It gained new popularity after 1933, and with Roosevelt as maestro, the old macabre accents began to haunt every home. In 1941 his orchestra of death was anxiously waiting for the signal to begin the new symphony. He had hoped for a German motif but Hitler had refused to assist with a few opening martial notes. Perhaps some Japanese statesman would prove more accommodating! At any rate, after the *Reuben James* incident had fallen flat he turned his eyes towards the Orient and sought new inspiration from the inscrutable East. He found it at Pearl Harbor when Japanese planes sounded the first awesome notes in a chorus of war that is still vibrating throughout the world.

Viewpoint 2

"[Roosevelt] cooperated with Britain as far as he could short of war, but he drew back from the decisive steps urged on him by Churchill and his own militant advisers."

Franklin D. Roosevelt Resisted U.S. Involvement in World War II

Robert A. Divine (1929-)

American entry into World War II, which followed a decade of isolationist legislation and policies, has been widely studied and interpreted by historians. Some, such as Charles Callan Tansill, have accused Roosevelt of maneuvering the United States into the conflict against the wishes of the American people. Roosevelt scholar and historian Robert A. Divine, in his book *The Reluctant Belligerent: American Entry into World War II*, offers a radically different interpretation of Roosevelt's actions. He argues that Roosevelt, far from instigating war, instead responded cautiously to the actions of Germany and Great Britain. Divine concludes that Roosevelt's actions in this period, which resisted direct involvement in war but sought to prevent Germany from emerging victorious, reflected a more accurate reading of American public opinion than that of his isolationist opponents. Divine is the author and editor of numerous books on American foreign policy history, including *Causes and Consequences of World War II, Eisenhower and the Cold War*, and *The Age of Insecurity*.

Excerpted from Robert A. Divine, *The Reluctant Belligerent*. New York: John Wiley & Sons, 1965. Copyright © 1965 by John Wiley, renewed 1993 by Robert A. Divine. Reprinted by permission of McGraw-Hill, Inc.

The first few months of the Second World War bewildered most Americans. In September [1939] German armored divisions overran Poland with amazing ease. Hitler achieved this brilliant victory by leaving the western front undermanned, but the French, outnumbering the German forces facing them by more than two to one, limited themselves to a cautious advance into the Saar basin. Before they could mount a more ambitious offensive thrust, resistance in Poland had disintegrated and Germany had reinforced her troops in the west. Soon both sides had built up strength to the level of one hundred divisions, but neither Germany nor the western allies were willing to undertake a major offensive before the onset of winter. Thus there ensued a war of nerves in which both sides confined activity to routine patrols and occasional air raids dropping leaflets rather than bombs.

The war at sea was only slightly more active. The powerful British Navy swept German commerce from the world's oceans and instituted a blockade to cripple the German economy. Hitler had neglected to build up the submarine fleet on which Germany had relied so heavily in World War I, and during the first few months of the conflict German U-boats inflicted only minimal damage on Allied shipping. Even the vexing issues of neutral rights that had troubled the United States so deeply from 1914 to 1917 failed to emerge. German submarine commanders were instructed to avoid attacking American ships at all costs. In the first two months of the war, before the cash-and-carry policy removed American commerce from the combat zone in Europe, not a single American ship was torpedoed. Despite a few critical voices over the British blockade of Germany, the State Department confined itself to polite protests and legal reservations in its correspondence with the British Foreign Office.

Throughout this period of "phony war," the Roosevelt administration made every possible effort to insulate the United States from the European conflict. When Hitler made peace overtures in October, President Roosevelt remained aloof, not wishing to offer his services as a mediator in arranging a peace that would grant Germany the fruits of aggression. The major American diplomatic initiative was designed to keep the war out of the Western Hemisphere. . . .

The "phony war" came to an end on April 9, 1940. In a single day Hitler's forces occupied Denmark and the southern portion of Norway. Britain and France, preparing to meet a German offensive in northern France, were caught completely by surprise. The British rushed an expeditionary force to Norway, but these troops were unable to dislodge the Germans and were soon withdrawn. This stunning failure toppled Neville Chamberlain from power, and on May 10 Winston Churchill formed a new government in England to take charge of the war against Hitler.

The Scandinavian campaign was only the prelude to the all-out German offensive in the West. On May 10, Hitler unloosed his panzer divisions on the neutral countries of Belgium and the Netherlands. . . . In three weeks Hitler had conquered Belgium and the Netherlands, driven the British off the continent, and had his armies poised to destroy a demoralized France. By using modern weapons in a bold and novel way, Germany had achieved a revolution in the art of war which imperiled the security of every nation in the world.

French Appeals for Help

On the day that Dunkirk fell, Churchill delivered a stirring speech to the House of Commons; he reiterated his determination to fight on even if Germany conquered the British Isles "until, in God's good time, the New World, with all its power and might, steps forth to the rescue and liberation of the old." This veiled reference to eventual salvation by the United States was echoed in France. On June 5 Germany resumed its offensive against the ill-equipped and ill-led remnants of the French army. Six days later, with the advance German units approaching Paris, Prime Minister Paul Reynaud sent a personal telegram to Franklin D. Roosevelt asking him to give England and France "aid and material support by all means 'short of an expeditionary force.'" Promising that such aid would not be in a lost cause, Reynaud pledged: "We shall fight in front of Paris; we shall fight behind Paris; we shall close ourselves in one of our provinces to fight and if we should be driven out of it we shall establish ourselves in North Africa to continue the fight and if necessary in our American possessions."

A few hours before he received Reynaud's appeal, President Roosevelt spoke out bluntly at Charlottesville, Virginia, on the tragic events in Europe. In an address to the graduating class at the University of Virginia, Roosevelt ridiculed the policy of isolation and made clear his attitude toward the European struggle. "Overwhelmingly we, as a nation," the President proclaimed, "are convinced that military and naval victory for the gods of force and hate would endanger the institutions of democracy in the Western World, and that equally, therefore, the whole of our sympathies lies with those nations that are giving their life blood in combat against these forces." He then denounced Italy, which earlier that day had declared war against France. "On this tenth day of June, 1940, the hand that held the dagger has struck it into the back of its neighbor." Roosevelt concluded by promising to send to England and France all available material aid in their struggle against Hitler and Mussolini.

When Roosevelt received Reynaud's telegram, there was little more that he could say. He released the French plea for help to the public, and on June 13 he sent a reply to Reynaud encourag-

---

Roosevelt and the Polls

San Francisco State University professor Jerald A. Combs is the author of several books on American diplomatic history. In this passage from his 1986 book, The History of American Foreign Policy, *he argues that German aggression in Europe made the American public far less isolationist than it had been previously, and that Franklin D. Roosevelt probably acted to intervene in World War II too slowly.*

Prior to France's collapse, 82 percent of Americans expected the Allies to win the war and thus saw no particular reason for the United States to aid them. After Germany had swatted aside French resistance, a majority of Americans polled feared that Germany would win the war. Therefore 80 percent favored extending aid to Great Britain, even though 65 percent expected this to lead to American involvement. And yet 82 percent still opposed American military intervention.

Roosevelt read the message these polls delivered. Americans wanted Britain to win the war and were willing to aid it, but they did not want to enter the war themselves. Consequently, Roosevelt portrayed every action he took to aid Great Britain as designed to prevent American intervention by helping the British to win on their own. Roosevelt undoubtedly realized that Britain would require American military intervention to win, but he never said that directly to the American people. He would not take a divided nation into a major war. Instead, he urged aid to the Allies in hopes either that a miracle would allow them to win or that Hitler would retaliate and galvanize Americans into a united determination to fight and defeat the Nazis. . . .

Despite Roosevelt's deviousness and proclamations that he would never send Americans to fight a foreign war, polls showed that Americans had few illusions about what the president was doing. In fact, most historians who have criticized Roosevelt have accused him of moving too cautiously toward intervention. They argue that the polls show Roosevelt to have been behind public opinion rather than ahead of it. Hitler seemed to understand Roosevelt's intentions as well. He refused to respond to Roosevelt's provocations and create an incident that would bring America into the European war. He remembered too vividly the miscalculation Germany had made in World War I. In hopes of diverting the United States from Europe, he encouraged the Japanese to expand. Even if this led to war with the United States, America would have to fight on two fronts, and Hitler could continue his triumphant march of conquest.

---

ing him to fight on in North Africa if Germany overran France. Meanwhile, French resistance continued to crumble. Paris fell to the German forces and the government fled to the south. On July 14, Reynaud delivered a final appeal to Roosevelt. "The only chance of saving the French nation, vanguard of democracies, and through her to save England, by whose side France could then remain with her powerful navy," Reynaud pleaded, "is to throw into the balance, this very day, the weight of American power." Sorrowfully, Roosevelt replied the next day. He told Reynaud that he admired the courage of France; that he would make every effort to send additional supplies to England and France; that he would not recognize the legality of the German conquest of France; but that he could not commit the United States to military intervention in the war. "Only the Congress," Roosevelt concluded, "can make such commitments." Three days later Marshal Pétain replaced Reynaud as head of the French government and surrendered his country to Germany. Hitler was now master of Western Europe.

The great German blitzkrieg, culminating in the fall of France, transformed American attitudes toward the war in Europe. The months of military inaction had bred a complacency and cynicism which now gave way to a sense of urgency and intense concern. In January, 1940, Roosevelt had asked Congress to appropriate slightly less than $2 billion for national defense, a modest increase over the previous year. For the next three months, economy-minded Congressmen whittled away at the Presidential request in committee. A week after the German thrust into Belgium and Holland, President Roosevelt went before Congress to ask for an additional billion dollars to strengthen the nation's security. An alarmed Congress acted with amazing speed; in late May both Houses approved additional appropriations of one-and-a-half billion, and when Roosevelt sought another billion on May 31, Congress granted this sum in two weeks' time. Heartened by this sudden cooperation, the President sent in a request for nearly $5 billion on July 10 to meet the new situation created by the fall of France. In September Congress approved this expanded program, raising the total defense appropriations in 1940 to $10.5 billion. Fearful of the peril to American security from a victorious Germany, Congress had voted a five-fold increase in expenditures for national defense.

The changing American attitude toward the European war found expression in the formation of the Committee to Defend America by Aiding the Allies. William Allen White and Clark Eichelberger, the men responsible for organizing public support for the repeal of the [1935] arms embargo, became worried over the complacency of the American people in the spring of 1940 and they met to consider creating a new committee to arouse the public. When Hitler unleashed his great offensive in May, they decided it was time to act. On May 17 White sent a telegram to several hundred prominent American men and women. "As one democracy after another crumbles under the mechanized columns of the dictators," White declared, "it becomes evident that the future of western civilization is being decided upon the battlefield of Europe. . . . The time has come when the United States should throw its material and moral weight on the side of the nations of western Europe great and small that are struggling in battle for a civilized way of life." White asked the recipients of his telegram to join with him in appealing to the American people for increased aid for the Allies. Within an hour enthusiastic replies began flowing in from clergymen, university presidents, and distinguished public leaders from all walks of life. Heartened by this response, on May 20 White made public the existence of the committee and formally launched an intensive publicity campaign to convert the American people to the cause of all-out aid to England and France.

The White committee was an immediate success. Within six weeks over 300 local chapters were formed representing every state except North Dakota. Small donations from the rank and file financed the work of the committee, though there were larger contributions from such diverse individuals as J. P. Morgan and David Dubinsky, president of the International Ladies Garment Workers Union. White, who continued to edit his newspaper in Emporia, Kansas, supervised the over-all policy of the committee, but the larger task of organization and day-by-day direction was carried on by Clark Eichelberger in New York City, where the committee had its headquarters. Eichelberger employed every possible technique of public pressure to advance the viewpoint of the committee. Local chapters sent petitions, telegrams and letters to the President and Congress; the committee sponsored national radio broadcasts and mass rallies in major American cities; Robert Sherwood, the noted playwright, prepared a dramatic full-page advertisement, "Stop Hitler Now," which appeared in newspapers around the nation in early June.

The activities of the White Committee, together with the ominous news from Europe, led to startling changes in American attitudes. During the winter months the great majority of the American people saw no reason to extend aid to England and France, and perceived little danger to the United States from the fighting in Europe. In a poll taken just after the outbreak of the war, 82% of those surveyed believed that England and France would defeat Germany. In May, when the blitzkrieg began, a majority still foresaw an eventual Allied victory. But with the fall of France this confidence was shattered; now a majority answered that Germany was likely to win the war. This new estimate made most Americans receptive to the campaign of the White Committee for additional aid to England. In a poll taken in June, four out of five Americans questioned favored giving Britain more material support. And they realized where this aid might lead; in a poll in June 65% of those replying thought that the United States would enter the war before it was over. Yet despite the fear of a German victory, the desire to aid England engendered by the White Committee, and the belief in eventual involvement, the great majority of Americans clung to the policies of neutrality and isolation. In June 1940 82% opposed entry into the European conflict. Shaken by the German victories, the American people were willing to back the administration in a policy of all-out aid to Britain, but they insisted that this aid stop short of war.

The Battle of Britain

In the summer of 1940 Americans watched tensely as the Battle of Britain began. Lacking the naval strength to launch an immediate invasion of England, Hitler decided to subdue the British from the air. On July 10 the German *Luftwaffe* began a series of heavy bombing raids on British shipping and ports along the English Channel. In mid-August Hitler shifted the attack to airfields in southern England, hoping to destroy the R.A.F. [Royal Air Force]. Meanwhile, German submarines, now operating out of French ports, began an increasingly effective campaign against British shipping. In May the British lost only 75,000 tons of shipping, but in June the losses totaled 290,000 tons. Using wolfpack techniques, the German submarines penetrated British convoys and threatened to sever Britain's lifeline to the United States and the Empire. Under attack from the air and the sea, Britain's chances for survival seemed tragically slim to many Americans. For the first time in their lives, many realized that England was indeed America's first line of defense. If Germany was able to invade the British Isles and take the British Navy intact, the Atlantic would be transformed from a secure barrier into a broad highway for German penetration of the Western Hemisphere.

The United States could do little to help the British meet the attack from the air, but there were measures the Roosevelt administration could take to assist in the war at sea. On May 15, 1940, Winston Churchill had asked Roosevelt to give Britain 40 or 50 overage destroyers for convoy duty. Britain had begun the war with 100 destroyers in her home waters; by May nearly half had been lost. The United States had over 200 destroyers dating back to World War I. The United States Navy commissioned 172 of these vessels for active duty, but it could spare enough to meet the

British request. President Roosevelt was fearful that every available ship might be needed to protect the Atlantic approaches to the United States, and hesitated to fulfill Churchill's request. Moreover, Congress had decreed in the naval expansion bill of June 28 that the President could not transfer military equipment to a foreign country until the Chief of Naval Operations certified that it was "not essential to the defense of the United States." This legal obstacle worried Roosevelt. Mainly he feared the reaction of Congressional isolationists if he sanctioned such a clear-cut violation of neutrality. Roosevelt was planning to run for a third term and he did not wish to provide the Republicans with a campaign issue. Thus in his reply to Churchill, the President explained the difficulties he faced and promised only to give the matter further thought.

Despite a personal plea from King George, Roosevelt continued to procrastinate through June and July. At a meeting with William Allen White on June 29, Roosevelt outlined the problem and stressed the obstacles to a transfer of the destroyers. White felt that Roosevelt had "lost his cud," and he decided to have the Committee to Defend America by Aiding the Allies agitate on this issue in order to strengthen the President. Throughout July and August, the White Committee focused its energies on the destroyer issue, encouraging members to write to the President urging the transfer, sponsoring mass rallies, and printing newspaper advertisements with the bold headline, "Between Us and Hitler Stands the *British* fleet!" The Committee's most effective move came on August 4 when it sponsored a radio broadcast by General John J. Pershing, the American commander in World War I. "America will safeguard her freedom and security by making available to the British or Canadian governments at least fifty of the over-age destroyers, which are left from the days of the World War," Pershing declared. "If the destroyers help save the British fleet, they may save us from the danger and hardship of another war."

While the White Committee stimulated nationwide support for transfer of the destroyers, a faction inside the Committee, known as the Century group, met to consider how they could persuade Roosevelt to act. The Century group consisted of businessmen, lawyers, journalists, and intellectuals, primarily in New York City, who wanted to go beyond the moderate policy of the White Committee and advocate American entry into the war. Alarmed by the inaction on the destroyer issue, these men decided to approach the President with a novel suggestion—the United States would turn over 50 destroyers to England in return for bases on British possessions in the Western Hemisphere and a pledge by Britain never to surrender its fleet to Germany. On August 1 a three-man delegation presented the proposal to Roosevelt. The President listened noncommittally, but the next day he discussed the idea with his cabinet and decided to explore this possibility with the British.

The Century group had broken the logjam on the destroyer issue, but a month of tedious negotiation followed before the deal could be completed. Fearful of political opposition, the President insisted that the Republican candidate, Wendell Willkie, approve the transaction. William Allen White undertook this delicate mission, and after some early difficulty was finally able to report to Roosevelt that Willkie would not attack the destroyer deal publicly. The British raised objections, preferring not to link the transfer of bases with the destroyer issue, but they finally acquiesced. The legal obstacle was overcome when the Chief of Naval Operations declared the destroyers surplus on the grounds that the acquisition of bases meant a net strategic gain for the United States. Finally, on September 2, 1940, Cordell Hull and Lord Lothian, the British Ambassador, completed the destroyers-for-bases transaction with an exchange of letters. The next day the President transmitted this executive agreement to Congress for its information. The same day Great Britain gave public assurances that it would never permit the British Navy to pass into German hands.

The End of Neutrality

The destroyers-for-bases agreement marked the end of American neutrality. In giving 50 warships to Great Britain, the United States was openly declaring its support of England in the war against Germany. The acquisition of sites for eight naval and air bases in British possessions stretching from Newfoundland on the north to British Guiana on the south blunted the isolationist criticism, for if Roosevelt had not performed "the most important action in the reinforcement of our national defense that has been taken since the Louisiana Purchase," as he told Congress, he had clearly strengthened American security in the Atlantic. But this achievement was totally inconsistent with the status of neutrality. From this time forward the United States was a nonbelligerent, not yet at war with Germany, but clearly aligned with Britain in the struggle against Hitler.

At the time Roosevelt was bitterly assailed by isolationists for undertaking such a momentous step without the consent of Congress. Yet there could be little question that his action met with the overwhelming approval of the American people. A public opinion poll revealed that 70% of the people supported the destroyer deal. Indeed, Roosevelt could easily be accused of acting too cautiously. He had procrastinated on Churchill's request at a time when the fate of England hung in the balance; he had allowed a group of private citizens to solve his dilemma; he had not acted until he had made certain that it was politically safe for him to do so. Roosevelt's hesitation had led William Allen White to warn him in June "you will not be able to lead the American people unless you catch up with them." Moving too slowly for the internationalists and too swiftly for the isolationists, Roosevelt had carefully gauged the national temper before committing the country to a status of nonbelligerency. His moderation proved to be wise, for when he finally acted, he carried the nation with him. Roosevelt knew that the great majority of the American people were still torn between a desire to defeat Hitler and a determination to stay at peace. The destroyers-for-bases agreement came within the limits of this national consensus. . . .

The 1940 Election

By the end of the first year of the war, American foreign policy had undergone a startling transformation. The nation that had attempted to insulate itself from war was now committed to all possible aid to England and to economic pressure to restrain Japanese aggression in the Far East. Congress had taken some important steps, most notably in revising the Neutrality Act, voting increased defense expenditures, and approving of Selective Service in September, but the major policy decisions had been undertaken by the President. Both the destroyers-for-bases deal and a limited embargo on Japan were executive actions performed without the consent of Congress. Although public opinion polls showed that a substantial majority of Americans approved of these steps, the President was taking a very real gamble in an election year. The ultimate test would come in November with Roosevelt's bid for a third term in the White House.

The Republican party virtually ruled out a showdown on foreign policy when it chose Wendell Willkie, an outspoken supporter of aid to Britain, as its candidate in June, 1940. . . . The Republican candidate agreed with the administration's course of all-out aid short of war to Britain, and contended only that he could conduct such a policy more adroitly than Roosevelt. By supporting both the destroyers-for-bases deal and the Selective Service Act, Willkie removed the major issues of foreign policy from the political arena.

Barred from the presidential contest, the isolationists found a way to present their views to the public during the election campaign. In the summer of 1940, R. Douglas Stuart, Jr., a Yale Law School student, and General Robert E. Wood, Chairman of the Board of Sears Roebuck and Company, formed a nation-wide organization to counter the activities of the White Committee and place the isolationist viewpoint before the American people. On September 4, the day after the destroyer deal was made public, Stuart and Wood announced the creation of the America First

Committee, with headquarters in Chicago. The response was immediately favorable. Local chapters sprang up throughout the Middle West and the Northeast, and soon America First was waging an intense propaganda effort. Officially a nonpartisan group, the America First Committee was heavily weighted toward the Republican party, and during the presidential campaign the radio speeches and newspaper advertisements it sponsored represented a major attack on Roosevelt's foreign policies.

The major theme of the America First movement was that all-out aid to Britain could end only in American entry into the European War. Their spokesmen skillfully probed at the glaring inconsistency of American opinion in 1940: the popular belief that material aid to England was sufficient to defeat a Germany powerful enough to be a direct menace to American security. The isolationists maintained that Hitler did not imperil the United States, that Britain and Germany were simply engaged in another round of the age-old struggle for the balance of power in Europe, and that "American democracy can be preserved only by keeping out of the European war." Although the America First spokesmen were naive in their estimate of German strength, they made a valuable attempt to clarify the issues confronting the American people in 1940. If Hitler's Germany was as powerful and as ruthless as interventionists claimed, then both Willkie and Roosevelt were misleading the American people by asserting that the United States could maintain its security without entering directly into the war in Europe.

The candidates did little to clarify the issue raised by America First. Willkie began a vigorous campaign in early September, but he neglected foreign policy to hammer away at the third term issue. Roosevelt kept carefully aloof from politics until mid-October, giving only two speeches. In the first, to the Teamsters Union on September 11, he concentrated on domestic problems, but in one brief reference to foreign policy he proclaimed, "I hate war, now more than ever. I have one supreme determination—to do all that I can to keep war away from these shores for all time." A month later, in a Columbus Day speech at Dayton, Ohio, the President was more forthright, warning the nation of the peril it faced from the aggressors overseas. On this occasion he proclaimed his determination to continue aid to Britain in the face of grave danger. "No combination of dictator countries of Europe and Asia," the President declared, "will stop the help we are giving to almost the last free people now fighting to hold them at bay."

Roosevelt's conflicting statements, affirming his determination to keep the nation at peace while extending all possible aid to Britain, provided Willkie with an opening he could not resist. With his campaign going badly, he succumbed to the advice of party professionals and began an assault on Roosevelt's foreign policy. In speeches in late October Willkie questioned Roosevelt's sincerity in pledging to keep the nation out of war, and implied that the President had entered into secret understandings with the British. At Baltimore on October 30 he charged that if Roosevelt was returned to the White House, "you may expect we will be at war." These accusations angered Roosevelt, and he responded by scheduling a series of speeches to set the record straight. In addresses in Philadelphia and New York, the President repeated the theme of his Teamsters' speech, reaffirming his dedication to peace and ignoring the inconsistencies in the policy of all-out aid to Britain. Even these remarks did not reassure worried Democratic leaders, and when the President traveled to Boston to deliver a speech to the predominantly Irish population, strongly isolationist because of antipathy toward England, he was under heavy pressure to make a final guarantee that he would not lead the nation into war. Reluctantly, Roosevelt agreed, and in Boston he declared:

> And while I am talking to you mothers and fathers, I give you one more assurance. I have said this before, but I shall say it again and again and again: Your boys are not going to be sent into any foreign wars.

Even the Democratic platform had added the precautionary words, "except in case of attack," and when Roosevelt was reminded of this before the speech, he dismissed the omission with the comment, "Of course we'll fight if we're attacked. If somebody attacks us, then it isn't a foreign war, is it?"

A week later the American people returned Roosevelt to the presidency by a margin of 5 million votes. The third term issue, growing disenchantment with the New Deal, and Willkie's colorful personality had held Roosevelt to a modest victory compared to the landslide in 1936. But F.D.R. still won nearly 55% of the votes, and he could claim that he had a mandate from the people for his foreign policies. Although Roosevelt carefully equivocated on the crucial issue of aid to Britain and eventual involvement in the war, all interested parties interpreted the re-election of the President as a clear sign that the United States would continue to oppose Germany and Japan, even at the risk of war. Isolationists mourned; interventionists were jubilant. From England Winston Churchill commented that the election was "a message from across the ocean of great encouragement and good cheer." If Roosevelt had failed to clarify the ambiguity that continued to underlie American foreign policy, at least he had not misled the American people. They knew that they were moving down the road toward war; like their President, they moved reluctantly, hoping for a last-minute reprieve.

Lend-Lease

On December 2, 1940, President Roosevelt left Washington for a Caribbean cruise aboard the U.S.S. *Tuscaloosa*. Weary from the months of crisis touched off by the fall of France and the rigors of the recent presidential campaign, Roosevelt, accompanied only by his personal staff and his close adviser, Harry L. Hopkins, looked forward to two weeks of relaxation in the warm, tropical sun. The war in Europe had entered another lull, and there seemed to be no immediate danger. . . .

On the morning of December 9 a Navy seaplane delivered a long personal letter from Winston Churchill. In 4000 words he described the grave course of the war, emphasizing Britain's critical need for American supplies. He pointed out that German submarines were taking a heavy toll of shipping. And he informed the President that Britain was running out of money. By June England would exhaust her financial reserves and would no longer be able to pay for goods ordered from the United States. Promising that Britain would "suffer and sacrifice to the utmost for the Cause," Churchill expressed his confidence that the President would find the "ways and means" to continue furnishing England the material aid necessary to win the war. . . .

On December 16 the President arrived in Washington, tanned and rested. The next day, at his press conference, he revealed his bold and imaginative response to Britain's financial crisis. He began by telling the reporters that he was convinced England was America's first line of defense. Since Britain needed supplies to help protect American security, the simplest solution, the President suggested, would be to lease the materials. "Now, what I am trying to do," Roosevelt said, "is eliminate the dollar sign." Then in an apt parable, he compared his idea to lending a garden hose to a neighbor whose house was on fire. You didn't sell your hose to the neighbor, you loaned it to him, and he gave it back when the fire was out. So it would be with the munitions Britain needed to defeat Hitler.

The concept of lend-lease, first stated in these homey words, was Roosevelt's reply to Churchill's plea. The popular response was overwhelmingly favorable, and Roosevelt elaborated on the idea in a fireside chat to the American people on the evening of December 29. Again he stressed the importance of England to American security. "If Great Britain goes down, the Axis powers will control the continents of Europe, Asia, Africa, Australia, and the high seas," Roosevelt warned. "It is no exaggeration to say that all of us in the Americas would be living at the point of a gun. . . . " The President reiterated his campaign pledge to keep the nation out of the war, and he contended that increased aid to

England was the best means available to insure against American involvement. "Emphatically we must get these weapons to them in sufficient volume and quickly enough, so that we and our children will be saved the agony and suffering of war which others have had to endure. . . . We must be," the President concluded, "the great arsenal of democracy."

In early January [1941], Treasury Department lawyers translated Roosevelt's formula into appropriate legislation. The basic authority they would seek for the President was simple—the power "to sell, transfer title to, exchange, lease, lend, or otherwise dispose of" any defense article to "the government of any country whose defense the President deems vital to the defense of the United States." This lend-lease bill, shrewdly numbered H.R. 1776, was introduced into Congress on January 10. At committee hearings in both Houses administration spokesmen repeated the arguments that Roosevelt had made and revealed with embarrassing clarity the financial plight of Great Britain. Isolationists, led by Charles A. Lindbergh, appealed to Congressmen and Senators to defeat legislation which could lead only to American entry in the war. Let us "preserve one stronghold of order and sanity even against the gates of hell," pleaded historian Charles A. Beard. But the isolationists were in the minority. Americans from every walk of life and every shade of political opinion announced their support for the President's policy. When Wendell Willkie, titular leader of the Republican party, endorsed lend-lease in mid-February, he made it a bipartisan issue, and thus guaranteed favorable action by Congress.

After brief and responsible debate the House passed the lend-lease bill by a margin of 260 to 161. In the Senate a small band of opponents, led by Democrat Burton Wheeler of Montana and Republican Gerald Nye of North Dakota, spent more than two weeks denouncing both Franklin Roosevelt and Great Britain, but to no avail. The Senate passed the lend-lease bill by a vote of 60-31, and on March 11 the President signed the new act. Within the next month Congress appropriated $7 billion to insure the continued flow of supplies to Britain and her allies in the war against the Axis.

The enactment of lend-lease was a major turning point in American foreign policy. Congress approved the decision to render all-out aid to Britain, reached by the administration during the dark days of the German blitzkrieg in the spring of 1940. The overwhelming margins indicated that the nation was now firmly committed to the goal of defeating Hitler. The great majority of the American people still hoped to achieve this objective by peaceful means. Yet by giving Britain unrestricted access to America's industrial resources, the United States took a major step toward war.

While Congress deliberated over the lend-lease proposals, an equally significant discussion was taking place secretly in Washington. From January 29 until March 27 representatives of the British Chiefs of Staff met with their American counterparts to coordinate military strategy in the event the United States entered the war against Germany. These talks stemmed from a memorandum submitted by Admiral Harold R. Stark, the Chief of Naval Operations, to President Roosevelt on November 12, 1940. Worried over the lack of planning for national defense, Stark sketched out the alternatives confronting the United States and stated his belief that "the continued existence of the British Empire" was crucial for the defense of the Western Hemisphere. "I also believe," Stark continued, "that Great Britain requires from us very great help in the Atlantic, and possibly even on the continents of Europe and of Africa, if she is to be enabled to survive." Therefore, Stark recommended that if the United States should become involved in war against the three Axis powers, it should concentrate its efforts in the Atlantic against Germany and stand on the defensive toward Japan in the Pacific. Finally, to prepare for such a situation, Stark asked the President for permission to hold staff conversations with the British military and naval leaders.

Strategy Meetings

With characteristic caution, the President refused to sanction Stark's Atlantic policy, but he did permit the staff meetings to take place. In mid-January the British battleship *King George V* brought Lord Halifax, the new ambassador, to Washington; also on board were five senior English officers dressed in civilian clothes and listed as "technical advisers" to the British Purchasing Commission. For the next two months they met with American military and naval leaders to draw up plans for joint strategy in case of American involvement in the war. They quickly ratified the fundamental decision made by Stark in November: in a war with Germany and Japan, the United States and Britain would concentrate on defeating Germany first. Other points provoked disagreement, but the staff talks ended on March 27 with the adoption of a joint plan, "ABC-1," which the two nations would follow if the United States entered the war. This military coordination, together with the passage of lend-lease, signified that the United States, while still technically a neutral, had entered into what Robert Sherwood so aptly termed a "common law alliance" with Great Britain.

The adoption of ABC-1 provided for future cooperation between the United States and Great Britain, but the immediate problem facing the two nations in the winter and spring of 1941 was the renewed German submarine onslaught. When Hitler was compelled to give up his plans to invade Britain in the fall of 1940, he adopted the advice of Admiral Erich Raeder, Commander in Chief of the German Navy, and began an intensive campaign to sever England's supply lines to the United States and the Empire. German submarines, now operating out of bases on the French coast near the Atlantic sea lanes, developed new wolfpack techniques to penetrate British convoys and take an ever-heavier toll of merchant shipping. Groups of from eight to ten submarines would patrol together, and once a convoy was sighted, they would wait until nightfall to make a surface attack, thereby eluding the sensitive sonar gear aboard the British escort vessels. The German commanders submerged after firing the torpedoes, and would surface again to renew the attack. These tactics were strikingly successful; British shipping losses rose from 320,048 tons in January to 653,960 in April. "The situation is obviously critical in the Atlantic," wrote Admiral Stark on April 4. "In my opinion, it is hopeless except as we take strong measures to save it."

Throughout the lend-lease debate American naval leaders wrestled with the problem of overcoming the German submarine attacks and insuring the safe delivery of supplies to Britain. On February 1 Admiral Stark directed that the naval units engaged in patrolling the hemisphere neutrality belt in the Atlantic be designated as the Atlantic Fleet. Two weeks later he ordered the commander of the new fleet, Rear Admiral Ernest J. King, to create a Support Force which would take over the task of escorting trans-Atlantic convoys from the over-burdened British Navy. For the next few weeks, 27 destroyers, four squadrons of Catalina patrol planes, and a number of minesweepers and tenders underwent intensive training in antisubmarine warfare. On March 20 the Navy informed President Roosevelt that it was now prepared to undertake convoy duty in the North Atlantic.

The Convoy Debate

The Navy's statement presented the President with a critical political decision. During the lend-lease debate the administration had barely been able to avoid an amendment prohibiting the use of American naval vessels in convoying supplies to Britain. When the Committee to Defend America by Aiding the Allies started calling for such convoys in mid-March, isolationists in the press and Congress made a loud outcry. Senator Burton K. Wheeler of Montana declared that he realized that as soon as lend-lease was enacted, "the warmongers in this country would cry for convoys, and everyone recognizes the fact that convoys mean war." On March 31 Senator Charles W. Tobey of New Hampshire introduced an anticonvoy resolution in Congress which touched off a long debate. At the same time public opinion polls revealed that a majority of the American people opposed employing the United States Navy to insure delivery of war materials to Britain.

The President hesitated to act in the face of such strong public resistance, but members of his administration warned that without American convoys, the lend-lease supplies would never reach Britain. On March 24 Secretary of the Navy Frank Knox and Secretary of War Henry L. Stimson agreed that convoying was "the only solution." The next day Adolf Hitler intensified the problem by extending the war zone in which he permitted his submarines commanders to operate several hundred miles westward to include the waters adjacent to Greenland. For the next two weeks the President studied the problem, torn between a desire to aid Britain and fear of public disapproval.

On April 2, urged on by Stimson and Knox, Roosevelt approved Hemisphere Defense Plan No. 1, which authorized the Navy to undertake aggressive action against German submarines in the Western Atlantic. The question of convoys still had to be faced, and at a White House meeting on April 10 attended by Harry Hopkins and four cabinet members, including Stimson and Knox, the President compromised. Announcing that Congressional hostility precluded the use of the American Navy for convoys, Roosevelt said that instead he would authorize the extension of naval patrols beyond the 300-mile neutrality belt out into the mid-Atlantic. . . . In effect, Roosevelt decreed that the Western Hemisphere began halfway across the Atlantic at longitude 25°. American naval units would patrol this area, but their precise mission remained undefined. Roosevelt did not make his new policy public, but later the same day the White House announced that on April 9 the United States government had signed an executive agreement with the Danish minister in exile placing Greenland under the protection of the United States and authorizing the construction of American air and naval bases there. The President justified this bold step, taken to prevent Germany from using Greenland as a supply depot for its submarines, as a measure for the defense of the Western Hemisphere. The next day Roosevelt sent a cable to Winston Churchill notifying him of the new patrol zone in the Atlantic and stating that the American Navy would inform the British of the presence of "aggressor ships or planes" that ventured into this area.

The decision to occupy Greenland and to patrol the western half of the Atlantic completed Roosevelt's response to the Battle of the Atlantic in the spring of 1941. His advisers, especially Stimson and Knox, continued to press for convoys, but at a White House meeting on April 15 the President ruled out this alternative by rescinding Hemisphere Defense Plan No. 1, which sanctioned aggressive action against German submarines in the patrol zone and would have made convoying permissible. In its place, Roosevelt ordered Admiral Stark to limit naval activity in the Atlantic to intensive patrols. The President specifically stated that American ships were not to shoot at German submarines. Under these limitations it would be impossible for the Navy to provide escorts for British convoys. This compromise policy failed to provide England with all the help she needed to bring lend-lease supplies across the Atlantic safely, but it did quiet the uproar in Congress. On April 30 the Senate Foreign Relations Committee tabled the Tobey anticonvoy resolution. The isolationists had been unable to enact a legislative restriction on American foreign policy, but they had succeeded in preventing Roosevelt from using American ships to convoy supplies to Britain.

Meanwhile, spring brought to the continent of Europe another massive German offensive. Striking from bases in Bulgaria, Hitler's forces moved swiftly through Yugoslavia and Greece despite fierce resistance in this mountainous terrain. . . .

In the Atlantic, despite the new American patrol, the outlook was equally gloomy. Hitler's naval leaders had discovered a gap in the British convoy system—escort vessels based in Canada left the eastbound convoys in mid-Atlantic—and the merchant ships were easy targets until they were met by naval units from England. In April and May German wolfpacks converged on this vulnerable zone south of Iceland and took a heavy toll of British shipping. . . .

[On May 27, 1941] President Roosevelt spoke to the nation over the radio. His speech, the first major policy address in five months, had been postponed because of illness, and public interest in the President's words . . . was intense. Eighty-five million people heard him review the course of the war in Europe and point out the dangers German victory posed for the United States. Focusing on the Battle of the Atlantic, Roosevelt warned that Nazi success on the sea "would jeopardize the immediate safety of portions of North and South America." Announcing that naval patrols were already helping to protect the flow of goods to England, he bluntly declared, "The delivery of supplies to Britain is imperative. This can be done; it must be done; it will be done." Roosevelt then concluded his address by proclaiming a state of "unlimited national emergency."

The President's speech evoked an enthusiastic response from the American people, but many thoughtful observers were puzzled over his failure to discuss the convoy issue. At a press conference the next day reporters asked the President if his determination to use all possible measures to deliver supplies to Britain meant that he planned to have the Navy begin convoying. To the dismay of interventionists, Roosevelt said no, indicating in a vague way that naval escorts were outmoded. He then astonished the press by commenting that he had no plans to issue the executive orders necessary to implement his declaration of an unlimited national emergency.

The speech of May 27, often hailed as a major turning point in American foreign policy, confirmed rather than altered the drift of Presidential policy. The passage of the Lend-Lease Act had raised the question of using American naval vessels to convoy supplies to Britain. Caught in a crossfire between isolationists and internationalists, the President hesitated, realizing that if American destroyers accompanied British ships across the Atlantic, they were bound to become engaged in naval action with German submarines. He was convinced that the American people were not yet ready for such direct involvement in the European war. . . .

Germany Invades Russia

The German decision to invade Russia [in June 1941] had a profound impact on the European war. . . .

The Roosevelt administration, sharing the widespread doubt of Russia's ability to survive, did not launch any immediate program to assist the Soviet Union. Instead, Roosevelt's advisers urged taking advantage of the breathing space to increase its aid to Britain. . . .

Even before the German invasion of Russia, the President had approved plans to land American troops in Iceland and take over from Britain the job of protecting this key island from potential German aggression. . . . On July 1 the United States and Iceland reached an agreement, and a force of 4000 American marines set out for Iceland. The President then began preparation of a message to Congress announcing the new operation. He planned to justify this action on grounds of defending the Western Hemisphere, but many of his advisers, most notably Secretary Stimson, urged him to take a broader position. The nation should be told, urged Stimson, that the United States was taking control of Iceland to forestall German invasion, and that once in Iceland, the United States would use its position there to escort British convoys across the Atlantic.

The President was not yet willing to go so far. On June 30 Senator Burton K. Wheeler had introduced a resolution in Congress demanding that the Naval Affairs Committee investigate rumors that American ships were already escorting British convoys. Worried by this Congressional sniping, and aware that recent public opinion polls revealed that the American people were still evenly divided on the convoy issue, Roosevelt refused to sanction convoys. In his message to Congress on July 7 he justified the sending of troops to Iceland on the need to forestall German occupation, which would give Hitler bases "for eventual attack against the Western Hemisphere." The President added that German seizure of Iceland would endanger all shipping in the Atlantic and interrupt the flow of supplies to Britain, but he did not announce any additional steps to protect the Atlantic supply line.

Although a few commentators criticized Roosevelt for straining the limits of the Western Hemisphere to include Iceland, the public response to the President's message was very favorable. Roosevelt was so encouraged that he decided to begin using American naval units for limited convoy duty in the Atlantic. On July 11 he approved Hemisphere Defense Plan IV, which provided for "escort convoys of United States and Iceland flag shipping, including shipping of any nationality which may join such convoys, between United States ports and bases, and Iceland." By this rather devious means, British ships could join the relatively small number of Icelandic and American ships traveling between the United States and Iceland, and receive the protection of the American Navy better than halfway across the Atlantic. Operations plans to this effect were issued on July 19, but before they went into effect on July 25 the President had changed his mind. Worried over the public reaction, at the last minute Roosevelt suspended the provision permitting "shipping of any nationality" to travel with American convoys. Once again, the President had drawn back from the momentous step of escorting British vessels across the hazardous waters of the North Atlantic. Despite repeated pleas from activists in his cabinet and polite promptings from Churchill, Roosevelt refused to make a move toward war with Germany which did not have the strong backing of the American people. . . .

Ideologically and emotionally, Americans strongly desired the defeat of Hitler and identified themselves with Britain in a common struggle. But at the same time they were not willing to enter fully into the conflict. With great political sensitivity Roosevelt observed the limits of this public mood. He cooperated with Britain as far as he could short of war, but he drew back from the decisive steps urged on him by Churchill and his own militant advisers. He continued to procrastinate on the convoy issue; he refused to commit the United States to oppose Japanese aggression against Britain or the Netherlands. The closeness of the [August 1940] vote on Selective Service extension confirmed his judgment and caused him to continue to move with extreme caution in giving aid to Britain and Russia. Roosevelt had led the nation to the brink of war by the summer of 1941, but he refused to take the final step until the nation was ready. . . .

German Attacks

The submarine menace eased somewhat in July and August [1941] following the American occupation of Iceland. Nine eastbound British convoys carried over 4 million tons of supplies across the North Atlantic during the summer, and not a single ship was lost. But in September the U-boats again found their targets. On September 8 twelve German submarines attacked a slow British convoy south of Iceland and over a three-day span sank fifteen merchant ships. Britain had badly overtaxed her limited destroyer strength in escorting the heavy run of summer convoys, and the strain on ships and crews was reaching a critical point. Supply shipments to Russia, which had to go around the German-occupied coast of Norway to Murmansk, added a new and very heavy burden that Britain could not handle alone. Unless the United States Navy shared the escort duty, Great Britain would lose the battle of the Atlantic by default.

Roosevelt, fully aware of the British plight, had promised at the Atlantic Conference that American naval units would escort convoys of British ships as far as Iceland. Yet despite this pledge, he held back, uncertain how he would justify such a policy to the American people. On September 1 Admiral Ernest King drew up an elaborate operation plan for convoy duty by the Atlantic fleet, but still Roosevelt hesitated. Then on September 4 Germany provided the pretext the President was seeking. The American destroyer *Greer*, carrying passengers and mail to Iceland, was attacked by a German submarine in the North Atlantic. The submarine fired two torpedoes; both missed the *Greer*, which responded with depth charges that also missed. Later reports revealed that the *Greer* had been trailing the submarine for over three hours in cooperation with a British patrol plane which dropped four depth charges on the U-boat. The submarine commander, far from being guilty of an unprovoked assault, had turned in desperation on his pursuer in an effort to escape destruction.

President Roosevelt, however, did not wait to ascertain the full story of the *Greer* episode. At a press conference on September 5 he called the attack deliberate. Later that day he met with Secretary of State Hull and Harry Hopkins and decided to institute the long-delayed convoys by the American Navy. He asked Hull to prepare a draft of a speech he would deliver to the American people about this momentous decision. When Hull cautiously sent in a weak statement, Hopkins and Judge Sam Rosenman, the President's chief speech writer, prepared a much stronger draft, which Roosevelt strengthened even more. On September 10 Roosevelt read the speech to Secretaries Hull, Knox and Stimson, who warmly endorsed it, and the next day he went over it with a bipartisan group of Congressional leaders.

Roosevelt delivered his address, one of the boldest speeches of his long career, to a nationwide radio audience on September 11. In blunt, biting phrases, he accused Germany of piracy in the *Greer* incident and called U-boats "the rattlesnakes of the Atlantic." Germany, he warned the nation, was seeking to secure control of the seas as a prelude to conquest of the Western Hemisphere. "This attack on the *Greer* was no localized military operation in the North Atlantic," declared Roosevelt. "This was one determined step towards creating a permanent world system based on force, terror, and murder." Therefore, the President continued, American ships would no longer wait to be attacked, implying, but not clearly stating, a new policy of shoot-on-sight for American destroyers. Then, in unambiguous language, he announced the beginning of American convoys: ". . . our patrolling vessels and planes will protect all merchant ships—not only American ships but ships of any flag—engaged in commerce in our defensive waters." "From now on," he concluded," if German or Italian vessels of war enter the waters the protection of which is necessary for American defense they do so at their own peril."

This "shoot-on-sight" speech, as it has been deceptively labeled by many historians, marked a decisive step toward war. Ever since the passage of the Lend-Lease Act in March, Winston Churchill, along with many of the President's own advisers, had been urging Roosevelt to insure the delivery of supplies by authorizing the United States Navy to undertake escort duty. Repeatedly, the President had given in to this pressure only to reverse himself on the grounds that the American people were not yet ready to face the risk of war involved in convoying. Now he had committed himself publicly.

Yet Roosevelt's boldness was misleading. Even in taking a momentous step, he acted deviously, seizing on a questionable incident and portraying it as a simple case of aggression, which it clearly was not. Roosevelt evidently still believed that he could not be honest with the American people. The public opinion polls, however, indicate that he seriously overestimated the strength of isolationism. Surveys in September showed that nearly 80% of the people opposed participation in the war; but such results were to be expected—rarely do people respond positively to a simple query about entering a major conflict. In early October, when George Gallup asked the more realistic question, Do you think it more important to defeat Hitler than to stay out of the war?, over 70% answered that it was better to insure defeat of Hitler. The American people wanted to stay at peace, but not at the cost of a German victory. Thus, to the President's relief, they responded enthusiastically to his convoy decision, taking in

287

stride its risk of war. Indeed, the public reaction was so favorable that Roosevelt could have begun convoys months earlier with solid public support. . . .

Revising the Neutrality Act

The next problem confronting Roosevelt was the prohibition on arming American merchant vessels and the ban on their entry into war zones contained in the 1939 Neutrality Act. With American cargo ships now traveling to Iceland to supply the American garrison there, it was essential that they be permitted to carry deck guns for protection against surface attacks by German submarines. In addition, if the United States was fully committed to the policy of insuring the delivery of lend-lease supplies to Britain, it would be very helpful to have American ships carry these goods across the Atlantic and thus relieve the over-burdened British merchant marine. When Roosevelt's advisers had pressed this question on him in July, he had consulted with Congressional leaders, and their negative reaction had caused him to defer the issue. Encouraged by the favorable response to his convoy speech, the President decided to ask for revision of the Neutrality Act. Yet again he acted with indirection. On October 9 Roosevelt asked Congress to repeal only Section VI of the Act, which prohibited the arming of merchant ships, a step he knew most Congressmen favored. Then, in less specific terms, he urged Congress to "give earnest and early attention" to other phases of the Neutrality Act. With studied vagueness, he suggested that Congress reconsider "keeping our ships out of the ports of our own friends," but he never specifically asked for repeal of the combat zone provisions of the Neutrality Act of 1939.

The House of Representatives considered the President's ambiguous requests in late October. Fearful of defeat by the isolationists, Congressional leaders restricted the legislation to repeal of Section VI, and thus the issue was confined to arming American merchant ships. As the debate reached its climax, news arrived that a German submarine had torpedoed an American destroyer, the *Kearney*, while it was attempting to beat off a wolf-pack raid on a British convoy. The *Kearney* managed to limp back into Iceland, and the next day the House voted to arm American merchant ships by the impressive margin of 259 to 138. In the tally Democratic Representatives backed the administration overwhelmingly, while three out of every four Republicans voted no.

The attack on the *Kearney* and the vote in the House led to public demands that the Senate repeal the entire Neutrality Act. The administration, however, remained cautious, and finally decided to ask only that the Senate expand the legislation to strike out the ban on American ships entering combat zones. Even this request caused a bitter debate in the Senate. The sinking of the American destroyer *Reuben James* with the loss of 115 lives on October 31 intensified the isolationist opposition, and lent support to the America First charge that Roosevelt was "asking Congress to issue an engraved drowning license to American seamen." If Britain needed American ships, suggested the administration's opponents, why not give them to her under lend-lease and thus avoid risking American lives on the high seas? However, on November 7, the Senate voted 50 to 37 to permit the administration to arm American merchant ships and send them into the war zone. The bill was then referred back to the House, which concurred in the combat zone provision by 18 votes, 212 to 194. . . .

Despite the closeness of the vote, the meaning of the Congressional action was clear. The United States had finally abandoned the major portions of neutrality legislation adopted in the prewar years. The only meaningful restrictions left in force were the ban on American travel on belligerent ships and the prohibition on loans, which had long since been circumvented by the Lend-Lease Act. All that remained then was a hollow shell which stood as a monument to the naive belief of the American people in the mid-1930's that they could find safety behind a legislative barricade when the world went to war. As long as it lasted intact, the Neutrality Act had served its purpose of keeping the nation out of war. But in the interval the American people had been taught by events overseas that the security of the nation, not avoidance of hostilities, was the true goal of American foreign policy.

The revision of the Neutrality Act, together with the even more important convoy decision, brought American policy in the Atlantic in line with the stand taken in Asia. In both regions the United States had exhausted the techniques of peaceful diplomacy and had challenged the Axis powers to a showdown. Just as Japan had to face the issue of peace or war over the freezing order of July 26, so Nazi Germany had to decide whether to accept the provocative American policy in the North Atlantic. In essence, Roosevelt surrendered the decision for war to Tojo and Hitler. It was now only a question of who would strike first.

For Discussion

Chapter One

1. How would you summarize George Washington's advice? Could his policy be described as isolationism? Why or why not?

2. What interpretation does Richard Olney give to George Washington's words? How does he support his interpretation?

3. Why has the continuing influence of George Washington's Farewell Address been harmful, according to Olney? In what respects does Olney criticize the United States?

Chapter Two

1. Woodrow Wilson has been characterized as both an isolationist and as an interventionist on the issue of American entry into World War I. How and why might he be seen as both? Using information from the two Wilson viewpoints in this chapter, explain why his interventionist side finally prevailed.

2. What crucial issues divided those who favored aid extending to the Allied Powers in World War I from those who opposed such aid? Why was William Jennings Bryan so opposed to extending such support?

3. William Gibbs McAdoo stresses economic factors in his arguments for American support of the Allies. Do his arguments support the theory that the United States entered World War I for economic reasons? Why or why not?

4. Why do you think Woodrow Wilson's war message to Congress has often been characterized as a classic statement of American idealism? Could those who opposed American entry into war, such as George W. Norris, also be seen as idealists? Why or why not?

5. What did James D. Phelan believe was the purpose of World War I? How might his views on World War I help explain his support for the League of Nations? How do his views differ from those of Lawrence Sherman?

6. What does Lawrence Sherman find threatening about the League of Nations? What distinctions does he draw between the United States and the rest of the world?

Chapter Three

1. What was the main purpose of the arms embargo, according to Bennett Clark? Does Cordell Hull fundamentally agree or disagree with Clark? Explain your answer.
2. What assumptions does Louis Ludlow make about the causes and prevention of wars? Why does he want to take decisions concerning war away from Congress?
3. Does Franklin D. Roosevelt fundamentally break with isolationism with his "quarantine" speech? How exactly does he propose to change foreign policy?
4. On what basis does the *New Republic* find Roosevelt's "quarantine" speech objectionable? Do the authors of this viewpoint approve or disapprove of Roosevelt's goals? of his methods? Explain your answer.
5. How much did World War I affect the foreign policy attitudes of American political leaders of the 1930s? What evidence can you present to support your answer?

Chapter Four

1. How would you describe the fundamental differences of opinion between Henry Stimson and William R. Castle? On what grounds does Stimson argue that isolationism is obsolete? How does Castle respond to this charge?
2. Franklin D. Roosevelt argues that the 1939 revision of the neutrality laws passed during the 1930s restores traditional American neutrality. William E. Borah argues that Roosevelt's proposed revisions would change America from being neutral to being on the side of the Allies. Who do you think is right? Explain your reasoning.
3. James F. O'Connor charges that lend-lease aid to Great Britain would inevitably lead to full U.S. participation in World War II. What response does Cordell Hull make to this concern? Explain your answer, using information from these two viewpoints.
4. How would you summarize the essential dispute between Franklin D. Roosevelt and Charles A. Lindbergh concerning the United States, Germany, and Great Britain?
5. Do the arguments in Lindbergh's viewpoint constitute racism or anti-Semitism? Why or why not? Might other viewpoints in this chapter or book be open to similar charges? Why or why not?
6. How was the controversy over American entry into World War II different from the controversy over entry into World War I? How was it similar?

Chapter Five

1. What does Wendell L. Willkie believe was the main lesson of World War I? How does his view differ from the views of isolationists?

2. Compare the arguments made by William P. Elmer against a new United Nations with the arguments in Chapter Two by Lawrence Sherman against a League of Nations. What parallels do you find? How are the arguments different? Why do you think Elmer was in the minority, while Sherman was in the majority?

3. What ties between the United States and Europe does Dean G. Acheson stress? Why do you think he emphasized these bonds in arguing for the North Atlantic Treaty Organization (NATO)?

4. How did Robert A. Taft make his case for returning to a foreign policy of isolationism after World War II? What concessions does he think are required by new, post–World War II realities?

5. Both Robert A. Taft and Dean G. Acheson refer to Senate Resolution 239 to buttress their arguments about joining NATO. How do they differ in their interpretation of that resolution?

Chapter Six

1. How do Charles Callan Tansill and Robert A. Divine portray the isolationist movement during the first two years of World War II? Were Americans willing or not to support and/or fight for the Allies, in Tansill's view? in Divine's view? How might the historians' differing answers to this question color their description of this period of U.S. history?

2. Select descriptive adjectives that Tansill and Divine use to characterize Franklin D. Roosevelt and his diplomacy. How would you characterize each historian's slant in describing Roosevelt?

General Questions

1. George Washington's Farewell Address has often been quoted by isolationists. How was the advice in his address used by some of the authors of the viewpoints in this volume? Cite examples. In your opinion, have people misunderstood and/or misused Washington's advice? Explain your answer.

2. Which arguments by isolationists seem relevant today, given the current world situation? Which seem quaint or dated? Defend your answer.

Chronology

August 1914	World War I begins in Europe. President Woodrow Wilson proclaims American neutrality and suggests that the United States act as mediator for the conflict.
August 15, 1914	Wilson bans loans by American bankers to any warring nation as being "inconsistent with the true spirit of neutrality."
February 4, 1915	Germany declares a war zone around the British Isles.
May 1915	The British passenger liner *Lusitania* is sunk without warning by a German submarine. President Wilson responds by declaring that the United States is "too proud to fight," even as he upholds as "indisputable" the right of American citizens to travel on belligerent ships.
June 1915	The German government issues secret orders to spare enemy passenger liners from submarine attacks.
September 1915	President Wilson reverses his previous position and permits private American firms to lend money to the Allies.
November 7, 1916	Wilson, campaigning on a "He kept us out of war" slogan, is reelected to a second term.
January 22, 1917	Wilson delivers his "peace without victory" speech calling upon the warring nations of Europe to settle their differences amicably.
January 31, 1917	Germany resumes unrestricted submarine warfare, meaning that American and all other neutral ships traveling within war zones are liable to attack without warning.
February 3, 1917	The United States breaks off diplomatic relations with Germany.
February 26, 1917	President Wilson asks Congress to pass legislation arming American merchant ships.
April 2, 1917	Wilson asks for an American declaration of war against Germany.
April 4, 1917	The Senate votes for war, 82-6.
April 6, 1917	The House of Representatives votes for war, 373-50.
January 8, 1918	President Wilson delivers his "Fourteen Points" speech setting out American terms for peace.

November 11, 1918	An armistice ending the fighting of World War I is reached after Germany asks for peace on the basis of Wilson's Fourteen Points.
January 18, 1919	The peace conference to settle World War I opens in Paris.
June 28, 1919	The Treaty of Versailles is signed. The treaty, which features the creation of the League of Nations as its centerpiece, needs Senate ratification to take effect in the United States.
September 3, 1919	President Wilson embarks on a nationwide tour to gain support for the Treaty of Versailles and for the League of Nations.
September 25, 1919	An exhausted President Wilson cancels the remainder of his tour just before suffering a debilitating stroke.
November 19, 1919	The Senate votes on the Treaty of Versailles, submitted with reservations added by Senator Henry Cabot Lodge; the Senate rejects the treaty by a vote of 39-55.
March 19, 1920	The Senate rejects the Treaty of Versailles once more. The vote is 49-35, a simple majority approval but short of the two-thirds majority needed.
November 2, 1920	Warren G. Harding is elected president, signaling a rejection of "Wilsonian" dreams of a new international order and American involvement in European affairs.
January 27, 1926	The Senate approves American membership on the World Court by a vote of 76-17 but conditions that membership with American reservations that prove unacceptable to the international body.
October 1929	The stock market crash marks the beginning of the Great Depression in the United States and other nations.
1931–32	Japan invades and conquers the Chinese province of Manchuria; it withdraws from the League of Nations after receiving criticism from that organization. The United States, like other nations, refuses to back up its diplomatic protests against Japan with economic sanctions or other actions.
November 8, 1932	Franklin D. Roosevelt, promising a "New Deal" to help Americans in the Great Depression, is elected president.
November 16, 1933	The United States extends formal diplomatic recognition to the Soviet Union.
September 1934	The Nye Committee, organized to investigate American entry into World War I, begins two years of investigative hearings.

August 1935	Congress passes and Roosevelt signs the first of four Neutrality Acts, which sets limits on U.S. economic activities with warring nations and is designed to prevent American entry into future European wars.
October 1935	Italy invades Ethiopia. The League of Nations responds ineffectually.
March 7, 1936	Germany reoccupies the Rhineland in open defiance of the Treaty of Versailles.
July 7, 1937	Japan, having conquered Manchuria, attacks the rest of China.
October 5, 1937	President Roosevelt delivers his "quarantine speech" to warn Americans of the dangers presented by aggressor nations.
March 1938	Germany under Adolf Hitler seizes Austria.
September 29, 1938	Great Britain, France, and Germany sign the Munich Pact, which transfers the Sudetenland from Czechoslovakia to Germany.
March 1939	Germany takes the rest of Czechoslovakia.
August 23, 1939	Germany and the Soviet Union sign a ten-year nonaggression pact, thereby assuring Hitler that Germany will not face a two-front war.
September 1, 1939	World War II begins in Europe with the German invasion of Poland.
September 3, 1939	Great Britain and France declare war against Germany
September 5, 1939	President Roosevelt proclaims the United States neutral in the conflict spreading in Europe.
November 4, 1939	Roosevelt signs the Neutrality Act of 1939, which revises the neutrality laws to permit Germany's enemies to buy American goods on a "cash-and-carry" basis.
April 1940	Germany invades the Scandinavian countries.
June 1940	Germany conquers France. President Roosevelt, in a June 10 speech, says U.S. policy is changing from "neutrality" to "non-belligerency," which means that the United States will openly support the Allies, short of going to war against the Axis.
September 3, 1940	Great Britain and the United States announce the "destroyers-for-bases" deal, in which the United States lends Great Britain fifty destroyers in exchange for the rights to construct U.S. military bases on British possessions in the Western Hemisphere.
September 16, 1940	Roosevelt signs into law America's first peacetime program of compulsory military service; because of isolationist opposition, draftees are limited to one year's service within the Western Hemisphere.

November 2, 1940	President Roosevelt is reelected to a third term.
December 1940	Roosevelt outlines his program of "lend-lease" to a beleaguered Great Britain.
March 1941	Congress passes the lend-lease legislation.
April 1941	The United States occupies Greenland.
May 21, 1941	The *Robin Moor* is torpedoed by a German submarine.
June 22, 1941	Hitler invades the Soviet Union; the U.S. response is to extend lend-lease aid to the Soviets.
July 1941	American troops are sent to Iceland and American ships begin to convoy goods to Great Britain.
August 14, 1941	President Franklin D. Roosevelt and Prime Minister Winston Churchill of Great Britain draft the Atlantic Charter outlining general Allied war aims.
August 18, 1941	A bill extending the army service of draftees for eighteen months is approved by Congress; the vote in the House is 203-202.
September 11, 1941	President Roosevelt delivers his "shoot on sight" address pledging to aggressively defend against attacks by Axis ships and submarines.
October 30, 1941	The American destroyer *Reuben James* is torpedoed and sunk while on convoy duty off the coast of Iceland.
November 1941	Talks between the United States and Japan break down as the two sides reject each other's peace proposals.
December 7, 1941	Japan bombs Pearl Harbor. The United States declares war on Japan the following day.
December 11, 1941	Germany and Italy declare war on the United States.
September 21, 1943	The House of Representatives approves the Fulbright Resolution to begin preparations for American participation in a postwar international peacekeeping organization. The Senate follows suit in November.
July 1944	Delegates from forty-four nations meet at Bretton Woods, New Hampshire, to plan the monetary and financial foundations of the postwar world economy.
February 1945	At an Allied summit at Yalta in the Soviet Union, President Roosevelt secures Soviet leader Joseph Stalin's pledge of Soviet participation in a postwar United Nations.
April 12, 1945	Franklin D. Roosevelt dies, five months after his reelection to a fourth term as president. Vice President Harry S. Truman succeeds him.

April 25–June 26, 1945	The founding conference of the United Nations is held in San Francisco.
May 8, 1945	Americans celebrate the end of war in Europe the day after Germany's surrender to the Allies.
July 28, 1945	The Senate approves the United Nations Charter by a vote of 89-2.
August 6, 1945	The United States drops an atomic bomb on Hiroshima, Japan. A second atomic bomb is dropped on Nagasaki on August 9. The Japanese surrender five days later.
September 2, 1945	The final terms of surrender are signed in Tokyo Bay, ending the war against Japan.
February 1947	British diplomats ask the United States to come to the rescue of the Greek government in its war against communist guerrillas.
March 12, 1947	President Harry S. Truman announces his intention to aid the Greek government in a speech declaring the Truman Doctrine, which pledges American support for victims of "totalitarian regimes" everywhere.
June 5, 1947	Secretary of State George Marshall announces the Marshall Plan of American economic aid to Europe.
July 21, 1949	The Senate approves the formation of the North Atlantic Treaty Organization by a vote of 82-13, thereby binding the United States to support militarily the member states and ending America's historic isolation from Europe.

Annotated Bibliography

Books Published 1950 and After

Dean G. Acheson, *Present at the Creation*. New York: Norton, 1969. The memoirs of Truman's secretary of state between 1949 and 1953 that describe his role in the decisions to reject isolationism and prosecute a Cold War against the Soviet Union.

Selig Adler, *The Isolationist Impulse*. New York: Free Press, 1966. A general survey of American isolationism with special emphasis on the years between World War I and World War II.

Howard Beale, ed., *Charles A. Beard: An Appraisal*. Lexington: University of Kentucky Press, 1954. Essays on the ideas of the scholar-activist who became an outspoken critic of Franklin D. Roosevelt's foreign policy of intervention in World War II.

Michael Beschloss, *Kennedy and Roosevelt: The Uneasy Alliance*. New York: Norton, 1980. A study of the relationship between President Franklin D. Roosevelt and his ambassador to Great Britain, Joseph P. Kennedy, who broke with the administration over its pro-British foreign policies.

Dorothy Borg, *The United States and the Far Eastern Crisis of 1933-1938*. Cambridge, MA: Harvard University Press, 1964. An important study of the American response to Japanese ambitions in the Pacific.

James MacGregor Burns, *Roosevelt: Soldier of Freedom, 1940-1945*. New York: Harcourt Brace Jovanovich, 1970. A pro-Roosevelt study of Roosevelt's diplomacy before and during World War II.

Mark Chadwin, *The Warhawks*. Chapel Hill: University of North Carolina Press, 1968. A study of the pre–World War II interventionists and their propaganda battles with the America First Committee.

Richard D. Challener, ed., *From Isolation to Containment, 1921-1952*. New York: St. Martin's Press, 1970. A collection of primary sources tracing the development of American foreign policy from Presidents Warren G. Harding through Harry S. Truman.

Charles Chatfield, *For Peace and Justice*. Knoxville: University of Tennessee Press, 1971. A scholarly study of pacifism in the United States from World War I through the onset of World War II.

Warren Cohen, *The American Revisionists: The Lessons of Intervention in World War I*. Chicago: University of Chicago Press, 1967. A study of scholarly and popular historians and their revisionist assessments of the American decision to enter World War I in 1917.

Wayne S. Cole, *America First: The Battle Against Intervention, 1940-41*. Madison: University of Wisconsin Press, 1953. A pioneering study of the most significant organized challenge to American entry into World War II.

Wayne S. Cole, *Charles A. Lindbergh and the Battle Against Intervention in World War II*. New York: Harcourt Brace Jovanovich, 1974. Less a biography of Lindbergh than a study of his role in the effort to block American entry into World War II.

Wayne S. Cole, *Roosevelt and the Isolationists, 1932-1945*. Lincoln: University of Nebraska Press, 1983. A highly detailed, comprehensive look at the sometimes stormy relationship between the president and his foreign policy critics.

Wayne S. Cole, *Senator Gerald P. Nye and American Foreign Relations*. Minneapolis: University of Minnesota Press, 1962. A study of Nye's foreign policy ideas and his role in investigating American entry into World War I and in attempting to prevent American entry into another European war.

David Culbert, *News for Everyman*. Westport, CT: Greenwood Press, 1976. A study of the role that radio played in the foreign policy debates of the 1930s.

Robert Dallek, *Franklin Roosevelt and American Foreign Policy, 1932-1945*. New York: Oxford University Press, 1979. The most comprehensive treatment of the full range of Rooseveltian diplomacy.

Richard Darilek, *A Loyal Opposition in Time of War*. Westport, CT: Greenwood Press, 1976. A study of the role of the Republican Party in the foreign policy debates during the period between the attack on Pearl Harbor and the Yalta conference.

Alexander De Conde, *Entangling Alliance*. Durham, NC: Duke University Press, 1958. A history of Federalist Party foreign policy before and after George Washington's Farewell Address.

Patrick Devlin, *Too Proud to Fight*. New York: Oxford University Press, 1975. A detailed examination of Wilsonian neutrality written by a British historian.

Robert A. Divine, *The Illusion of Neutrality*. Chicago: University of Chicago Press, 1962. A study of the thinking behind the passage of the neutrality laws of the 1930s and their subsequent impact on American foreign policy.

Robert A. Divine, *Roosevelt and World War II*. Baltimore: Johns Hopkins Press, 1969. A brief history of Rooseveltian diplomacy, which argues that the president was not fully committed to intervention prior to Pearl Harbor.

Robert A. Divine, *Second Chance*. New York: Atheneum, 1967. A history of the American role in the creation of the United Nations, which argues that World War II saw the triumph of internationalism in the United States.

Justus D. Doenecke, *Anti-Intervention: A Bibliographical Introduction to Isolationism and Pacifism from World War I to the Early Cold War.* New York: Garland Press, 1987. A detailed survey of the literature relating to all varieties of American anti-interventionism.

Justus D. Doenecke, *In Danger Undaunted: The Anti-Intervention Movement of 1940-1941 as Revealed in the Papers of the America First Committee.* Stanford: Hoover Institution Press, 1990. A comprehensive collection of documents relating to the work of the main organized effort to block American entry into World War II.

Justus D. Doenecke, *The Literature of Isolationism: A Guide to Non-Interventionist Scholarship, 1930-1972.* Colorado Springs: Ralph Myles, 1972. A bibliography of scholarly writings concerning isolationism from the 1930s through the height of the Cold War.

Allen Drury, *A Senate Journal, 1943-45.* New York: McGraw-Hill, 1963. Diary recording the author's impressions of the Senate and Senate debates as the United States moved away from isolationism and toward acceptance of internationalism.

Herbert Feis, *The Road to Pearl Harbor.* Princeton, NJ: Princeton University Press, 1950. A history of the events leading to Pearl Harbor that generally defends the policies of Franklin D. Roosevelt.

Gilbert Fite and H.C. Peterson, *Opponents of War, 1917-1918.* Madison: University of Wisconsin Press, 1957. A study of the opposition to World War I within the United States.

John Lewis Gaddis, *The United States and the Origins of the Cold War.* New York: Columbia University Press, 1972. A history that charts the decline of isolationism as the United States prepared to wage a Cold War against the Soviet Union.

Felix Gilbert, *The Beginnings of American Foreign Policy.* New York: Harper's, 1961. An intellectual history of the roots of American isolationism from the colonial period to George Washington's Farewell Address.

Norman Graebner, *The New Isolationism.* New York: Ronald Press, 1956. A scholarly study and a contemporary critique of those Americans who preferred unilateral American action in Europe and Asia to a foreign policy of international cooperation.

Thomas Guinsburg, *The Pursuit of Isolationism in the United States Senate from Versailles to Pearl Harbor.* New York: Garland, 1982. A careful study of a segment of the Senate and its thinking and voting on key foreign policy issues during the time between World War I and World War II.

Michael Hogan, *The Marshall Plan: America, Britain, and the Reconstruction of Western Europe, 1947-1952.* New York: Cambridge University Press, 1987. A comprehensive history of one of the crucial American programs that helped spell the end of traditional American isolationism.

Paul S. Holbo, ed., *Isolationism and Interventionism, 1932-1941*. Chicago: Rand McNally, 1967. A documentary history of this crucial period of change in American foreign policy.

Manfred Jonas, *Isolationism in America, 1935-1941*. Ithaca, NY: Cornell University Press, 1966. A critical study of isolationist-minded politicians, intellectuals, and pamphleteers in the years immediately preceding American entry into World War II.

Burton Ira Kaufman, ed., *Washington's Farewell Address: The View from the 20th Century*. Chicago: Quadrangle Books, 1969. A collection of essays by historians showing how opinions over what George Washington meant in his famous address have changed over time.

George F. Kennan, *Memoirs, 1925-50*. Boston: Little, Brown, 1967. The first volume of the memoirs of the professional American diplomat who was the architect of the doctrine of Soviet Union containment.

David Kennedy, *Over Here*. New York: Oxford University Press, 1980. A history of the homefront during World War I, which provides important information on the shift from isolationism to interventionism between 1914 and 1917.

Thomas Kennedy, *Charles A. Beard and American Foreign Policy*. Gainesville: University of Florida Press, 1975. A study of the foreign policy thinking of the historian-isolationist during the 1930s and 1940s.

Warren Kimball, *The Most Unsordid Act: Lend-Lease, 1939-1941*. Baltimore: Johns Hopkins University Press, 1969. A study of the rationale behind, the debates over, and the early implementation of lend-lease.

Walter LaFeber, *The Origins of the Cold War, 1941-47*. New York: Wiley, 1971. An important general history of the move away from isolationism and toward the decision(s) to prosecute a Cold War.

Joseph Lash, *Roosevelt and Churchill, 1939-1941: The Partnership That Saved the West*. New York: Norton, 1976. A laudatory study of the personal and political relationship of the World War II leaders.

N. Gordon Levin, *Woodrow Wilson and World Politics*. New York: Oxford University Press, 1968. A diplomatic and intellectual history of Wilsonian foreign policy.

Leonard Liggio and James Martin, *Watershed of Empire*. Colorado Springs: Ralph Myles, 1976. A series of essays highly critical of American liberalism generally and New Deal foreign policymaking specifically.

Charles A. Lindbergh, *An Autobiography of Values*. New York: Harcourt Brace Jovanovich, 1978. The posthumously published autobiography of the symbol and spokesman of the America First Committee's fight against American entry into World War II.

Charles A. Lindbergh, *The Wartime Diaries of Charles A. Lindbergh*. New York: Harcourt Brace Jovanovich, 1970. The daily reflections of one of the leading isolationists following Pearl Harbor and the American decision for war.

James Martin, *American Liberalism and World Politics, 1931-1941*. New York: Devin-Adair, 1964. A dense but nonetheless important study of the transformation of American liberalism from anti-interventionism in the early 1930s to interventionism by 1941.

Ernest May, *The World War and American Isolation, 1914-1917*. Cambridge, MA: Harvard University Press, 1959. A diplomatic history of the American road to World War I written on the basis of American, British, and German sources.

Arno J. Mayer, *The Politics and Diplomacy of Peacemaking*. New York: Knopf, 1967. A detailed study of the background to and drafting of the Versailles treaty after World War I.

George Nash, *The Conservative Intellectual Movement in America Since 1945*. New York: Basic Books, 1976. An intellectual history of conservative intellectuals, some of whom were "old isolationists" critical of the new American empire of the early Cold War.

Robert Osgood, *Ideals and Self-Interest in America's Foreign Relations*. Chicago: University of Chicago Press, 1953. An interpretive study of American foreign policy in the first half of the 20th century and the American oscillation between isolationism and interventionism.

James Patterson, *Mr. Republican*. Boston: Houghton Mifflin, 1972. A thorough and thoroughly readable biography of Senator Robert A. Taft, a leading Senate isolationist.

Ronald Radosh, *Prophets on the Right*. New York: Simon and Schuster, 1975. Essays on key isolationists of the 1930s, including Charles A. Beard, Oswald Garrison Villard, and John T. Flynn, who eventually became critics of American globalism in the Cold War.

Leroy Rieselbach, *The Roots of Isolationism*. Indianapolis: Bobbs-Merrill, 1966. A study of congressional voting patterns as they related to the development of American isolationism.

Elliott Roosevelt, ed., *FDR, His Personal Letters, 1928-1945*. New York: Duell, 1950. A two-volume collection of President Roosevelt's correspondence edited by his son.

Bruce Russett, *No Clear and Present Danger*. New York: Harper and Row, 1972. A scholarly study that is highly critical of American diplomacy prior to Pearl Harbor.

James Schneider, *Should America Go to War?* Chapel Hill: University of North Carolina Press, 1989. A detailed study of the foreign policy debate as it unfolded in the city of Chicago, which was a center of isolationism, between 1939 and 1941.

Paul Schroeder, *The Axis Alliance and Japanese-American Relations*. Ithaca, NY: Cornell University Press, 1958. A critical study of American foreign policy that places a heavy share of the blame for eventual war between the countries on the Roosevelt administration.

Ralph A. Stone, *The Irreconcilables*. Lexington: University of Kentucky

Press, 1970. A history of the movement against the Treaty of Versailles and biographical sketches of those senators who were irreconcilably opposed to a League of Nations in any form.

Robert A. Taft, *A Foreign Policy for Americans*. Garden City, NY: Doubleday, 1951. A statement of early Cold War foreign policy aims written by a leading Senate isolationist.

Charles C. Tansill, *Back Door to War*. Chicago: Regnery, 1952. A piece of scholarship that attacks Roosevelt for plotting to get the United States into World War II.

Robert Smith Thompson, *A Time for War*. New York: Prentice Hall Press, 1991. A study of Franklin D. Roosevelt's foreign policy, which argues that the president actively involved the United States in World War II prior to Pearl Harbor.

Arthur Vandenberg, ed., *The Private Papers of Senator Vandenberg*. Boston: Houghton Mifflin, 1952. A collection of primary sources relating to the Senate career of an isolationist of the 1930s who became a cold warrior after World War II.

Frank Waldrop, *McCormick of Chicago*. Englewood Cliffs, NJ: Prentice-Hall, 1966. A biography of the publisher of the Chicago *Tribune*, who was a leading isolationist during the years between the two world wars.

H. Bradford Westerfield, *Foreign Policy and Party Politics*. New Haven: Yale University Press, 1955. A study of congressional voting patterns on key foreign policy issues from Pearl Harbor through the Korean War.

Burton Wheeler, *Yankee from the West*. Garden City, NY: Doubleday, 1962. The autobiography of the senator from Montana who became one of the most outspoken and anti-Roosevelt isolationists of the 1930s.

William A. Williams, *The Tragedy of American Diplomacy*. New York: Delta, 1972. An extended essay on 20th-century American foreign policy, written from the perspective of a left-oriented diplomatic historian in sympathy with those on the left and right who have been critical of American interventionism.

John Wiltz, *From Isolationism to War, 1931-1941*. New York: Crowell, 1968. A brief study of American diplomacy in the 1930s with special emphasis on the work of the Nye Committee.

Lawrence Wittner, *Rebels Against War*. New York: Columbia University Press, 1969. A study of the American pacifist movement from before World War II through the 1960s.

Books Published Prior to 1950

Thomas Bailey, *The Man in the Street*. New York: Macmillan, 1948. A history of the road to World War II that is also a defense of President Roosevelt's strategy of manipulating an essentially isolationist-minded country into war.

Charles A. Beard, *The Devil Theory of War*. New York: Vanguard Press, 1936. A highly selective documentary history of critical decisions that eventually brought the United States into World War I.

Charles A. Beard, *A Foreign Policy for Americans*. New York: Knopf, 1940. An extended essay on the limits of American power, written at the time of the German attack on Scandinavia and the Low Countries of Belgium and the Netherlands.

Charles A. Beard, *Giddy Minds and Foreign Quarrels*. New York: Macmillan, 1939. A pamphlet attacking what Beard regards as the uniquely American brand of interventionism, which presumes wickedness at the heart of other nations.

Charles A. Beard, *President Roosevelt and the Coming of the War*. New Haven: Yale University Press, 1948. A highly critical history of Rooseveltian foreign policy that contends that Roosevelt violated the Constitution with both his destroyers-for-bases deal and lend-lease.

Phillips Bradley, *Can We Stay Out of War?* New York: Norton, 1936. A dispassionate analysis of the problems and possibilities of American neutrality and an argument against collective security as a means of maintaining that neutrality.

Earl Browder, *Fighting for Peace*. New York: International Publishers, 1939. A collection of articles and speeches by the leader of the American Communist Party from early 1939 that argue for American intervention in a war against fascism.

Earl Browder, *The Second Imperialist War*. New York: International Publishers, 1940. A collection of articles and speeches by the leader of the American Communist Party after the Nazi-Soviet pact that argue against American intervention in the war in Europe.

Boake Carter, *Why Meddle in Europe?* New York: R.M. McBride, 1939. An accounting of the costs of World War I, an attack on the New Deal, and a statement against American involvement in future European wars.

Merle Curti, *Peace or War*. New York: Norton, 1936. An instant history of the battle over neutrality legislation in the mid-1930s.

Theodore Dreiser, *America Is Worth Saving*. New York: Modern Age Books, 1941. An extended essay by the famous American novelist written to advance American isolationism and criticize an American foreign policy of cooperation with Great Britain.

John Foster Dulles, *War, Peace and Change*. New York: Harper's, 1939. A study, written by a future secretary of state, reflecting his doubts about intervention in World War II.

H.C. Engelbrecht and Frank Hanighen, *Merchants of Death*. New York: Dodd, Mead & Company, 1934. A popular investigation of the role of the munitions industry in bringing the United States into World War I.

John T. Flynn, *As We Go Marching*. New York: Doubleday, 1944. An extended essay that sought to make the case that a foreign policy of interventionism was leading the United States toward fascism.

Jerome Frank, *Save America First*. New York: Harper's, 1938. A classic statement of pre–World War II isolationism.

C. Hartley Grattan, *The Deadly Parallel*. New York: Stackpole Sons, 1939. A warning against future American intervention in Europe, written by a critic of American intervention in World War I.

Quincy Howe, *Blood Is Cheaper Than Water*. New York: Simon and Schuster, 1939. A satiric look at American foreign policy written by one of the most prolific isolationists of the 1930s.

Cordell Hull, *The Memoirs of Cordell Hull*. New York: Macmillan, 1948. The two-volume autobiography of the man who was President Roosevelt's secretary of state between 1933 and 1944.

Walter Johnson, *The Battle Against Isolationism*. Chicago: University of Chicago Press, 1944. A contemporary history of the fight between the America First Committee and the Committee to Defend America by Aiding the Allies.

Walter Millis, *Road to War*. Boston: Houghton Mifflin, 1935. A critical examination of Wilsonian foreign policy, which led—unnecessarily, in the author's view—to war in 1917.

George Seldes, *Iron, Blood and Profits*. New York: Harper's, 1934. An exposure of the munitions industry and its role in the making of American foreign policy.

Robert Sherwood, *Roosevelt and Hopkins: An Intimate Biography*. New York: Harper and Row, 1948. A firsthand account written by a Roosevelt speechwriter who was highly critical of the "savage campaign" of the isolationists who forced Roosevelt to wait to be pushed into war.

Wendell L. Willkie, *One World*. New York: Simon and Schuster, 1943. A plea for the United States to join a new world organization, written by the defeated Republican presidential candidate of 1940, who had undertaken an international goodwill tour for his victorious opponent, President Franklin D. Roosevelt.

Index

311